D1130417

# The Devious Dr. Franklin, Colonial Agent:

Benjamin Franklin's Years in London

*Benjamin Franklin* (1767), by David Martin

# The Devious Dr. Franklin, Colonial Agent:

Benjamin Franklin's Years in London

David T. Morgan

MERCER UNIVERSITY PRESS
Macon, Georgia • 1996

ISBN 0-86554-525-1

# The Devious Dr. Franklin, Colonial Agent:
## Benjamin Franklin's Years in London
### by David T. Morgan

Copyright © 1996
Mercer University Press, Macon, Georgia 31210-3960 USA
All rights reserved.
Printed in the United States of America.
The paper used in this publication meets the minimum requirements
of American National Standards for Information sciences—
Permanence of Paper for printed Library Materials,
ANSI Z39.48-1984.

Library of Congress Cataloging-in-Publication Data

Morgan, David T.
    The Devious Dr. Franklin : Benjamin Franklin's years in London/
David T. Morgan.
        xii + 273 pp.       6x9"
    Includes bibliographical references and index.
    ISBN 0-86554-525-1 (alk. paper)
        1. Franklin, Benjamin, 1706–1790.  2. Colonial agents—England
—London—Biography.  3. Statesmen—United States—Biography.
4. Americans—England—London—Biography. 5. Franklin,
Benjamin, 1706–1790—Homes and haunts—England—London.
6. United States—Politics and government—To 1775.  7. United
States—Foreign relations—Great Britain.  8. Great Britain—
Foreign relations—United States.  I. Title.
E302.6.F8M85   1996
973.3'092—dc20
[B]                                       96-7709
                                          CIP

Cover art: *Benjamin Franklin* (1767), by David Martin. Courtesy of the Museum of American Art of the Pennsylvania Academy of Fine Arts, Philadelphia. Gift of Maria McKean and Phebe Warren Downes through the bequest of their mother, Elizabeth Wharton McKean.

96-136

# Contents

To the memory of my maternal grandmother, Mary Jane Deal Herring, who believed in me and always made me feel special— even when I did not deserve it.

# Acknowledgments

Perhaps the time will soon be upon us, in this high-tech age, when virtually all research materials will be available to an author via the Internet. If so, it will be far less expensive, yet far less enjoyable, than journeying to distant archives and libraries and combing through manuscripts, public records, and books and meeting some of the fine people who work in those depositories. In doing research for this book I visited many splendid archives and libraries, and in all cases I was given access to needed materials and treated kindly. I came to know some of the members of the staff at a few of the places, and I appreciate their helpfulness and friendship. On two different occasions (six years apart) I spent days at the Benjamin Franklin Collection, located at the Yale University Library. Jonathan Dull and Claude-Anne Lopez, as well as others on the staff, were very gracious and helpful. Thomas Adams and his staff at the John Carter Brown Library of Brown University also lent kind assistance. The staff at the Library of the Pennsylvania Historical Society assisted me in locating sources and in making them available to me. Roy Goodman at the Library of the American Philosophical Society did likewise. People on the staff at other depositories—the British Museum, the Georgia State Library and Archives, the Library of the Georgia Historical Society, and the Rare Book Room of Duke University's Perkins Library —all willingly lent me kind assistance.

Besides the help I received at the hands of some delightful people at various depositories, I was fortunate to have the support of many people at the University of Montevallo where I teach. Several times I received research grants from the University's Research and Special Projects Committee, as well as a sabbatical leave through the Academic Development Committee. Without the support of my colleagues on those committees, I would not have been able to do my research. I am grateful to all who supported my applications for research funds and for my sabbatical leave. Mrs. Carlye Best, then our departmental secretary and now executive assistant to the president of the university, typed the manuscript in its entirety when I first began to seek a publisher for it; she did a superb job. Our current departmental secretary, Mrs. Judy Morris, helped me with computer questions during the final revision of the manuscript. I heartily thank each of them.

I thank my wife, Judy, for her patience while I was off chasing down the ghosts of Benjamin Franklin and his friends and enemies. Oftentimes

I left her at home to keep family matters on track. Unlike Deborah Franklin, who refused to cross the Atlantic with her husband, Judy accompanied me to England in 1986 during one of my longest research jaunts. She also made one trip to New Haven with me. Her company was always appreciated and comforting. I also thank my grown children, Cindi and Brian, for their interest in their father's work. I regret any neglect of them that my work might have caused.

Finally, I am grateful to Jon Peede of Mercer University Press for the enthusiasm he has shown for the manuscript from the outset. He has worked diligently in putting it into shape for publication. I sincerely appreciate his efforts. And let me not forget John Belohlavek of the University of South Florida and John B. Frantz of Pennsylvania State University. Both of them believed in the manuscript when some did not, and both offered me welcomed encouragement. Professor Belohlavek read the manuscript in its initial stages and offered valuable suggestions. A faulty memory no doubt keeps me from recalling others who helped me along the way, and I regret not being able to include them, but I sincerely appreciate everyone, mentioned and unmentioned, who gave me assistance and encouragement of any kind.

# Preface

Long before today's politicians and sports heroes knew that image is of the utmost importance to their continued fame and fortune, Benjamin Franklin, one of the most highly acclaimed among America's founding fathers, understood that image is crucial to a person in public life. For that reason he worked hard to project a favorable public image to his contemporaries and to create such an image for posterity. While other great men of his day left the matter to chance, Dr. Franklin meticulously cultivated his image. For the most part, his effort succeeded, since he has occupied a place in the higher echelons of the founders of our country for over two centuries. Even though he could not completely cover up his indiscretions and misdeeds, he was able to touch them up in much the same way that modern photographers hide the worst flaws of their subjects. Consequently, the best biographers of Franklin have, generally speaking, been kind to him, even when dealing with his shortcomings.

Franklin, of course, did have a dark side, but just how dark is hard to determine—mainly because of the heroic public relations campaign he waged in his own behalf. He had an illegitimate son, William, but to this day no one knows for sure who "Billy" Franklin's mother was. Benjamin Franklin did not really marry Deborah Read. Theirs was a common-law union. Since they lived as man and wife for over forty years and since Franklin was careful to create the image of a devoted family man, posterity has chosen to overlook the famous man's failure to show proper regard for convention and ceremony. Franklin admitted to some youthful sexual encounters and considered himself fortunate that he did not contract any social diseases as a result of them. Most biographers have chalked up those flings to just being young and human. The truth is, however, that not all of Franklin's indiscretions were committed while he was a young adult.

During the fifteen-and-a-half years he spent in England—1757–1762 and 1764–1775—as a colonial agent, America's best known citizen of those pre-Revolutionary years kept most people guessing with regard to his position on issues like the hated Stamp Act and concerning his intentions of staying in England or returning to America. In the matter of the Stamp Act he was thoroughly devious. First he protested against it only mildly before acquiescing in its enactment and trying to help his friends benefit from it through political appointments. Finally—after he was vilified for accepting the hated tax—Franklin came out strongly in favor of its repeal and had the audacity to give himself credit for Parliament's repealing it.

With regard to his intentions of returning to Philadelphia or remaining in London, he told the people who wanted to hear that he would soon be going home, mainly Deborah, that he would return soon. Over and over he assured his wife he would be home in the spring, then the fall, then the next spring, and so on for years. She died in late 1774, not having laid eyes on her husband for the last ten years of her life. Just as he deceived Deborah, Franklin did the same with his son William, the royal governor of New Jersey. And while he was assuring Deborah, William, and others that he would soon leave London for home, he was dropping hints in England that if the right government post were offered him there, he would be happy to stay forever.

Franklin was even deceptive about why he left England when he did depart. He stated that he returned to Philadelphia to straighten out his affairs because of his wife's death; in truth, he was virtually forced to leave. His indiscretions as a colonial agent in the service of Massachusetts made his departure necessary, if he were to escape being brought to justice for the role he played in making public the famous "Hutchinson-Oliver letters." Securing the letters by doubtful means and sending them to recalcitrant Boston whigs destroyed Franklin's credibility as a colonial agent in London, since his doing so made him a pariah to British officials and a criminal in the eyes of British jurists. Thomas Hutchinson, Andrew Oliver, and other New England officials wrote the letters to a mutual friend in England during the Townshend Duty crisis, and in them they called upon officials in the mother country to take stern measures against the colonists. For secretly obtaining the letters and shipping them off to Boston, Franklin was praised in America and condemned in England. Some in the mother country were quite serious about prosecuting the American agent for what they regarded as his theft of the letters and his intention of sowing seeds of sedition by turning them over to defiant Bostonians. Thus ruined beyond redemption in England, where he probably preferred to stay, Dr. Franklin demonstrated his amazing resilience by using the wrath heaped upon him in the mother country to make himself a hero in the eyes of the American colonists.

Thomas Hutchinson no doubt overstated the case when he blamed the American Revolution on Franklin's handling of the Hutchinson-Oliver letters, but the agent's action probably did hasten the break between the mother country and her colonies in North America. Sending those letters to Boston definitely determined Franklin's future. Finished in England, he could no longer keep people guessing about whether or not he preferred to live out his life in London or Philadelphia. As luck would have it, though, his star had begun to rise to new heights in America.

While Franklin was not actually a traitor to the American cause nor a man who had allegiance solely to his own selfish interests, as Cecil Currey has maintained in his *Road to Revolution* and *Code 72*, Philadelphia's most publicized citizen was clearly a man who kept his options open, and he let no one know what his true intentions were. Perhaps he sometimes did not even know himself. He never closed one door without being sure that another was open to him. Although not the villain Currey has made him, Franklin was, on the other hand, not exactly the selfless statesman Carl Van Doren's prize-winning, classical biography makes him out to be either. Franklin was shrewd man who knew well the value of a public image and how to make sure that he would have a secure place no matter where the consequences of his devious actions landed him.

All of the acclaimed doctor's character flaws were clearly exhibited by him during the fifteen-and-a-half years he served in London as colonial agent for Pennsylvania (1757–1762 and 1762–1775), Georgia (1768–1774), New Jersey (1769–1775), and Massachusetts (1771–1775). Up until now this is the only part of Franklin's career that has not been the focal point of an in-depth examination by historians. Because those years in London reveal much about the character of a man who has been counted among America's greatest early leaders, such a study is not only needed but long overdue.

# 1. "To Plays and Other Places of Amusement": Enjoying Life in London

Benjamin Franklin, the most famous man in America by 1757, lived slightly more than one-fifth of his long life in London. During most of the years he spent there, he lived on Craven Street, first at number 7 (later renumbered 36) and then in another house just across the street. Franklin's years on Craven Street were important for him and for the American colonies. The Pennsylvania Assembly had good reason to choose him to go to England in 1757 on the essential business of settling differences between the province's angry citizens and the Penn brothers, Thomas and Richard, who were the colony's proprietors. Franklin already knew something of London, for as a young man he had spent two years there. Also, he was well known in England, and indeed throughout Europe, because of his highly publicized experiments with electricity. Moreover, he would depart for London with considerable support among Pennsylvanians, since he was the most popular political figure in the province. His powers to charm and persuade were well known and undoubted. Surely the proprietors would listen to such an emissary and reach some sort of accord with him, or so it seemed in early 1757.

No one expected Franklin to be gone long. His was only a temporary mission with a single objective. Hence there was no need, at that juncture, to weigh the Philadelphia printer's qualifications for serving as a colonial agent. After the mission turned into a five-year sojourn, however, he would clearly possess the qualifications for becoming a permanent agent when he would return to England for a second mission in 1764. Even so, when he did go back it would be as co-agent with the heralded British barrister Richard Jackson to help secure the ouster of the proprietors in favor of a royal charter for Pennsylvania. To Franklin's surprise and that of many others, he would ultimately emerge as *the* Pennsylvania agent and would remain on the Pennsylvania Assembly's payroll until 1775. Thus, Franklin stumbled into the position that would change his life dramatically and eventually affect the course of the British Empire. The Pennsylvania Assembly had no way of knowing in 1757 or 1764 that its decision to send the creator of "Poor Richard" to London would play a part in launching the American Revolution.

Eventually, through on-the-job training and observation of how established agents went about their work, Franklin learned the art of being a colonial agent and, to some degree, brought his own personal style to the job. An agent was a combination of a lobbyist and an ambassador. Some of his specific tasks included: lobbying with British officials to secure the interests of his colony, writing propaganda, appearing personally before the Board of Trade, the Privy Council, and sessions of Parliament, gaining compensation from the treasury when his colony helped England win a war and then investing the funds that he might be able to obtain. In Parliament he was expected to fight proposed laws that would harm his colony and work to secure bounties on the raw materials it produced. The agent, in short, was at Westminster to win every possible advantage for the colony he represented.

Unfortunately agents did not always enjoy prestige and honor for their efforts and pains, as they were sometimes treated as clerks and lackeys instead of ambassadors. Although Franklin performed his share of piddling tasks, he was not the typical agent who kept a low profile. He gradually pushed himself forward until he assumed the role of unofficial spokesman for all the colonies. This seemed appropriate, since Franklin was the American who came to know more about England than any other American and knew more about America than anybody else in England.[1]

As Franklin, accompanied by his twenty-six-year-old son William and two slaves, King and Peter, sailed toward England in 1757, the memories of his first voyage across the Atlantic some thirty-three years before must have flooded his mind. What a naive lad he had been in 1724 when he became the victim of a practical and somewhat cruel joke played on him by the strange, and perhaps even unbalanced, governor of Pennsylvania, Sir William Keith. The governor promised to set Franklin up as a printer in Philadelphia and sent him off to England on a wild goose chase, ostensibly to purchase the necessary printing equipment for opening the

---

[1]Rachel Welles Carroll, "Benjamin Franklin, Colonial Agent to Great Britain, 1757-1762," unpublished M.A. thesis, University of North Carolina at Chapel Hill, 1937, 11; Michael Kammen, *A Rope of Sand: The Colonial Agents, British Politics, and the American Revolution* (Ithaca NY: Cornell University Press, 1968) 8, 41; Ralph Ketcham, *Benjamin Franklin* (New York: Washington Square Press, Inc., 1965) 17; Ella Lonn, *The Colonial Agents of the Southern Colonies* (Chapel Hill: University of North Carolina Press, 1945) 387-88; Thomas Wendel, *Benjamin Franklin and the Politics of Liberty* (Woodbury NY: Barron's Educational Series, 1974) 87-88.

young man's shop. The gullible young Franklin sailed merrily away, believing that in the governor's bag of dispatches that he carried were the letters of credit needed to buy the equipment. On 24 December 1724, just before the ship reached England, Franklin searched the bag in vain for letters of credit. Years later he would write that Governor Keith was "liberal of promises which he never meant to keep."[2]

That first voyage had been a long time ago. Franklin's circumstances in 1757 were far different. After "a smooth, swift voyage of twenty-seven days" he and his small entourage docked at Falmouth on 17 July 1757, and, following an appearance at church to thank God for a safe journey, set out immediately for London. On the way they stopped to see Stonehenge, a few miles out of Salisbury, and then went by the famous house of Lord Pembroke at Wilton. Taking nine days to reach London, they traveled seventy miles on the last day, 26 July. Franklin's expenses from Falmouth to London totaled £32 and thirteen shillings for himself and his three fellow travelers. Once in London the Franklin party lodged briefly at the Bear Inn near old London Bridge on the Southwark side. Four years later this establishment, which had been a favorite of the diarist Samuel Pepys and which charged Franklin £2, thirteen shillings, and six pence, would be torn down. Through arrangements made by Robert Charles, one of Pennsylvania's regular agents, Franklin soon took up residence in Margaret Stevenson's home at 7 Craven Street, apparently moving in there on 30 July. He would live on Craven Street off and on for the next eighteen years. It was an ideal location. Craven was a short street running from the bustling Strand down to the Thames River. It was within easy walking distance of Whitehall, the political nerve center of the British Empire.[3]

---

[2]Leonard W. Labaree and others, eds., *The Autobiography of Benjamin Franklin* (New Haven and London: Yale University Press, 1964) 78-93; Leonard W. Labaree and others, eds., *The Papers of Benjamin Franklin*, 29 volumes to date. (New Haven: Yale University Press, 1994) VII, 273 n. 8.

[3]George Simpson Eddy, ed., "Account Book of Benjamin Franklin kept by him during his First Mission to England as Provincial Agent, 1757-1762," *Pennsylvania Magazine of History and Biography* 55 (1931): 99-102; *Franklin Papers*, VII, 243, 245, and 245 ns. 8, 9; James H. Hutson, *Pennsylvania Politics, 1746-1770: The Movement for Royal Government and Its Consequences* (Princeton: Princeton University Press, 1972) 41; Henry C. Shelley, *Inns and Taverns of Old London* (Boston: L. C. Page and Company, 1923) 14-16, 19; Sheila L. Skemp, *Benjamin and William Franklin: Father and Son, Patriot and Loyalist* (Boston and New York: Bedford Books of St. Martin's Press, 1994), 30.

By the time the new agent had moved into his permanent quarters on Craven Street he had already—on 27 July—sought out William Strahan, a London printer and publisher with whom Franklin had corresponded for fourteen years. Having already become friends through their letters to one another, the two men soon forged a close friendship that would last the rest of their lives. "Straney," Franklin's nickname for Strahan, and the newly arrived agent probably talked about London and how it had changed since Franklin had left it in 1726. Numerous changes had certainly occurred, but one thing had changed little, if at all. London was still a dirty, unhealthy city with a multitude of social problems. As soon as he had opportunity to suggest it, Franklin recommended to London officials that regular street-cleaning be undertaken, a project much like one he had already successfully promoted in Philadelphia.[4]

As it had been in 1726, so it was in 1757. London teemed with poor people who lived in squalor. Buildings were dirty and dilapidated, and roads around the city were neither attractive nor safe. On the outskirts of the city, hogs fed on the city's garbage. Ditches along the roads were full of nastiness, and their dirt emitted a powerful stench. In the city itself numerous old houses, though literally falling down in many cases, were patched together and turned into tenement houses, common lodging houses, or brothels. Not a few were left empty and came to be inhabited by vagrants, beggars, and runaway apprentices. Most poor people, however, lived in furnished rooms, paying a weekly rent, but so did many people of good financial circumstances. The standard rent for a London artisan, until a precipitous jump in rents around 1795, was two shillings to three shillings and six pence weekly, although cellars and garrets could be had for less.[5]

Franklin's return to London in 1757 coincided with a great deal of expansion with regard to new streets and residential developments, as well as a steady influx of newcomers to the city. One estimate of the period claimed that as many as two-thirds of the adults in London had

[4]*Franklin Papers*, VII, 317-18; Robert Dale Harlan, *William Strahan: Eighteenth Century London Printer and Publisher* (Ann Arbor MI: Microfilms, Inc., 1960) 41-44, 158, 174; Dorothy Marshall, *Dr. Johnson's London* (New York: John Wiley and Sons, 1968) 35; Richard B. Schwartz, *Daily Life in Johnson's London* (Madison: University of Wisconsin Press, 1983) 16, 126; Skemp, *Patriot and Loyalist*, 30.

[5]M. Dorothy George, *London Life in the XVIII Century* (New York: Alfred A. Knopf, 1925) 73, 86-89, 91-92, 95, 97.

"come from distant parts." Unfortunately many of the young women, unable to find work, ended up as prostitutes. At Charing Cross, along the Strand, in Fleet Street, and near Covent Garden they were easily found. There was even a guidebook called *New Atlantis* for sale, a book that listed the names, addresses, physical characteristics, and specialties of the prostitutes. The median age of these unfortunate women was eighteen, but some were mere girls as young as ten![6]

Unemployed young men from the country, coming to London in search of work, were frequently carried away by army recruiters or the death angel. London attracted all kinds of people, the best and the worst, but always there were the poor and seemingly forever in preponderant numbers.[7]

The filthiest streets, courts, and houses were those where the Irish lived, for large numbers of the Irish poured into London during the eighteenth century, and most of them were unskilled laborers who were perpetually down on their luck. Their willingness to work for less than prevailing wages caused fights with angry Englishmen, and from time to time riots were provoked over the issue. Not a few of the Irish who arrived in London were fleeing from the law, and once in the city they became a serious problem for the police and the people who tried to administer the Poor Law. In 1763 some Irishmen would engage in a pitched battle with English sailors at Covent Garden—a battle that turned into a general melee and led to considerable destruction of property.[8]

London was not very tolerant of foreigners. The Irish caused the most problems, but Londoners despised Jews, too, and the French most of all. Actually the number of French residents was relatively small. The number of Jewish inhabitants fluctuated, but the trend was upward. In 1734 it was estimated that there were six thousand Jews in the city; in 1753 only five thousand. By 1800, however, the number would climb to between twenty and twenty-six thousand. Most of them were Ashkenazic (i. e., German or Eastern European) Jews and, like the Irish, uneducated and poor. By the time of Franklin's second arrival in London in 1757 anti-semitic feelings ran deeply and were pervasive. The Jews clustered in "Petticoat

---

[6]Ibid., 110-11, 113; Schwartz, *Johnson's London*, 39, 77-80.
[7]George, *London Life*, 110-11, 113.
[8]Ibid., 105, 113-14, 117-21.

Lane and its purlieus." In the Houndsditch area some of them competed with English "fences" in disposing of stolen goods.[9]

One mid-eighteenth-century observer claimed that in London there was nothing but "anarchy, drunkenness, and thievery" among the lower classes, while in the country there was "good order, sobriety, and honesty." The observer's biases are quite obvious and make his description somewhat suspect, but he was not wrong about the drunkenness in the city. During much of the eighteenth century excessive drinking and a passion for gambling were common, but among all classes, not just the poor. London social life centered around the tavern, the alehouse, and the club. The city had a history of alcoholic consumption that was and is almost beyond belief. For the most part, the poor drank gin because it was cheap. The gin shops, far too numerous before 1751, in many cases offered more than gin, as they often served as low-class brothels and places for receiving stolen goods. The drunkenness and poverty caused, at least partially, by the gin shops also promoted crime and violence and helped make many parts of London unsafe. One took a huge risk in wandering among the courts off Holborn and Gray's Inn Lane, the rookeries of St. Giles and those between St. Martin's Lane, Bedford Street, and Chando Street. Even in Westminster, where the nation's government was housed, there were dangerous places: Petty France, Thieving Lane, Orchard Street, Peter Street, Pye Street, and the many courts and lanes around the Haymarket and St. James's Market. Covent Garden and many courts off the Strand were also places not to walk alone.[10]

Compared to Philadelphia, London was indeed a dangerous place in 1757, but as bad as it was, conditions were improving. Actually a popular campaign against gin drinking had been launched as far back as 1721. Franklin must have heard and read much about that effort during his London sojourn of the mid-1720s. In those years he had proved to be an exceptional young man, refusing to drink strong beer and gin and referring to his fellow workers as "great guzzlers of beer." Responding to a public outcry, the government passed laws in 1736, 1743, and 1747 to curb the consumption of alcoholic beverages. Although the act of 1743 reduced the number of gin shops, the good it did was reversed by the act of 1747 that once more allowed the distillers to retail their product.

---

[9]Ibid., 128-33.
[10]Ibid., 16-17, 30, 40-43, 83, 156, 277-74.

Apparently the act of 1743, passed because of the enormous volume of liquor sold that year—eight million gallons!, was judged to be too strict after it went into force, but volume swelled again when that law was superseded by the new act of 1747. Finally, in 1751, a statute resurrecting the principles of the 1743 act was passed and rigorously enforced. Excessive drinking was curbed. This does not mean that London was sober after 1751—only more sober than was traditional.[11]

Besides the decline in drunkenness, London was undergoing other improvements. Streets were being widened, squares were being built, and new streets and roads were being cut. Cavendish, Grosvenor, and Hanover squares and New Bond Street with its adjacent streets had already been completed by 1757. Fashionable London was creeping westward from Covent Garden, Soho, and St. Giles. New Road from Paddington to Islington had been started the year before Franklin arrived to carry out his mission for the Pennsylvania Assembly, and this opened up the parish of St. Pancras to much new growth. By the time the Seven Years' War ended in 1763 eastward expansion, which would become significant, began, and in some areas dignified Georgian homes were built. Thus, the East End did not consist solely of working-class houses, shops, and pubs. Moreover, London officials had awakened to the need for educating the public on matters of hygiene, land reclamation, and the prevention of disease. Even so, it would be 1769 before the "dispensary movement" would provide centers where the poor received free medicine and medical advice.[12]

Another improvement had been the elimination of "Fleet Marriages." Before the Marriage Act of 1753 Fleet Street had been notorious as the place where clergymen who ignored episcopal authority made extra money performing unpublicized marriages. Women were often lured into these secret marriages by persuasion, force, or fraud and then stripped of their fortune and deserted. After 1753 no marriage was legal without securing banns and a license prior to the ceremony.[13]

Little by little London was becoming safer, more sanitary, more attractive, and, in general, a more pleasant place in which to live. Coffeehouses provided a less boisterous alternative to the taverns. There was

---

[11]Ibid., 20, 30-38, 40-41, 290-91; Marshall, *Dr. Johnson's London*, 252-53.

[12]George, *London Life*, 50-51, 57-58, 64-65, 99-100; Marshall, *Dr. Johnson's London*, 31-33.

[13]George, *London Life*, 314-15; Schwartz, *Johnson's London*, 26-27.

entertainment at the theatres. Covent Garden Theatre, which had opened on 7 December 1733 with its production of "The Way of the World," was open all the years Franklin served as a colonial agent. The Haymarket Theatre had also opened in 1733. Thousands of people per week attended these and the theatre in Drury Lane. Also providing interesting diversions were "gardens" like Vauxhall and Ranalegh, which were really places "to see and be seen." Another place to be seen was the Mall in St. James's Park, but at night the park could be dangerous, for it became a place of "indecency," the "haunt of soldiers and their molls." Another place of recreation was Marleybone Gardens, noted for its peddlers of delicious plum cake and evening concerts. Those with intellectual curiosity could visit the British Museum, erected at mid-century and built at first around a collection of curiosities owned by Sir Hans Sloane to whom Benjamin Franklin sold an asbestos purse during his first sojourn in London. The coarse and cruel among London inhabitants sometimes visited Bedlam and curiously observed the hospital's insane patients or looked for a place where they could watch a cockfight or a bear baiting. In London there was amusement for all—the most civilized and sophisticated and the crudest and most barbarous.[14]

More important than the places of diversion that London offered was the fact that the city's standard of living was rising among all classes. Wheat bread, which only the rich had been able to afford for countless years, was now within the financial reach of the lower classes. Meat was usually cheap and plentiful in London, while fruits and vegetables were easily obtainable. The misery and want so long characteristic of London were gradually slipping away. Not only were Londoners eating better, they were better clothed. Quite a few of the city's inhabitants were very "clothes-conscious," and there were abundant places to shop. The Strand was London's principal shopping street. It offered some fancy shops, but the wealthy looked primarily to the shops in Pall Mall and St. Paul's

---

[14]E. Beresford Chancellor, *The Pleasure Haunts of London* (Boston and New York: Houghton Mifflin Company, 1925) 88-92, 96-99; M. Dorothy George, *English Social Life in the Eighteenth Century* (London: Sheldon Press; New York and Toronto: Macmillan Company, 1923) 108-109, 112-13; George, *London Life*, 26-28, 274-75; Marshall, *Dr. Johnson's London*, 69, 150-56, 189; Schwartz, *Johnson's London*, 55, 57, 66-67, 80; Shelley, *Inns and Taverns*, v, 77-78.

Churchyard, and, of course, there were other shops in various parts of London, some to fit the pocketbook of all classes.[15]

The signs were hopeful, but, still, London had a long way to go, for its death rate was nothing short of appalling. Between 1720 and 1750 the death rate rose. Children died in horrifying numbers. In 1726, when Franklin first lived in London, it was not uncommon for twenty people a week to starve to death there. At mid-century the city's annual death rate was estimated at fifty per thousand. Burials consistently outnumbered baptisms. In 1720 baptisms totaled 18,906, while burials were numbered at 25,976. It was worse in 1730 and still bad in 1760 when there were 18,880 baptisms and 22,001 burials. The year 1770 was far worse than 1760. Not until 1790 did christenings exceed burials for the first time. Throughout most of the century diseases of all kinds killed thousands per year, with consumption, convulsions, and smallpox claiming the most victims. In spite of its frightening mortality rate, London's population was steadily augmented by newcomers, and the trend was upward. The city's numbers grew from around 674,000 in 1700 to about 900,000 at the end of the century and to 1,274,000 by 1820. Although death occurred with shocking regularity, it was to an alive, growing, and more attractive city that Franklin returned in 1757 after an absence of thirty-one years. For a man of his intellectual curiosity and literary interests, it was the city that offered greater opportunities than any other in the world at the time.[16] Perhaps he compared for Strahan, London as he remembered it in 1726 with the London he found in 1757.

Franklin had another occasion to reminisce about his first visit to London when he renewed his friendship with James Ralph, a constant companion in 1724. The two young men sailed to England together that year, both leaving women waiting in Philadelphia. Ralph left a wife and daughter, while Franklin left Deborah Read to whom he had made "promises." Having had problems with his wife's relatives, Ralph, a ne'er-do-well poet, probably never planned to return, but Franklin

---

[15]George, *London Life*, 26-28, 274-75; Marshall, *Dr. Johnson's London*, 149; Schwartz, *Johnson's London*, 35.

[16]George, *London Life*, 22-23, 25, 43-48, 170, 405; Marshall, *Dr. Johnson's London*, 24, 219; Schwartz, *Johnson's London*, 127.

The figures given include regular Anglicans only. Estimates for dissenter births and deaths could not be located, meaning that these numbers provide only a general picture of the total situation.

departed fully intending to purchase equipment for his printing business and then hasten back to Philadelphia to set up shop and marry Deborah Read. What a pity that he discovered Keith's cruel joke too late. And the nonexistent letter of credit that Franklin thought he was carrying with him was not the end of the governor's mischief. Upon reaching London, acting on Keith's instructions, Franklin presented a letter to a stationer, presumably on the governor's behalf. The letter, however, was not written by Keith, as the young would-be printer had been led to believe. Instead it had been written by a conniving Philadelphia attorney named Walter Riddleston, whom the stationer despised. When he examined the letter, the stationer abruptly walked away, leaving the young American stunned and embarrassed.[17]

Completely baffled by Governor Keith's behavior, Franklin went to Thomas Denham, a Quaker merchant, who had been a fellow passenger on the voyage to London. Denham quickly assured the young man that he had been victimized by a totally unreliable man. The governor could send no letter of credit because he had no credit to give, Franklin was told. The Quaker advised his young friend to find a job in the printing business, learn all he could, and then return to America to use his experience to advantage.[18] This was sound advice, and the young Philadelphian acted on it. The two men became close friends in the days that followed, and a year-and-a-half later they returned to Philadelphia together.

Meanwhile, Franklin and James Ralph became inseparable—at least for awhile. The two young men roomed together in "Little Britain," paying three shillings and six pence per week. Franklin paid the rent and lent his friend money, while Ralph supposedly looked for employment. In little time at all Franklin found work at Palmer's Printing House in Bartholomew Close and spent his earnings taking Ralph and himself "to Plays and other Places of Amusement." Both of them soon forgot the women they had left behind in Philadelphia. Franklin did write Deborah one letter to tell her that he would probably not return anytime soon. He proceeded to spend his money, saving little for a return passage.[19] The budding young printer had not yet discovered the wisdom of Poor Richard with regard to saving pennies, but he soon would.

---

[17]*The Autobiography*, 89-94.
[18]Ibid., 94.
[19]Ibid., 95-96.

Soon Ralph became a burden too heavy to bear. Not only did the would-be poet contribute nothing to the rent or other expenses, he hurt other people and used Franklin. First, Ralph became involved with a young woman who lived in the house where he and Franklin roomed. When she moved out, Ralph moved with her and lived with her. Unable to find work that he deemed worthy of him, Ralph finally accepted a job as a country schoolmaster. Fearing this might damage his reputation in the future, he assumed Franklin's name. He then wrote and asked Franklin to look after his girlfriend who, as it turned out, had lost her friends and her millinery business because of Ralph. If Ralph was not aware that his request was the equivalent of asking a fox to watch a hen, he was terribly naive. Franklin visited the woman, lent her money, and, because he was then "under no Religious Restraints," tried to seduce her. Not only did the young woman, already a victim of Ralph's confidence games, reject Franklin's advances, she told Ralph all about it. The aspiring poet proceeded to play the part of the betrayed for all it was worth, informing Franklin that *all* obligations between them were ended. That the money he had lent Ralph was gone forever hardly bothered Franklin, for he realized that the end of the friendship marked the end of a "Burthen."[20]

Franklin worked at Palmer's for almost a year. While there he was called upon to set type for the third edition of the Reverend William Wollaston's *The Religion of Nature Delineated*. Disagreeing with Wollaston, Franklin answered his work with a piece of his own called *A Dissertation on Liberty and Necessity, Pleasure and Pain*. He printed one hundred copies, gave a few to his friends, and destroyed the rest, for he was soon sorry he had written what amounted to a frontal assault on conventional religion. In his *Dissertation* he set forth the classical assumptions of Deism. He argued that evil does not exist because God is the author of all events and, since God is wise, good, and powerful, he can only let good happen. Interestingly enough he dedicated this effort to James Ralph, whose religious principles Franklin blamed himself for destroying.[21]

Not long after breaking with Ralph, Franklin left Palmer's to go to work at Watts' Printing House near Lincoln's Inn Fields. There he would work until he left London. Watts' employed about fifty workers, and

---

[20] Ibid., 98-99.
[21] Ibid., 96; *Franklin Papers*, I, 57 n. 6, 58-60, 58-59 n. 1, 70-71.

Franklin mixed well with them—in spite of the fact that he drank water instead of beer and was referred to as the "Water-American." When some observed how much stronger Franklin was than his fellow workers, they followed his advice and abandoned beer in favor of his water-gruel diet. Those who continued their drinking ways frequently borrowed money at interest from Franklin, when their credit was used up at the alehouse. He was not at Watts' very long before he was moved from the press room to the "Composing Room." Because of his "uncommon Quickness at Composing," he made more money than most of the other workers. This, plus the extra money he made lending at interest, gave him a good income.[22]

When Franklin took the job at Watts' his lodgings in Little Britain became "too remote," and so he moved to Duke Street, a few blocks from his new place of employment. A widow, her daughter, and a maid kept the house where Franklin now rented a room. It was not until after she checked on Franklin's character where he had lived previously that the widow accepted the young printer, charging him the same rent he had paid in Little Britain. Once he had gained her favor Franklin tricked the widow into reducing his rent by talking about moving closer to his work and taking a room for two shillings less. Liking her new roomer and wanting to have a man in the house for protection, the woman reduced Franklin's rent from three shillings and six pence per week to one shilling and six pence.[23]

Franklin demonstrated considerable shrewdness in looking after himself financially. Not only did he find jobs that paid him well, lend money to fellow workers at interest, and trick a gout-stricken widow into lowering his rent, he also sold "Curiosities" from America—on at least one occasion to a man numbered among the high and mighty. Sir Hans Sloane, royal physician and soon-to-be president of the Royal Society, purchased from Franklin a purse made of the "Stone Asbestus." Sloane, according to Franklin, paid a handsome price for the unusual purse, which the famed doctor later put on display at the British Museum.[24]

For a time Franklin enjoyed London immensely. He had fun, he made friends, he earned good money. He also showed off his strength and skill

---

[22]*The Autobiography*, 99-101.

[23]Ibid., 102; George, *London Life*, 93.

[24]*The Autobiography*, 98; Benjamin Franklin to Sir Hans Sloane, 2 June 1725. *Franklin Papers*, I, 54, 54 ns. 3 and 4.

as a swimmer and taught friends like John Wigate to swim. On one occasion he swam over three miles in the Thames—from "near Chelsea to Blackfriars." Wigate proposed that he and Franklin tour Europe together and then return to London to open a swimming school. The young printer considered it. He might well have done it, too, if Thomas Denham had not persuaded him to return to Philadelphia. Denham planned to go back and open a store. He wanted Franklin to be his bookkeeper and, eventually, his partner. The Quaker merchant held out prospects of a bright future, and Franklin, a little tired of London and perhaps homesick as well, prepared to go home. On 22 July 1726, he and Denham sailed down the Thames. Contrary winds caused the *Berkshire*, the ship that was to carry the two men back to America, to put into one English port after another until 10 August, when the transatlantic voyage finally got underway. On the way across Franklin revealed signs of his curiosity in things scientific when he carefully observed a lunar eclipse. He also made some resolutions concerning his future behavior. When he finally reached Philadelphia on 11 October 1726, he called it "the most joyful day I ever knew." As planned, he went to work for Denham, lived with him, and got along well with him, but the Quaker merchant became ill and died the next year. Franklin was again in search of work. As he walked the streets of Philadelphia, he sometimes encountered William Keith, now the ex-governor, but Keith, no doubt ashamed, passed in silence. The young returnee might have been just as ashamed at meeting Deborah Read, if she had not already given up on him and married a man named John Rogers.[25]

Strangely enough, Franklin never felt much ill will toward James Ralph—even in 1725 when they parted ways in anger. The two men, middle-aged in 1757, were delighted at being reunited, and they must have had more than one good laugh when they remembered and reminisced about those experiences so many years ago. Like Franklin, Ralph had found the road to success during the thirty-odd years of their separation. Some thought Ralph was among the "best political Writers in England." His career as a poet had been dealt the death blow by criticisms from Alexander Pope in the *Dunciad*, but his "Prose was thought to be as good as any Man's." Besides political polemics he had written a history of England covering the period encompassed by the

---

[25]*The Autobiography*, 103-108; *Franklin Papers*, I, 72-81, 83, 86-87, 93-100.

reigns of William III, Queen Anne, and George I. He had also helped the noted writer Henry Fielding manage the Little Theatre at the Haymarket. Since 1753 he had been retired, enjoying a pension of £300 per year.[26]

In spite of his worldly success, however, Ralph's basic character seemingly remained the same. He was as self-centered as ever. Franklin had brought a letter from Mary Garrigues, the daughter Ralph had abandoned in 1724. Mary wrote of herself and her ten children and expressed a desire to exchange communications, but, because he did not want his English wife and daughter to learn "of his having any connections in America," Ralph was unwilling to do more than express privately to Franklin "his great affection for his daughter and grandchildren."[27] There is no evidence suggesting that Ralph went beyond asking Franklin to pass these sentiments along to Mary.

Exactly how Ralph felt about his reunion with Franklin is not clear, but it appears that he was less excited about it than was his old companion. In any case, they seem to have seen little of each other after the initial meeting. Perhaps Ralph remembered with embarrassment his longstanding debts to Franklin, and maybe the Pennsylvania agent, because of pressing business, did not have much time to spend with Ralph. Besides, Franklin had cemented his friendship with William Strahan, a man with whom he had much more in common now and a man who could put him in touch with important Englishmen. At "Straney's" home the two men played cribbage, discussed politics, and visited with mutual friends. Soon Strahan was urging Franklin to make London his permanent residence and vowing to persuade Deborah to join her husband—even though Franklin had warned him that Deborah was utterly afraid of sea voyages and would never agree to cross the Atlantic. Strahan was thoroughly charmed by the Philadelphia printer and wanted to keep him in London forever. Thus a friendship that had been developing since 1743, when Strahan had written Franklin to introduce him to a young printer named David Hall, had reached full maturity. Hall, who had subsequently become Franklin's partner in the printing business, was, like Strahan, a lifelong friend of the congenial Franklin.[28] As the main shareholder and printer of the *London Chronicle*, a popular evening

---

[26]*The Autobiography*, 248; *Franklin Papers*, I, 58 n. 1.

[27]Benjamin Franklin to Deborah Franklin, 22 November 1757. *Franklin Papers*, VII, 274, 274 n. 3.

[28]Harlan, *Strahan*, 41-44, 158, 174.

newspaper, Strahan was in a position to help Franklin promote his causes, and he did so time and again.[29]

Besides Ralph and Strahan, Franklin already had two other friends in London at the time of his arrival in 1757. There was Peter Collinson, Quaker merchant and botanist, who had supplied Franklin with an electrical tube in the 1740s and who brought Franklin's electrical experiments to the attention of the Royal Society. There was also Dr. John Fothergill—physician, botanist, and influential English Quaker—to whom Franklin carried a personal letter of introduction from Israel Pemberton, a powerful Quaker political figure in Pennsylvania and Fothergill's close friend. Fothergill advised the Pennsylvania emissary on how to proceed with the Penns and also treated him when he became ill within a few weeks of his arrival in London. Through Collinson, Fothergill, and Strahan, Franklin would soon make new friends, some of them in high places.[30]

This was just the beginning, as the newly arrived agent continuously found his way into sophisticated circles. In 1756 he had been accepted for membership in the Royal Society, and on 24 November 1757, he was formally inducted as a fellow. This exalted honor enabled him to meet some of England's greatest "natural philosophers." One of them, Dr. John Pringle, the royal physician, became Franklin's intimate friend and traveling companion on several European tours. The Pennsylvania agent also joined the club that called itself the "Honest Whigs," and this put him in contact with Joseph Priestly, Richard Price, and Jonathan Shipley, the Bishop of St. Asaph. Only Strahan, among people who lived in England, was closer to Franklin than these three men, all known for their commitment to a somewhat radical Whig ideology and later for their defense of American revolutionary principles. In a relatively short time, then, Franklin was moving easily about in London society, hobnobbing with philosophers, publishers, and a few politicians of mainly the middling and lower ranks. He tried in vain to arrange a meeting with the great William Pitt, whose elevation to the peerage by George III was still nine years in the future. Knowing how important contacts among the

---

[29]Verner W. Crane, ed., *Benjamin Franklin's Letters to the Press, 1758-1775* (Chapel Hill: University of North Carolina Press, 1950) xv.

[30]Israel Pemberton to John Fothergill, 4 April 1757. *Franklin Papers*, VII, 173; VIII, 356-57; Leonard W. Labaree, "Benjamin Franklin's British Friendships," *Proceedings of the American Philosophical Society* 108 (20 October 1964): 423-27.

influential were to his mission, Franklin frequented the coffeehouses where he usually met lesser, but not always unimportant, members of English society. He received mail at the Pennsylvania Coffeehouse in Birchin Lane and dropped in on various occasions at the "Virginia and Maryland," the "New York," the very popular "New England" at 60 Threadneedle Street, the "Jamaican," and "Waghorn's."[31] The stranded young printer of 1724–1726 had, in 1757, become the fashionable American agent about London.

Just how much did Franklin come to love England and his life on Craven Street? Did he prefer living in London at Margaret Stevenson's to residing in Philadelphia with his wife "Debby" and daughter "Sally"? Answering these questions is difficult because of Franklin's devious nature. While he never forgot that he was at heart an American, he truly enjoyed the more intellectually stimulating atmosphere of English society and the interesting people he met who applauded his accomplishments. He had been in England only a few months when he wrote Deborah that "Men of Learning" and "Persons of Distinction" took notice of him in England and that this helped ease the pain caused by his absence from "Family and Friends." In England his ego was stroked, and at last he felt appreciated for his contributions in the field of electricity. Even so, he claimed it was duty to his country and nothing more that kept him from leaving immediately for home.[32] One can only wonder if he were fooling his wife and perhaps even himself.

Franklin's letters to Deborah, who was usually greeted as "Dear Debby" or "Dear Child," were fairly regular for awhile, beginning with his letter of 22 November 1757. He had been prevented from doing much writing before that because of an eight-week illness, the symptoms of which included a "humming Noise" in his head, the seeing of "little faint twinkling Lights," and a feeling of tenderness around his head. Dr. Fothergill gave him several medical concoctions made of a tropical American aromatic root and the shavings of a deer horn, among other ingredients. The Quaker physician also bled him from the back of the head. As late as 14 January 1758, Franklin was still feeling the effects of the disease—and possibly the remedy, too—although he felt better and

---

[31]Kammen, *Rope of Sand*, 16, 19, 22, 69-70; Labaree, "Franklin's British Friendships," 427-28; Shelley, *Inns and Taverns*, 173-75.

[32]Benjamin Franklin to Deborah Franklin, 22 November 1757. *Franklin Papers*, VII, 279.

stronger than he had in October and November. He referred to the ordeal as his time of "seasoning."[33]

In his 14 January 1758 letter, Franklin told his wife how much he missed his "little Family" and talked of his return home, but at the same time he informed her that Strahan was trying to persuade him to move to England permanently. The English publisher, Franklin reported, had offered to bet his American friend that he could convince Deborah to cross the Atlantic with one letter. The Pennsylvania agent told Deborah that he refused to bet Strahan, not wanting to "pick his pocket," for he knew that she would never cross "the Seas." He was not sure when he would return home, Franklin said—a strong hint that Deborah should not expect him anytime soon. A week later on 21 January he wrote that he would probably be in England *at least* another year, but he made an effort to sound homesick. Franklin's letters to his wife sent conflicting signals regarding where he would rather be, writing in one line about missing his family and in the next about enjoying the company of so many interesting and important people.[34] Deborah, who was neither educated nor interesting, must have wondered if her husband would ever return to Philadelphia.

From time to time Franklin wrote letters that were loving and tender, thanking Deborah for keeping him informed of happenings at home and complaining of the soot and smoke-filled air of London and the colds he caught from too much walking around the city. Peter, his slave, was minding his manners and had learned London well enough to run errands anywhere. (King, the other slave, had run away.) Franklin had bought and sent presents, "something from all the China Works in England," to Deborah and Sally, he reported, and he was shopping for more china and silver which he planned to take home upon his return.[35]

---

[33]Benjamin Franklin to John Fothergill [October 1757]; Benjamin Franklin to Deborah Franklin, 14 January 1758. *Franklin Papers, VII*, 271-74, 271 ns. 5-8, 359-60.

[34]Benjamin Franklin to Deborah Franklin, 14 January 1758; 21 January 1758. *Franklin Papers*, VII, 359-60, 363-65.

On 13 December 1757 Strahan wrote Deborah to say that the ladies of London had their eye on Franklin, and, since he was far from home and might get lonely, she had better come to England and protect her interests. As it turned out, Franklin knew his Debby, for she was not moved by the "warning" Strahan wrote in jest. See: William Strahan to Deborah Franklin, 13 December 1757. *Franklin Papers*, VII, 295-98.

[35]Benjamin Franklin to Deborah Franklin, 19 February 1758. Ibid., VII, 379-84.

After a year-and-a-half passed, Franklin's letters changed slightly. He wrote that the mail ships were not very reliable and that Deborah should not expect a letter every month. If a ship arrived without a letter from him, she should rest "easy" and look for a long letter on the next packet boat. In letter after letter he talked of going home next spring or sometime soon, but the years rolled by. This pattern of constant promises of returning and always postponing it came to characterize all the years Franklin spent in England as a colonial agent. One can only wonder if even he knew where he would rather be. Surely he loved his family and Philadelphia, but there were so many allurements in England. It became easy during both of his "temporary" missions as Pennsylvania's agent to continue finding reasons for remaining. At the end of August 1759 he intended to return to Philadelphia "early the next spring," but nearly three years passed before he actually reached home. And during his second mission on 14 February 1765 he wrote Deborah that he hoped to be home in a few months. In May of the same year he wrote Sally, his daughter, that he would see her in the fall. Two years later, on 22 June 1767, he told his wife that he needed to stay "another Winter." Promises of an impending departure were written in 1768 and then every year until Deborah, whose health had long since begun to fail, passed away in December 1774.[36]

The year 1768 seems to have been one of genuine confusion for Franklin. For a time he thought he would find favor with the British ministry and secure an important political appointment through the Duke of Grafton. In May he wrote Deborah that he was impatient to go home and be with her, but a few weeks later he told Grey Cooper, a minor English official, that he was willing to remain with his friends in England "some time longer, if not for the rest of my life." He made it clear that a good position in the government could entice him to stay in England indefinitely. He confided to his son William, however, that he would have no regrets if no such position were offered, for he had grown too old to have much ambition! Knowing that the elder Franklin had already expressed some apprehension over possibly losing his position as head of the colonial postal service because of his pro-American stance, William

---

[36]Benjamin Franklin to Deborah Franklin, 6 and 29 August 1759; 14 February and 4 June 1765; 22 June 1767; Benjamin Franklin to Sarah Franklin, 30 May 1765; and Benjamin Franklin to William Strahan, 23 August 1762. *Franklin Papers*, VIII, 423, 431-32; X, 149, 237; XII, 62-64, 152, 168-69; XIV, 192-95; XV, 139, 159-64, 292-93.

must have laughed aloud at his father's profession of losing his political ambition. And surely Deborah had come to doubt her husband's sincerity, even when he claimed that he considered "no future Prospect except one, that of returning to Philadelphia there to spend the Evening of Life with my Friends and Family." She probably remembered the eagerness with which he returned to England in 1764, and she perhaps knew that he promised Strahan to return to England forever, if he could prevail upon her to join him.[37] Deborah must have considered the possibility that her husband had decided to stay in England without her, while merely holding out promises of his return to Philadelphia. As late as 1773, several years after she had begun to fail physically, Franklin was using "Prudential Algebra" in London to decide whether he should go home or remain in England. There was nothing in his algebraic formula about wife, family, and friends back home.[38]

Life was good in London. Margaret Stevenson catered to Franklin's every need, and her perspicacious daughter Mary (affectionately known as "Polly") adored the American philosopher and became his student. She read various works he recommended and discussed them with him at length.

Besides the pleasure of residing on Craven Street with the ladies Stevenson, Franklin found much else to keep him occupied. In the early days his meetings with the Penns were sporadic, as he made proposals and awaited their response. There was time to discuss with the Rev. John Waring, Secretary of the Bray Associates, the possibility of establishing a Negro school in America.

Not a little time was spent shopping, as the Philadelphian purchased brass casters for a chair, a shovel, tongs, coal, butter, cream, spices, steel spindles for the "armonica" he invented in 1761, leather breeches, spectacles, candles, Madeira wine, books, and a variety of articles to send home to Deborah, Sally, and Jane Mecom, his favorite sister who lived in Boston. Franklin made numerous purchases for his friend Isaac Norris, and he invested money for Norris. He also, through his correspondence with a variety people who were conducting electrical experiments,

---

[37]Benjamin Franklin to Deborah Franklin, 25 May and 21 December 1768; Benjamin Franklin to William Franklin, 2 July 1768. Ibid., XV, 139, 159-64, 292-93.

[38]Benjamin Franklin to Deborah Franklin, 4 July 1771; "Prudential Algebra"; Ibid., XVIII, 161-62; XX, 336-38.

discussed electricity in order to keep up with the latest developments in that field.

Too, there was business pertaining to the colonial post office to which he had to attend, for he continued to hold the office of deputy postmaster general of the colonies—a position he had taken in 1753 and had held along with William Hunter ever since. While in England Franklin relied on his printer friend James Parker to take charge of the postal system and perform the daily duties associated with the office, but he was careful to keep a check on developments.

Along with all his other activities, Franklin accepted numerous dinner invitations. What he did infrequently, if at all, was attend church services. He declined to attend even those conducted by dissenting clergymen who were numbered among his closest friends. Actually he was not even sure where the churches of most of them were located.[39]

On both occasions when the Pennsylvania Assembly sent Franklin to England, he and members of the Assembly expected him to be there only briefly, and both times he remained for years. Each time he went to work jointly with regularly appointed agents, and each time he soon overshadowed them. He had been in England only a few months in 1757 when the Assembly, on 18 October, reappointed him as agent and made Robert Charles and Richard Partridge his assistants, although the two men had served for years as the regular agents.[40]

Franklin had a way of taking charge and finding ways to do what he wanted done, but always in the name of service to his country. As an agent he worked reasonably hard for Pennsylvania and later Georgia, New Jersey, and Massachusetts. London, he came to believe, was the place where he could do the most good for Pennsylvania and the other American colonies. That he greatly enjoyed living there made it all the better—and all the easier to find reasons to remain as long as he could. In the early months of 1775, with the threat of arrest hanging over his head, he refused to leave and stubbornly worked to heal the breach between colonies and mother country. Not until the sad news that Deborah, his wife of nearly forty-five years, had died did he finally take ship for Philadelphia. One can only wonder what might have happened

---

[39]Verner W. Crane, "The Club of Honest Whigs: Friends of Science and Liberty," *William and Mary Quarterly* 23 (April 1966): 218-19, 222; *Franklin Papers*, I, 211; VII, 98 n. 2, 191-94, 298-316, 321-25, 377-79; VIII, 147-49, 149 n. 1, 169-72, 230.

[40]Ibid., VII, 269 n. 7.

to the devious Dr. Franklin if Deborah had lived awhile longer. He could well have marked the beginning of the Revolutionary War in a London jail, if he had continued his negotiations with British officials.

# 2. "The Heads of Complaint":
## Confrontation at Spring Garden and Whitehall

Benjamin Franklin did not emerge suddenly as a political leader in Pennsylvania. He served for fifteen years as clerk of the provincial assembly before being elected to that body in 1751. There was no controversy surrounding his first political victory. Indeed, at that juncture he was all things to all men, trying to act as conciliator in the long-standing power struggle between the Assembly and the Pennsylvania proprietors for domination in the colony. For five years he tried to work with men he liked on both sides of the proprietary/anti-proprietary party dispute. Two Quaker leaders, Isaac Norris and Israel Pemberton, were anti-proprietary in sentiment and ruled the roost in the Assembly.

After five years as a member of that body Franklin's political star began to rise. In 1756, with the help of his son William, Franklin saved the colony from disaster during the French and Indian War in the face of old-line Quaker foot-dragging and Governor Robert Hunter Morris's bungling. Once before the Philadelphia printer had played an important part in the defense of Pennsylvania. In 1747, during King George's War, he had proposed a voluntary "Association" to defend the colony, since the pacifist Quakers opposed a provincial militia. The governor had called the Association an attack on constituted authority, while the proprietors were suspicious of it because they did not control it. Yet, because the Association was voluntary, many Quakers unofficially supported it. The proprietary party liked it, too, for it offered a way of circumventing the pacifist roadblocks often erected by the old-line Quakers during times of military crisis. Thomas Penn, the leading proprietor (because he owned three fourths of the Pennsylvania proprietary and his brother Richard owned only one fourth), took note of the popularity Franklin reaped as architect of the Association. Since the dominant proprietor was about as popular as smallpox with most Pennsylvanians, he began to see the creator of Poor Richard through a jaundiced, and perhaps jealous, eye.[1]

---

[1]*Franklin Papers*, VIII, 3-4, ns. 1-6; William S. Hanna, *Benjamin Franklin and Pennsylvania Politics* (Stanford: Stanford University Press, 1964) 22, 24-25, 33-34, 48-49, 51; Joseph J. Kelley, Jr., *Pennsylvania: The Colonial Years, 1681-1776* (Garden City NY:

During the disasters of the French and Indian War Governor Morris came to rival Thomas Penn in unpopularity. After deserting the frontier and returning to Philadelphia with his troops, the governor called a special session of the Assembly for February 1756 in order to deal with the crisis. Franklin, who had remained on the battlefront, hurried back to the provincial capital to take his seat. He was furious with Morris for what he regarded as inadequate leadership. Claiming that Morris had nearly provoked a civil war in Pennsylvania, Franklin asked the Assembly to oppose the ruinous policies of the governor and the proprietary party. This, plus the fact that all the old-line Quakers save one quit the Assembly in the summer of 1756, seemed to prepare the way for a more vigorous defense policy. Franklin's common-sense proposals and forceful leadership won him enough support among the Norris faction to control the Assembly. Governor Morris had refused to sign a defense bill unless it exempted the estates of the proprietors from taxation, but he was now out of office. In his place, taking office 20 August 1756, was William Denny. Before long Franklin and the Assembly learned that Denny, like Morris, intended to abide by his instructions, and that meant no taxation of proprietary property.[2]

For years the Penns and their supporters had justified the tax-dodging of the proprietors by claiming that the Quakers, angry over the Penns' defection to the Anglican Church, were out for revenge. Thomas Penn insisted that the Quakers wanted nothing more than to ruin him through taxation. Penn supporters in Philadelphia contended that the proprietors were willing to pay a fair share of taxes, if they could be certain that the Assembly would not gouge them. The evidence suggested an opposite conclusion to the anti-proprietary forces, for the Penn brothers consistently resisted every effort to tax their estates.[3]

---

Doubleday and Company, 1980), 316-30; Willard S. Randall, *A Little Revenge: Benjamin Franklin and His Son* (Boston and Toronto: Little, Brown and Company, 1984) 79-91; William R. Shepherd, *History of the Proprietary Government of Pennsylvania* (New York: AMS Press, 1967; first published 1896) 222, n. 1.

[2]*Franklin Papers*, VII, 106-109; Hanna, *Franklin and Pennsylvania Politics*, 10-11, 103, 113, 115; Hutson, *Pennsylvania Politics*, 27; Randall, *A Little Revenge*, 98-102, 111-14.

[3]Hutson, *Pennsylvania Politics*, 118; Theodore Thayer, *Pennsylvania and the Growth of Democracy, 1740-1776* (Harrisburg: Pennsylvania Historical and Museum Commission, 1953) 42-45.

Refusal by Governor Morris and then Governor Denny to approve a defense bill that included taxation of the proprietary estates prompted the Assembly to send Franklin to England to negotiate with the Penns. If the printer-politician could not reach a settlement, he was to petition the king against the proprietors "for man[a]cling their Deputies with instructions inconsistent not only with the Privileges of the People, but with the Service of the Crown." Isaac Norris, the Assembly's speaker, was appointed to accompany Franklin as co-agent, but he decided not to go. Although Franklin's appointment was made on 29 January 1757, a variety of problems delayed his departure until June. He sailed on the *General Wall*, captained by Walter Lutwidge.[4]

Franklin's mission to England troubled some people in Pennsylvania, notably Richard Peters, secretary to the governor's Council. He contended in a letter to Thomas Penn that Franklin meant "to effect a change of Government" and could "prove a Dangerous Enemy." He cited Franklin's popularity and prestige associated with his electrical experiments as the way the newly appointed agent might make influential friends in England. Unlike Peters, Penn was not worried. He was convinced that few people in England were even aware of Franklin's work in electricity. Besides, the would-be scientist from Philadelphia did not know the influential political figures who would settle the dispute. Penn did.[5]

No doubt Penn was right. Franklin was indeed at a disadvantage when it came to political in-fighting at Whitehall, the seat of the British Empire's bureaucracy, but the new agent, without hesitation, went right to the task. Through his friend Peter Collinson, Franklin soon met John Hanbury, an influential Quaker tobacco merchant, who in turn introduced him to Lord Granville, the president of the Privy Council. Unfortunately, Franklin got off to a shaky start with his lordship. They quickly disagreed over how binding upon a colony the king's instructions to a governor were. Granville insisted that such instructions were tantamount to law, while Franklin argued that colonial laws, once given royal assent, could not be altered by a governor's instructions. This was a gloomy beginning

---

[4]*The Autobiography*, 248-52. 225 n. 7, 250 n. 9, 256; Eddy, "Account Book," 96-97; *Franklin Papers*, IV, 173, 173 ns. 9-10; VII, 109-111, 117 n. 2, 121-42, 133 n. 7, 142 n. 9.

[5]*Franklin Papers*, VII, 110-11 n. 9; Hanna, *Franklin and Pennsylvania Politics*, 119; Labaree, "Franklin's British Friendships," 424; Thomas Penn to [Richard] Peters, 15 March 1757 and 14 May 1757. Penn Papers, Historical Society of Pennsylvania.

for the Pennsylvania Assembly's emissary, and, for awhile, it would be little better. The inexperienced and little-known agent found it impossible to obtain an audience with the high-ranking ministers, and the lesser ones who would bother to talk to him gave him little encouragement, mainly because Thomas Penn was hard at work poisoning many officials against him.[6]

Not long after Franklin's spat with Lord Granville, Dr. Fothergill arranged a meeting between the agent and the Penn brothers at Thomas's house "in Spring Garden." The meeting took place sometime between 13 and 17 August 1757. Both Franklin and the Penns expressed hope that a reasonable accommodation could be worked out, but it quickly became obvious that such an outcome was highly unlikely. The agent vigorously defended the Assembly's actions, while the proprietors spiritedly defended their position. Franklin's enemies had already accused him of going to England to effect the overthrow of proprietary government in favor of a royal one. The evidence suggests, however, that the agent negotiated in good faith, at least in the beginning. He responded to the proprietors' request that he put the Assembly's position in writing by delivering to them on 20 August a document labeled "The Heads of Complaint."[7]

Not surprisingly, the Penns found Franklin's document unacceptable, and the negotiations broke down. This was as much the fault of the proprietors as it was of the agent. In fact, the sincerity of the Penns in expressing hope for an amicable settlement through negotiations is clearly open to doubt. Thomas Penn had started to undermine Franklin's mission before the agent reached England. First, he tried to persuade Postmaster General Sir Everard Fawkener to withhold support from Franklin as deputy postmaster general of the colonies, and then he turned regular agent Richard Partridge against the Pennsylvania Assembly's emissary. Moreover, Penn had already stated in a private letter that he and his brother had been so abused by Pennsylvania's anti-proprietary party that they would be unable to "accommodate the matters in Dispute privately." All indications are that the proprietor closed his mind to a settlement

---

[6]*The Autobiography*, 261-62, 278, 285; *Franklin Papers*, VII, 63-68, 67 n. 9, 249-50; Hutson, *Pennsylvania Politics*, 49-50.

[7]*The Autobiography*, 262-63; *Franklin Papers*, VII, 247-52, 250 n. 7; Thomas Penn to [Richard] Peters, 5 September 1757. Penn Papers, HSP.

through negotiations with Franklin more than a month before first talking to him at Spring Garden.[8]

The "Heads of Complaint," which the Penns found highly objectionable, was based on a report made to the Pennsylvania Assembly by a seven-member committee on 22 February 1757. That report was saturated with Franklin's ideas, for six of the committee's seven members were his allies. The basic problem highlighted in the committee report and in the "Heads of Complaint" was that the Pennsylvania governors were unduly restricted by the proprietors' instructions. Because the proprietors were so far from the scene and could not authorize changes quickly, the king's cause had been damaged in time of war more than once. Also, the governors were too limited in the kind of money bills they could approve, and this, too, had interfered with the defense of the colony. Furthermore, the Assembly objected to the proprietors' insistence that their estates be exempted from taxation. Although Thomas Penn promised a speedy response to the "Heads of Complaint," it was well over a year before the agent received an answer. First, the Penns turned the negotiations over to their attorney, Ferdinand John Paris, a former Pennsylvania agent. Franklin regarded this proud man, a man well-known for his high fees and low tactics, as his mortal enemy. He refused to treat with Paris, insisting upon direct talks with the Penns. Paris, apparently hoping to slow the negotiations to a snail's pace, advised the proprietors to turn the "Heads of Complaint" over to the king's attorney general, Charles Pratt, and solicitor general, Charles Yorke, for a legal opinion regarding proprietary authority.[9]

That opinion was not forthcoming until early November 1758, and it was 27 November 1758 before Paris sent a reply to Franklin on the "Heads of Complaint." What Paris had to say—and Franklin justifiably considered it as unsatisfactory—was entirely predictable and should have required but a few days, or perhaps only hours, to draft. But now, after fifteen months, Paris could assert with the support of the Crown's legal advisers that the proprietors had every right to instruct their governors as they saw fit and that they could continue to do so. He and the Penns did not doubt this in August 1757, and surely they knew that Pratt and Yorke

---

[8]*Franklin Papers*, VII, 248-49; Thomas Penn to James Hamilton, 7 July 1757. Penn Papers, HSP.

[9]*The Autobiography*, 263-64; *Franklin Papers*, VII, 136-42, 142 n. 9, 247 n. 6, 251-52; VIII, 178-86.

would confirm their position. It is not surprising that Franklin suspected them of stalling.

Following his emphatic assertion of proprietary authority to instruct governors, Paris claimed the proprietors were badly hurt by the insinuation that "they would not contribute their Proportion to the Defense of the Province." While it was true, he said, that they would not allow their quit rents to be taxed, they had ordered £5,000 to be paid for the public service "out of the Arrears of that very Fund." The Assembly, the proprietors believed, had been "unjust and cruel" to accuse them of not contributing to defense simply because they had not done it in the way the Assembly demanded. They wanted harmony restored and the public service provided for, they claimed, but they reserved "the Right of disposing of their own Estate." They hinted that they might be willing to have their estates "enquired into" and to contribute their fair share to defense. Compromise was possible, they said, but only if the Assembly sent someone besides Franklin to negotiate—"some Person of Candor." The Penns left no doubt that in their eyes Franklin was *persona non grata.*[10]

The proprietors were unhappy with the Assembly's agent for several reasons. After he had submitted the "Heads of Complaint" to them and refused to negotiate with Ferdinand John Paris, Franklin, to the proprietors' way of thinking, had behaved obnoxiously while waiting for the Penns' answer. As news of events in Pennsylvania reached him (mainly through correspondence with Isaac Norris), he proposed that the proprietors take this action or that and make this concession or another. For example, Franklin contended that both Indian and military matters were being mismanaged in the colony, and he urged Thomas Penn to make some basic changes. Through the agent and in letters from people in Pennsylvania, the proprietor learned that a naval vessel that had been promised by the British government had not been sent to Delaware Bay to protect Pennsylvania's trade. When Penn petitioned the Admiralty about the matter, he was informed that "his Majesty's Frigate the Beaver" would soon be sent. The proprietor asked Franklin to inform the

---

[10]Ibid., VIII, 178-86; *Pennsylvania Colonial Records*, 16 volumes. (Harrisburg: State of Pennsylvania, printer Theo. Penn & Co., 1838–1853) VII, 276-81.

Assembly of this and expressed hope that the *Beaver* would furnish all the protection needed.[11]

While Thomas Penn gave the appearance of cooperating with the Assembly and its special agent, it was not long before articles criticizing Pennsylvanians in general and the provincial legislature in particular began showing up in the English press. Franklin was convinced that the proprietors were behind the negative articles, but his belief was never substantiated. William Franklin labeled the newspaper pieces "scandalous and malicious Falsehoods" and spoke of the "Obstinacy and Wickedness of the Proprietors" for having them published. Since the elder Franklin, still trying to negotiate with the Penns, could not answer the articles in his own name, he answered them through his son who published rebuttals in the short-lived newspaper called *The Citizen* and also the *London Chronicle*. In William's letters the proprietors came under attack for tax-dodging and maligning the Quakers in the Pennsylvania Assembly. The Quakers, his response contended, had in the past granted large sums of money for the "King's Use" (the Quakers' euphemism for defense funds) and had selflessly resigned from the Assembly in 1756 to keep from being stumbling blocks to the war effort. It was not the fault of the Quakers that military bills had failed but that of the proprietors who consistently forbade their governors to sign bills that taxed their estates. William Franklin was right; the proprietors had refused to budge even slightly on the tax issue, and they were continuing to maintain their intractable stance in early 1758. This would force the Assembly, because of the military emergency, to pass in the spring of 1758 a £150,000 Supply Bill that exempted the proprietary estates from taxation.[12]

By the early months of 1758 the proprietors, who never really wanted to negotiate with Franklin in the first place, were becoming thoroughly annoyed with him, while, at the same time, he was losing all patience with them. There was little doubt in the agent's mind that the Penns were stalling, even though they insisted that they were merely waiting to hear

---

[11]Isaac Norris to Benjamin Franklin, 17 October 1757, and 24 November 1757; Thomas Penn to Benjamin Franklin, 25 November 1757. *Franklin Papers*, VII, 264-70, 279-85; Thomas Penn to William Denny, 14 November 1757; Thomas Penn to William Allen, 12 January 1758. Penn Papers, HSP.

[12]*The Autobiography*, 265-66; William Franklin to Elizabeth Graeme, 9 December 1757; Isaac Norris to Benjamin Franklin, 29 April 1758. *Franklin Papers*, VII, 255-63, 288-92; VIII, 54-59.

from the attorney and solicitor generals. Thomas Penn argued that he and his brother made concessions and tried to cooperate, only to have Franklin make more and more demands.

In a sense it is remarkable that the Penn brothers carried on the pretense of negotiations as long as they did, for they differed fundamentally with Franklin on the rights Pennsylvanians had under the colony's charter. According to the agent, the Pennsylvania Assembly was to Pennsylvania what the British House of Commons was to Great Britain. Thomas Penn asserted that there was nothing in the Pennsylvania charter that granted the Assembly any such privilege. Franklin countered that the privilege was granted by William Penn in the 1701 Charter of Privileges. Thomas responded that the charter from the Crown had given his father no power to grant such privileges, and, if Pennsylvanians had been taken in by promises his father could not legally make, then that was their mistake. This statement infuriated Franklin, causing him to feel the utmost contempt for the proprietor and to liken him in a letter to Isaac Norris to a "low jockey" who laughed at a purchaser who claimed he had been cheated in a horse trade.

Franklin's enemies in the proprietary party back home obtained the letter, copied it, and sent a copy to Thomas Penn. Upon reading it, Thomas claimed that the agent had misrepresented their conversation and declared that he would no longer talk to Franklin "on any pretence." He also showed the letter to Lord Halifax who, as president of the Board of Trade, was a powerful force in the British government. The Penns, too, took note of the "many imprudent things" William Franklin had said in the press, but they resolved not to engage in a public war of words for fear of alienating the British ministry. "Let them write what they please," said an irate Thomas Penn of the Franklins' newspaper campaign.[13]

Amidst the Franklin-Penn negotiations, which soon resembled a feud more than diplomacy, the Pennsylvania agent was making himself fashionable by spending considerable sums at the wig-maker and tailor shops. He seems to have used Robert Christopher regularly as his tailor.

---

[13]Benjamin Franklin to Isaac Norris, 14 January 1758; Thomas Penn and Richard Penn to Benjamin Franklin, 28 January 1758; Benjamin Franklin to Joseph Galloway, 17 February 1758. *Franklin Papers*, VII, 361-64, 366, 370, 372-74; Hutson, *Pennsylvania Politics*, 46-47, 58-59; Thomas Penn to Richard Peters, 14 January 1758, 10 February 1758, and 13 May 1758; Thomas and Richard Penn to William Denny, 28 January 1758. Penn Papers, HSP.

He also spent a fair amount on wine and for the room and board of himself and his "Servants." After a few months of London's high prices, the £1,500 appropriated for him by the Pennsylvania Assembly prior to his departure from Philadelphia began to appear inadequate. Franklin already realized he would be in London far longer than he had anticipated at the time he undertook the mission. The Assembly said nothing about more money, but the agent carried on, confident that the assemblymen would provide just compensation when he completed his work and returned to Philadelphia.[14]

Blame for the agent's lack of progress was rightly laid at the proprietors' door. After writing to people in Pennsylvania about settling matters with Franklin at the earliest possible moment for the good of the colony, Thomas Penn began to hedge on the promise and defend the delays. On 14 November 1757, he wrote Richard Peters to say that Franklin had only been in London *a few months* and that members of the government were away on holiday. He hoped to hear from his majesty's legal experts soon and give the agent an answer by the end of the month. Why was Franklin in such a hurry? the proprietor wondered. Had he not been so sick for two months that he could not have settled matters even if the Penns had been ready? Penn professed to be puzzled by the anxiety of Franklin and his Pennsylvania allies over the delay in developments.[15]

Although various people told the Pennsylvania agent that matters involving the government took time and that the Penns were not necessarily stalling, he was highly skeptical. Writing to Joseph Galloway on 17 February 1758, Franklin said:

> My Patience with the Proprietors is almost tho' not quite spent. They continue to profess a sincere Desire of settling everything with the Assembly amicably on Reasonable Terms, but that they may act safely they would have the Attorney and Solicitor General's Opinion on some Points that relate to the Prerogative of the Crown . . .

---

[14]Benjamin Franklin, "Account of Expences of my Voyage to England, 1757–1762." Original manuscript, Library of the American Philosophical Society, 3, 5, 12, 26; Kammen, *Rope of Sand*, 48; J. Bennett Nolan, *Benjamin Franklin in Scotland and Ireland, 1759 and 1771* (Philadelphia: University of Pennsylvania Press, 1956) 13.

[15]Thomas Penn to [Richard] Peters, 14 November 1757. Penn Papers, HSP.

He made it clear to Galloway that he suspected a stall, but indicated that he could do nothing about it without being accused of "Rashness." For more than a month Franklin had felt utter contempt for Thomas Penn. To Galloway he revealed how furious he was by remarking that the proprietors deserved to be "gibbeted up" and left "to rot and stink in the Nostrils of Posterity."[16]

Franklin's patience, which was "almost . . . spent" in February, was completely exhausted by September. During the months following the agent's letter to Galloway, the Penns aired the quarrel between them and the Pennsylvania Assembly in public. This was brought about through an appeal to the Privy Council by the Reverend William Smith, the provost at the Philadelphia Academy and a strong Penn supporter. Isaac Norris informed Franklin in a letter dated 21 February 1758 that Smith, "Our old Inviterate Scribbler," had libeled the Assembly and was in jail for doing so. According to Norris, Smith had become "a Tool to narrow Presbyterian politicks."[17]

Franklin had met Smith a couple of years before undertaking his mission to England. The two men started out as good friends, but ended up as irreconcilable enemies. They worked together at the academy until a bitter quarrel resulted in Franklin's removal as president of the school's board of trustees. Thereafter he remained a member of the board, albeit one with little or no influence. By November 1756 the two men had stopped speaking to one another, and Franklin was convinced that he had made an enemy of Smith by "doing him too much Kindness."[18]

Smith's troubles with the Assembly began on 6 January 1758, when that body's sergeant-at-arms arrested him for publishing "The Humble Address of William Moore, One of the Justices of the Peace, for the County of Chester." Nineteen days later, on 25 January, Smith was tried for libeling the Assembly, found guilty, and incarcerated.

---

[16]Benjamin Franklin to Joseph Galloway, 17 February 1758, *Franklin Papers*, VII, 374.

[17]Isaac Norris to Benjamin Franklin, 21 February 1758. *Franklin Papers*, VII, 385-89, 385 n. 9, 386 n. 3.

[18]Benjamin Franklin to Ebenezer Kinnersley, 28 July 1759. *Franklin Papers*, VIII, 415-16; Ralph L. Ketcham, "Benjamin Franklin and William Smith: New Light on an Old Philosophical Quarrel," *The Pennsylvania Magazine of History and Biography* 88 (1964): 142-43, 153.

About two weeks after being jailed, Smith appealed to the King in Council and Parliament for relief. The Privy Council received his petition on the first day of April and ordered hearings on the matter for 20 and 27 April. Franklin, with help from his co-agents and several lawyers, managed the case for the Assembly, while the Penns brought out a team of lawyers, led by Ferdinand John Paris, to argue the case on Smith's behalf. Paris lost no time in turning the proceedings into something much bigger than a libel case. He heaped vituperation on the Pennsylvania Assembly, alleging that it was persecuting a well-meaning citizen to cover up its own transgressions. According to Paris, Smith was being oppressed by the Assembly's Quaker members because he advocated strong defense measures for the colony, while they opposed any kind of military action. The Penns' attorney went from that allegation to questioning some of the privileges that the Assembly claimed for itself.[19]

The attorneys hired by Franklin—Joshua Sharpe, George Perrot, and William de Grey—responded to Paris a week later, using information furnished them by Franklin and fellow agent Robert Charles. First, they pointed out that most of the Quakers had left the Assembly and that the Assembly of 1758 was largely non-Quaker. In fact, the Quakers who held seats were outnumbered two to one, and those who were there were in favor of defense measures. Second, the Assembly's attorneys, with Franklin providing the material, made it clear that Smith had a history of making intemperate remarks in public. Franklin called him "a common Dealer in Libels and Disturber of the public Peace, contrary to the Duties of his Profession." Although claiming to be a minister of the gospel, Smith had "no Charge as a Clergyman" and had been denied a pulpit in Philadelphia. The agent claimed that the Penns were taking up Smith's cause only because he had often attacked the Assembly and because they saw an opportunity to lay down a smoke screen to disguise the "true Cause of the Disagreement between the Governor and Assembly." The Penns, Franklin argued, had merely seized the chance to blame the Quakers and make the disagreement appear to be "a religious Dispute about the Lawfulness of Defence," when, in fact, they were only trying to keep their property from being taxed.[20]

---

[19]Benjamin Franklin to Thomas Leech and the Pennsylvania Assembly's Committee of Correspondence, 13 May 1758. *Franklin Papers*, VIII, 60. Also see: Ibid., VIII, 28-29, 31, 34.

[20]Ibid., VIII, 35, 42-47, 61-62.

During the hearings on the Smith case Franklin asked the highly respected attorney Richard Jackson, known popularly as "Omniscient" Jackson because of his vast legal knowledge, for his opinion on the constitutional questions raised by the Penns' attorneys on 20 April. Especially well-versed in the legal provisions of American charters, Jackson offered an opinion that must have comforted Franklin greatly. In so many words the famed attorney contended that the Pennsylvania Assembly had to have a voice in any constitutional changes that involved that colony. In view of the fact that the proprietors' lawyers were urging the Privy Council to curtail certain privileges claimed by the Assembly, Jackson's opinion was good news indeed. But would the Privy Council agree? Jackson argued further that Quaker rights, which were more extensive in Pennsylvania than England, could not be taken away except by the Assembly. On the matter of taxes he believed that the proprietors should pay them to help with the colony's defense and that they should pay on unimproved as well as improved lands. He even went so far as to say that the Penns should lose their right to govern the province, although he was convinced that the Privy Council would not agree with him. Jackson's opinions seemed to support Franklin's idea that the Assembly was to Pennsylvania what the House of Commons was to England. In all probability Franklin, or his lawyers speaking for him, made this assertion at some point during the proceedings, for Paris expected a ruling favorable to the Penns—one that would condemn Franklin's contention that the Pennsylvania Assembly had "as full powers as the House of Commons had."[21]

Not until 26 June 1759 did the Privy Council finally render a decision in the Smith case, ruling that the libel was aimed at an expired Assembly and that the newly elected Assembly had no right to act for its predecessor. Meanwhile, Smith had long since been released from jail and protected from re-arrest by Pennsylvania's chief justice, William Allen. In a sense the Smith affair was much ado about a small matter, one of little importance in Pennsylvania or England. In another sense, however, it represented a turning point in Franklin's mission, for the hearings before the Privy Council confirmed the agent in his hatred for the Penns. Henceforth he would seek the ouster of the proprietors as rulers of Pennsylvania and lobby for the establishment of a royal government. In

---

[21]Ibid., VIII, 6-27, 62 n. 3; Benjamin H. Newcomb, *Franklin and Galloway: A Political Partnership* (New Haven: Yale University Press, 1972) 51-52.

a letter of 16 September 1758 to Joseph Galloway, Franklin excoriated the proprietors for abusing the Assembly openly during the Smith affair. This he regarded as "an open Declaration of War." He no longer had any hope of "an Accommodation" with them, nor, since the hearings, had he "desired an Audience of them." He would wait for instructions from the Assembly on how to proceed, he told Galloway, but he already knew how he wanted to proceed—if the Assembly would support him. On the same day he wrote Galloway, Franklin also wrote Isaac Norris and expressed the conviction that the British ministry stood ready to relieve the Penns of the Pennsylvania government. The agent asked Norris what his sentiments were on the matter of *"getting rid of the Proprietary Government."* Did Norris think such a step would be *"generally agreeable to the People?"*[22] This was no new idea. Norris could hardly have been shocked by it, for it had been suggested before on several occasions, mostly by Quaker leaders during earlier battles with the proprietors. While it was not a new idea, it had never been suggested before by anyone as determined and shrewd as Benjamin Franklin.

Without waiting for Norris's reply regarding the sentiments of Pennsylvanians on royal government, the agent embarked upon a campaign to turn British officials and the British public squarely against the Penns. William Franklin, now a law student at the Middle Temple seeking admission to the bar, had to be more circumspect in his public utterances than he had been the year before, and so he could no longer lend his name and pen to his father's cause. The elder Franklin, therefore, took up the pen himself under cover of pseudonyms. In September 1758, writing as "A. B.", he used the *London Chronicle* to put twenty-nine questions to Lord Baltimore, Maryland's proprietor. Taxation of proprietary estates was an issue in Maryland just as it was in Pennsylvania. The Baltimores (or Calverts) attempted to make it appear that their estates were taxed on the same basis as the estates of all other Marylanders. Franklin's queries showed the claim to be a deception and then raised the issue of whether or not there should be an inquiry "into the nature and conduct of these Proprietary Governments" in order to "put them on a better footing."

---

[22]Carroll, "Franklin, Colonial Agent," 68; Benjamin Franklin to Joseph Galloway, 16 September 1758; Benjamin Franklin to Isaac Norris, 16 September 1758. *Franklin Papers*, VIII, 38 n. 4, 149-52; Hanna, *Franklin and Pennsylvania Politics*, 135. Also see: *Acts of the Privy Council of England*, 6 volumes. Colonial Series. (London: His Majesty's Stationery Office, 1908–1912) IV, 375-85.

What he hoped, of course, was that such an inquiry would put the Baltimores and, more especially, the Penns out of business as proprietors. These queries, as historian Verner Crane has rightly concluded, were nothing more than a flank attack on Thomas and Richard Penn.[23]

The queries in the *London Chronicle* marked only the first shots in Franklin's war against the proprietors. On 20 September 1758, and again on 6 February 1759, the Pennsylvania agent petitioned the King in Council concerning complaints the Delaware Indians and their chief, Teedyuscung, had against the Penns. The Indians were certain that the proprietors had defrauded them of considerable land through several tricky agreements, particularly the Walking Purchase of 1737. Franklin sided with the Delawares, but he did not stop at merely accusing the proprietors of theft. He argued that the proprietors' acts of "Jockeyship" had given the Indians the worst possible opinion of Englishmen and had been a major cause of the murders of whites by Indians during the current war.[24] Obviously Franklin, clawing after the Penns' jugular, was not being fair, for attributing murders in Pennsylvania to fraudulent land deals, some of which had been agreed upon twenty years earlier, was a vicious accusation that could hardly be proved.

The Privy Council referred Franklin's petition to the Board of Trade, which held a hearing on 15 May 1759. Franklin, represented by Joshua Sharpe, was there to face the Penns and their spokesman, Ferdinand John Paris. Just over two weeks later, on 1 June, the Board sent a report to the Privy Council, recommending that the matter be handed over for investigation to Sir William Johnson, the king's Indian agent north of the Ohio River. The report conceded that the Indians might have been cheated in Pennsylvania, as they had in other colonies, but the board members saw the whole matter of Indian lands and boundaries as a complex problem with no easy solution. Yet they hoped that somehow the Indians, who *were* British allies, might receive enough consideration to keep them on the British side.[25]

The results of William Smith's appeal in the spring of 1758 and Franklin's petition on behalf of the Delaware Indians at the end of the

---

[23]Crane, *Letters to the Press*, 3-7; *Franklin Papers*, VIII, 162-68; *London Chronicle*, 19 September 1758.

[24]*Franklin Papers*, VIII, 264-76.

[25]*Franklin Papers*, VIII, 379-89; Thomas Penn to [William?] Logan, 8 February 1759; Thomas Penn to Richard Peters, 10 February 1759. Penn Papers, HSP.

summer must have convinced the agent of something John Fothergill articulated to Israel Pemberton, Jr., about that time—namely, that Franklin's "obstructions" were next to "insurmountable," because "great pains had been taken and very successfully to render him odious." The people to whom he carried his appeals suspected the agent's integrity, and their suspicions could "only be worn off by time and prudence."[26]

By June 1758 Franklin knew he would be in England at least another year. Perhaps John Fothergill persuaded him that succeeding at his mission would require a great deal of patience—far more than he had demonstrated previously. Hence, Franklin, informed by his friends that little political business was conducted in London at the close of summer, made plans for some travel and relaxation. He and son "Billy" visited Cambridge where they were "kindly entertain'd" in "the Colleges." William was taking time off from his own studies at the Middle Temple. From Cambridge the Franklins journeyed into the Midlands, where they visited the ancestral homes of the Franklins and of Deborah's maternal forebears—the White and Cash families. They looked up relatives and made genealogical charts. Eyre Whalley, rector of Ecton parish in Northhamptonshire, gave them much helpful information on the "Francklines." At Wellingborough they visited Benjamin's cousin, Mary Franklin Fisher, who at age eighty-five would die before the year was over. In Banbury they met Robert Page who had been the husband of Jane Franklin, another cousin, and in the churchyard they found the grave of Thomas Franklin, Benjamin's grandfather. Slave Peter, who also made the trip, cleaned off tombstones in the search for the graves of the Franklins' relatives. At Birmingham, Benjamin and William talked to some of Deborah's relatives and found out as much as possible about them.

After seeking relatives and information about ancestors they headed south for Tunbridge Wells. Arriving there in mid-August, they joined Richard Jackson who frequented the fashionable spa. The elder Franklin remained at Tunbridge for two weeks, while his lawyer son and lawyer friend soon headed toward London. Located some thirty-six miles southeast of London, the vacation resort featured taking the waters, attending concerts, making excursions into the country, participating in promenades, and making frequent conversation. In a word, it was a place

---

[26]John Fothergill to Israel Pemberton, Jr., 12 June 1758, in Betsy C. Corner and Christopher C. Booth, eds., *Chain of Friendship: Letters of Dr. John Fothergill* (Cambridge MA: The Belknap Press, 1971) 195.

"to see and be seen." Franklin made it clear in a letter to Joseph Galloway that his summer activities in 1758 were undertaken to restore his health and "to improve and increase Acquaintance among Persons of Influence."[27] The ever-curious agent would take more trips during the next three summers, and his critics would accuse him of "parading" to "every nook and cranny of the realm while the provincial business suffered."[28] Such a charge was hardly valid, since Franklin traveled only when government officials abandoned London for their summer retreats.

Important developments followed Franklin's summer travels. William Franklin was "call'd to the Bar in Westminster Hall" on 10 November 1758. This happy event was quickly followed by disappointment, as Thomas Penn soon acknowledged that he had received the long-awaited legal opinion on the "Heads of Complaint" from the attorney general. In a letter to Richard Peters, the proprietor reported that he and his brother would presently give Franklin an answer to his "Paper." Their answer reached the agent via a letter from Ferdinand John Paris on 27 November. Franklin's response on the following day effectively ended his negotiations with the Penns. He asked probing questions, specific questions about the proprietary estates and what the proprietors meant with regard to having them "enquired into." When the agent made the mistake of noting in his response that he could settle nothing without first consulting with the Assembly, the Penns sent Paris in person to deliver their final word. Since Franklin was "not impowered to conclude proper Measures," they would deal directly with the Assembly and have no more correspondence with him. Paris reported that the agent looked disappointed when he was informed that the Penns' were slamming the door on further negotiations, but he said nothing.[29]

---

[27]Numerous letters that Franklin wrote to a variety of people, plus letters that some people wrote to him give considerable insight into his 1758 travels. See: *Franklin Papers*, VIII, 90-96, 114-15, 114 n. 4, 117-19, 120-21, 121 n. 3, 131-32, 131 n. 9, 132 n. 5, 133-47, 152-55, 152 n. 5, 172-74, 221-22, 288-89, 289 ns. 7 and 8, 414. Also see: Sheila L. Skemp, *William Franklin: Son of a Patriot, Servant of a King* (New York: Oxford University Press, 1990) 33-34.

[28]James H. Hutson, "Benjamin Franklin and the Parliamentary Grant for 1758," *William and Mary Quarterly* 23 (1966): 583.

[29]Benjamin Franklin to Jane Mecom, 11 November 1758; Benjamin Franklin to Thomas and Richard Penn, 28 November 1758. *Franklin Papers*, VIII, 172-74, 186-88, 187 ns. 1-3, 193-94; Thomas and Richard Penn to the Council of Pennsylvania, 10 November 1758; Thomas Penn to Richard Peters, 11 November 1758, and 8 December

The Penns' cutting off negotiations with Franklin amounted to little more than recognizing reality, for there had been no real negotiations for months. All that the two parties had been doing was going through the motions required by politeness and for the preservation of their respective public images. Each party seemed to be searching for a legitimate excuse for laying the blame on the other. Franklin had already verbally consigned the proprietors to perdition, and they were no less disgusted with him. Whether or not they had read Franklin's letter comparing Thomas Penn to a "low jockey" by 28 November is not ascertainable, but it is certain that they had seen it or heard about it by 9 December, when Thomas referred to it as "most infamous" in a letter to Benjamin Chew, one of the proprietors' staunch Pennsylvania supporters. On the same day, the senior proprietor wrote William Allen to say that he and his brother would confer with the Assembly's agents. They hoped, however, that Franklin, who was no longer acceptable to them, would not be reappointed to that post.[30]

As far as treating with the Penns was concerned, Franklin's usefulness in London was unquestionably over by early December 1758. He knew it and said so to Isaac Norris. If the Assembly wanted to continue negotiations with the Penns, it needed, said the agent, to send another person who was "more acceptable or more pliant." Franklin himself made it clear that he favored ending all talks and seeking a royal government for Pennsylvania. He waited to learn the pleasure of the Assembly, and, while he waited, he corresponded with relatives, lent his support to Dr. William Heberden (an English crusader calling for inoculation against smallpox), invested Isaac Norris's money in English banks, complained that his mail was being intercepted and read, made plans to use propaganda to improve Pennsylvania's image in the eyes of the British politicians, and schemed to undermine the Penns.[31]

Early in 1759 Franklin persuaded Richard Jackson to organize his thoughts on the Pennsylvania Charter and produce a pamphlet entitled *An Historical Review of the Constitution of Pennsylvania*. The agent arranged to have the pamphlet printed for the purpose of putting Pennsylvania in "a much fairer Light," but the 2,000 copies he had printed sold poorly in

---

1758, Penn Papers, HSP; *Pennsylvania Colonial Records*, VII, 299-300.

[30]Thomas Penn to William Allen, and Thomas Penn to Benjamin Chew, 9 December 1758. Penn Papers, HSP.

[31]See Franklin's letters to a variety of people in England and America, January-March 1759. *Franklin Papers*, VIII, 151, 223-24, 232-39, 281-86, 287, 290.

England and America. While the pamphlet seems to have had no measurable impact on public opinion, its joint production with Jackson did cement a long-lasting friendship between the two men. So close did they become that Franklin soon recommended the heralded barrister to be the successor to Richard Partridge, Pennsylvania's longtime agent who died on 6 March 1759, of "a suppression of urine." At this juncture, Franklin had become convinced that an agent should be a member of Parliament (which Jackson was about to be) and that he should have an assistant to do the "Drudgery of running about attending the Offices." Robert Charles, in Franklin's opinion, could do the legwork well enough.[32]

The attribute that probably recommended Jackson most to Franklin was his willingness to join in the frustrated agent's campaign to tarnish the public image of the Penns. Having failed so far to dent the Penns' armor, Franklin was willing to take help where he could find it and use all means at his disposal. He resorted mainly to his old ally, printed propaganda, smearing the proprietors for allegedly mistreating the Indians. Besides presenting Teedyuscung's claims about the Treaty of Easton and the Walking Purchase to the Privy Council, he had a pamphlet entitled *An Enquiry into the Causes of the Alienation of the Shawanese and Delaware Indians* published. Although several hundred copies of the work were sent to America, it was primarily produced for distribution in England. The pamphlet's author was Charles Thomson, a Franklin political ally in Pennsylvania. Thomson savagely attacked the Penns, and Franklin was convinced that his pamphlet helped correct the wrong impressions that the proprietors had made in England concerning their dealings with the Indians. According to the Pennsylvania agent, the Penn brothers had "artfully" misled such officials as Lord Granville and Lord Halifax. In addition to the Thomson pamphlet, Franklin saw to it that other damaging information about Indian affairs was published in the *London Chronicle*. This proved easy to do, since his good friend "Straney" was the newspaper's principal owner. While laboring to high-light the proprietors' alleged abysmal record in Indian relations, Franklin

---

[32]John Fothergill to Israel Pemberton, Jr., 9 April 1759. Corner and Booth, *Letters of Dr. John Fothergill*, 210; Benjamin Franklin to Isaac Norris, 19 March 1759; Benjamin Franklin to Joseph Galloway, 7 April 1759. *Franklin Papers*, VIII, 291-97, 309-10; Hutson, *Pennsylvania Politics*, 50-51.

worked hard to convince the British public that Pennsylvania had contributed its share and more to the current war effort.[33]

Franklin's attempts in the spring of 1759 to make the proprietors look
bad and Pennsylvania and its inhabitants look saintly marked the
beginning of his campaign to replace the propriety government of his
adopted colony with a royal one. His mind was made up. Proprietary rule
had to go. "For my Part, I must own that I am tired of Proprietary
Government, and heartily wish for that of the Crown," he wrote to Joseph
Galloway on 7 April 1759. The task before him was that of swinging
ministerial opinion in England and public opinion in Pennsylvania behind
him. Given the plodding, inefficiency, and often anti-American spirit that
Franklin had seen at work in the British government for a year-and-a-half,
one is compelled to conclude that the agent was moved by little more
than unalterable hatred for the Penns. In a letter to Isaac Norris on 19
March 1759, he told the Assembly's speaker that most of the current
powerful ministers—Granville, Hardwicke, and Halifax—were strict
adherents of the royal prerogative and thought the colonies had too much
freedom and too many privileges. All of them favored curtailing
American privileges and forcing the colonists to obey the king's orders
without question. There were some ministers, of course, who defended
the Americans, but the ones who made the decisions were more than a
little anti-American in their views. These same mixed views prevailed in
Parliament, where the ministry, Franklin admitted, could enact any
measure it was determined to carry.[34] Since Franklin knew all of this
about the British government, one must assume that he thought the respective agents of the colonies could change the attitudes of those in power
or that the next elections might bring into high office more people who
were pro-American. Throughout his years in London Franklin exhibited
a tendency to be overly optimistic about British politics. He seemed
always to believe that the next elections would put in power people who

---

[33]*Acts of the Privy Council*, IV, 402; Crane, *Letters to the Press*, 72-3; *Journals of the
Commissioners for Trade and Plantations, 1704-1782*, 14 volumes. (London: His
Majesty's Stationery Office, 1920–1938, XI, 32-36. (Hereinafter cited as *Journals of the
Board of Trade*.); Benjamin Franklin to Israel Pemberton, 19 March 1759; Benjamin
Franklin to Joseph Galloway, 7 April 1759. *Franklin Papers*, VIII, 297-300, 298 n. 7,
313-15, 333-38; Thomas Penn to Richard Peters, 10 May 1759. Penn Papers, HSP.

[34]Benjamin Franklin to Isaac Norris, 19 March 1759; Benjamin Franklin to Joseph
Galloway, 7 April 1759. *Franklin Papers*, VIII, 291-97, 315.

would see matters his way. In the spring of 1759 he wanted royal government for Pennsylvania, presumably because any other rulers would be better than the Penns. And, besides, the next election might well put Whitehall in the hands of men who sympathized with the colonists!

As Franklin mapped out his campaign to oust the proprietors in favor of royal government, the Assembly in Philadelphia was once more fighting with the governor over a supply bill. Again, it was taxation of the proprietary estates that blocked agreement. The Assembly passed a supply bill in the amount of £100,000 on 24 March 1759. Because it contained a provision for taxing the Penns' property, Governor Denny refused to sign it and returned it to the Assembly. A few weeks later, however, Denny offered to compromise, apparently because of pressure from General Jeffrey Amherst and, according to the proprietors and their supporters, because the Assembly bribed the governor. Whatever the reasons, Denny signed the Supply Act of 1759 on 17 April. The fact that the Assembly voted money for the governor's support at the same time he signed the Supply Act lent credence to the charge of bribery. The law did contain a provision for taxing the proprietary estates, but it also allowed credit for the gift of £5,000, which the proprietors made earlier. When word of the new Supply Act reached the Penns, they, acting on the advice of Ferdinand John Paris, petitioned for disallowance by the King in Council.[35]

Since it would take more than a year for the Privy Council to decide on the Penns' petition, Franklin found it necessary to remain in England. All chances for reaching an accommodation with the proprietors had vanished. Clearly he had failed in what he had been sent to do and would probably have felt compelled to return to Philadelphia in 1759, if it had not been for the controversy over the new Supply Act and if he had not fastened upon the opportunity to obtain Pennsylvania's share of a grant Parliament was about to make to the colonies for their support in prosecuting the French and Indian War. By April 1759 it was certain that Parliament would indeed make the appropriation (which it did on 30 April), and in a 7 April letter to Joseph Galloway, Franklin vowed to do whatever was necessary "to obtain a Share" of the grant. He warned, however, that the Assembly should not expect too great an amount, given

[35]Isaac Norris to Benjamin Franklin, 5 and 12 April 1759. *Franklin Papers*, VIII, 303-305, 311; *Pennsylvania Colonial Records*, VIII, 301-303, 318-20, 323-31, 353-62, 529-35, 554-55; IX, 10-11.

the depleted condition of the British treasury.[36] One can hardly escape the conclusion that Franklin was not ready to leave England in the spring of 1759, although his mission was over and was a failure. Indeed he was already on a new mission, a personal one, to overthrow the Penns, and it could be accomplished best in England—or so it appeared to Franklin at that moment. He needed valid reasons for remaining, and those reasons appeared in the form of the controversial Supply Act of 1759, which had to be defended before the Privy Council, and the Parliamentary grant of which Pennsylvania's share had to be secured and put to whatever use the Assembly determined.

Governor Denny had endeared himself to General Amherst and the Assembly by signing the Supply Bill of 1759 into law, but this deed and his subsequent cooperation with the Assembly deeply angered the proprietors. Denny's days in office were surely numbered. How could the Penns not have been suspicious and angry? After all, the Assembly *had* voted Denny £3,000 after he signed the Supply Act. Moreover, it was known that the governor had virtually retired to his forty-five-acre estate near the "Falls of the Schuylkill" River. Having been informed of all this, Thomas and Richard Penn were soon in search of a new governor. They found their man in former governor James Hamilton, a member of an influential Pennsylvania family, and a man long active in provincial politics. When the controversy over the Supply Act erupted, Hamilton was in England, having hand-carried the Reverend William Smith's petition to the Privy Council in 1758. He accepted a new governor's commission from the Penns in the summer of 1759, but he delayed his departure to America for several months. Not until 17 November 1759, did he appear in Philadelphia to assume office as the province's new governor.[37]

Almost two months before Hamilton arrived, the Assembly passed a bill on 26 September authorizing Franklin to take Pennsylvania's part of the Parliamentary grant and deposit it in the Bank of England. There it was to be subject to drafts and bills of exchange by the trustees who presided over the Pennsylvania Loan Office. Governor Denny signed the bill. When the Penns learned that Franklin had been named to manage

---

[36]Benjamin Franklin to Joseph Galloway, 7 April 1759. *Franklin Papers*, VIII, 326-27, 326 n. 4, 327 ns. 5-8.

[37]Isaac Norris to Benjamin Franklin, 31 July 1759, 22 August 1759, and 8 October 1759. *Franklin Papers*, VIII, 418-21, 421 n. 4, 427-30, 441-42.

Pennsylvania money over which they had no control, they were livid, and they immediately took steps to prevent the agent from receiving the money. They argued that it was improper for a man who had not been made agent by the "whole Legislature" to receive the province's money.[38]

Meanwhile, Franklin had worked through the spring of 1759, pursuing before the Board of Trade his petition in favor of Pennsylvania Indians. As business in London began to slow down with the onset of summer, the busy agent made plans for a trip to Scotland in early August. There were several reasons for the trip. Franklin's contributions in the field of electricity had prompted the University of St. Andrews to award him an honorary Doctor of Laws degree in February 1759. The degree had arrived at Craven Street by mail, totally unexpected. Now the Pennsylvania agent wanted to go in person to thank the university faculty for honoring him. Also, because of his friendship with William Strahan, he knew he could meet and converse with the great and near great men of Scotland, most of whom were "Straney's" personal friends. And, finally, Franklin was naturally curious to visit a country he had heard and read so much about but had not seen. As he prepared to make the journey northward, he had his and "Billy's" wigs refurbished and had his tailor make him a new suit.[39]

Just before the two Franklins and slave Peter set out, William learned that a woman with whom he had been keeping company was carrying his child, but this news did not deter the younger Franklin from his travels. Benjamin rented a chaise and off they went northward through Staffordshire and Derbyshire, down the Carlisle Road leading to Edinburgh. Once in Edinburgh the Franklins were soon in the company of printers, book dealers, and some of Scotland's greatest intellectuals. They visited with the likes of David Hume, the renowned Scottish philosopher, Lord Kames, one of Britain's brightest legal minds, Adam Smith, the incomparable economic thinker, and Sir Alexander Dick, Scotland's foremost physician—to name a few of the Scottish luminaries they met. One particularly fortunate contact made by the Pennsylvania agent was Dr. William Robertson, who would later become the "Principal" of the Uni-

---

[38]Hutson, "The Parliamentary Grant for 1758," 579; Thomas Penn to Richard Peters, 10 May 1759, and 3 August 1759. Penn Papers, HSP; *Pennsylvania Colonial Records*, VII, 524, 546-47, 552.

[39]Nolan, *Franklin in Scotland and Ireland*, 43-44, 49-51, 55-60, 62-63, 90; Skemp, *William Franklin*, 35-36.

versity of Edinburgh. Robertson was a highly esteemed historian who quickly became enchanted with the philosopher from Philadelphia. Because of the friendship that developed between the two men, Franklin was able during the ensuing years to obtain honorary doctorates for his American friends and to secure admission to the university's medical school for the sons of his Pennsylvania cronies. Besides Robertson, Franklin became bosom friends with two of the other Scots previously mentioned—Alexander Dick and Lord Kames. He and William were invited to be house guests at the homes of both men, and the elder Franklin carried on a regular correspondence with them for many years.[40]

In addition to meeting many of the Scottish elite and forming fast friendships with some of them, Franklin received several honors during his visit to Scotland. He was accepted into membership by the Guild Brethren in both Edinburgh and St. Andrews. Also, while in St. Andrews thanking the university for his honorary doctorate, he was formally invested with the doctorate and was the honored guest at a reception following the ceremony. When Franklin went to Glasgow he made friends with a number of faculty members who taught at the city's university. One of these new friends was the eccentric Professor John Anderson. Disdained by his colleagues because of his contempt for them, Anderson warmed to the Franklins and became their guide and traveling companion on their travels through the Highlands.[41]

After his pleasant trip to Scotland, which Franklin always remembered fondly, the Pennsylvania agent returned to London in late October or early November to deal with the petition concerning the Delaware Indians and to obtain the money coming to Pennsylvania from the Parliamentary grant. Tranquility had prevailed during his absence, for as late as 13 October Thomas Penn had written to James Hamilton, "The Offices continue shut up and no business will be done 'til the beginning of next Month, when I shall devote my whole time to oppose the several Bills [i.e., objectionable bills passed by the Pennsylvania Assembly and signed into law by Governor Denny], and Mr Franklin if he makes any motion."[42]

---

[40]Labaree, "Franklin's British Friendships," 426; Nolan, *Franklin in Scotland and Ireland*, 43-44, 49-51, 55-60, 62-63, 90; Randall, *A Little Revenge*, 156; Skemp, *William Franklin*, 34-35, 38.

[41]Nolan, *Franklin in Scotland and Ireland*, 49-51, 70-74, 76-79, 83.

[42]Thomas Penn to James Hamilton, 13 October 1759. Penn Papers, HSP.

The proprietor was prepared for a fight to the finish with the Pennsylvania agent whom he had come to detest. Franklin was no less ready to do battle. The war resumed. For the next ten months it raged between the Penns, represented first by Paris and then upon his death by Henry Wilmot, and the Pennsylvania Assembly, whose spokesmen were Benjamin Franklin and the battery of lawyers he retained. Franklin had failed in his attempt to settle matters with the Penns by negotiation, and now he was determined to defeat them in the councils of Whitehall as a prelude to depriving them of their power to govern Pennsylvania. Ever devious in his schemes, he made no public mention of his ultimate objective. That he shared with no more than a few intimate friends and with most of them only by innuendo.

# 3. "Alterations and Amendments":
## An Uneasy Compromise

As Franklin braced himself for the monumental struggle with the Penns in the closing months of 1759, he must have found his Craven Street residence a little less interesting. Polly Stevenson, his admirer and devoted disciple, had moved away in May to Essex to live with her Aunt Mary Tickell, a lady of means who apparently intended to leave her money to Polly—if Polly continued to please her. Hence the move to Essex, but Polly and Franklin corresponded regularly. He recommended books for her to study and wrote her in great detail on a variety of scientific subjects. She responded with her impressions of the books and his writings, in addition to offering commentary of her own regarding religion and philosophy. Franklin affectionately called her his "dear little Philosopher."[1]

The Pennsylvania agent doubtlessly needed a diversion of the sort that his correspondence with Polly provided in 1760, for it turned out to be a year of virtually constant contention. Not only was he engaged in a bitter fight with the proprietors over matters of great importance to Pennsylvania, he also involved himself in a great national debate. The issue was whether Britain should make peace with France without regard to advantage or whether the British ministry should demand Canada or the West Indian sugar island of Guadeloupe. On 24 November 1759, the *London Chronicle* published Franklin's "A Description of Those Who at Any Rate Would have a Peace with France," an article that condemned the peace-at-any-price advocates as "selfish wretches" and "enemies to their Country." The incensed agent claimed that the "sordid Views" of such people were rooted in a "lust for Power."[2]

Not only did Franklin want Britain to dictate the peace with France, he argued that the now almost-conquered Canada should not be restored

---

[1]Roger Burlingame, *Benjamin Franklin, Envoy Extraordinary* (New York: Coward-McCann, 1967) 38-39; letters between Benjamin Franklin and Mary Stevenson, beginning 4 May 1759. *Franklin Papers*, VIII, 338-40; IX 102-103, 117-22, 125, 247-52, 264-66, 297 n.8, 338-39.

[2]Crane, *Letters to the Press*, 13-16; *London Chronicle*, 27 December 1759.

to France under any circumstances. He worked hard to sway public opinion to his point of view. His first effort in the cause was a tongue-in-cheek article signed "A. Z.". It appeared in the *London Chronicle* on 27 December 1759. Entitled "Humorous Reasons for Restoring Canada," the piece asserted that retaining Canada would only mean an increase in British trade, too many beavers available for making beaver hats for Quakers, the prevention of future expensive wars, and a decrease in Indian massacres. The matter could be settled easily and simply, A. Z. contended, by halting military action immediately and not completing the conquest of Canada.[3] Of course, Franklin knew that few Englishmen would tolerate the idea of permitting France—already down on one knee—to stand up again to fight another round.

In less than a fortnight after Franklin's "Humorous Reasons" appeared in the *Chronicle,* he wrote his friends John Hughes in Pennsylvania and Lord Kames in Scotland to say that he was busy every day and everywhere, resisting the view that Canada should be returned to France. He believed he was having some success in overcoming the contention that Canada was too large to populate and not worth possessing. He told Lord Kames that the French would continue to harass the British colonies along the Atlantic seaboard if they were allowed to keep Canada. On the other hand, if the French were forced to relinquish Canada, British people would fill the country from the St. Lawrence River to the Mississippi within a century. Trade would expand, and British influence would "spread round the Whole Globe, and awe the World."[4]

By April 1760 Franklin was deeply involved in the debate over Canada. Writing anonymously (but not successfully hiding his authorship) he produced a pamphlet called *The Interest of Great Britain Considered,* which soon came to be known as the "Canada Pamphlet." In this fifty-eight-page effort Franklin drove home his conviction that Britain must keep Canada and forget any thought of returning it to France. He offered many reasons for such a course, which, he believed, was the only one that made sense. As long as French colonies bordered British colonies the

---

[3]Crane, *Letters to the Press,* 13-16; *London Chronicle,* 27 December 1759.

[4]Benjamin Franklin to Lord Kames, 3 January 1760; Benjamin Franklin to John Hughes, 7 January 1760. *Franklin Papers,* IX, 5-10, 13-15.

In this letter to Kames, Franklin raved about his visit to Scotland, praising Scottish hospitality and calling his stay "Six Weeks of the *densest* Happiness I have met with in any Part of my Life."

peace would be constantly in jeopardy, for "the refuse of both nations lived on the frontiers" and their low morals and lack of discretion would lead perpetually to hostile encounters. British possession would remove this potential for war. Moreover, the Indian threat would be reduced if the French were no longer in Canada to incite them to strike and then provide them with a place of refuge.[5]

Besides giving reasons for retaining Canada, Franklin refuted the arguments of those who wished to give it back to France and demand Guadeloupe instead. He also attacked the oft-repeated assertion that Great Britain had rushed to the rescue of the colonies and had spent untold blood and treasure to save them. On the contrary, it was the colonies, Franklin contended, that had been drawn into a British war in which they now fought for the glory of Great Britain.[6] On this point Franklin was being a little deceptive. Although British policy had prompted Governor Robert Dinwiddie of Virginia to send young George Washington into western Pennsylvania in 1754 to challenge French expansion there, the war began as an American war (at least in part for the benefit of Virginia land speculators) and remained one for two years before it became part of the much larger European conflict in 1756.

The combative agent also challenged British critics who contended that Americans would expand economically, produce their own manufactures, and leave British manufacturers without an American market if they no longer had to depend upon the mother country for protection from the French. Franklin claimed that America's abundance of land would keep the colonists from ever engaging in manufacturing to an extent great enough to threaten Britain in that area. He denied the assertion of many who claimed that the colonists, with the French gone, would spread out in all directions and become less dependent upon Britain. Franklin insisted that it would take many years for Americans to occupy the vast quantities of land west of the Appalachians. In the meantime, the

---

[5]Verner W. Crane, *Benjamin Franklin: Englishman and American* (Baltimore: Published for Brown University Press by The Williams & Wilkins Company, 1936) 90-93; *Franklin Papers*, IX, 47-110; [Benjamin Franklin], *The Interest of Great Britain Considered With Regard to her Colonies and the Acquisitions of Canada and Guadeloupe.* Second Edition. (London: Printed for T. Becket, at Tilly's Head near Surry-Street in the Strand, 1761) 1-15. Located in the Rare Book Room, Perkins Library, Duke University.

[6]Ibid., 16-17.

multiplying colonists would consume British goods, thus increasing British trade enormously.[7]

The Pennsylvania agent made it clear under his very thin cloak of anonymity that he was not unalterably opposed to taking Guadeloupe and capitalizing on its sugar production. He was sure, however, that the immediate returns would be far less than some expected, since the sugar planters would still be French and would continue to sell to their established connections. Those connections, of course, were French. Hence, Frenchmen would continue to reap the benefits of the sugar business in Guadeloupe, at least in the short term.[8]

The Canada Pamphlet, not surprisingly, produced strong reactions both pro and con. On 26 April 1760, the *London Chronicle* published a highly favorable review of it, but on 8 and 17 May the same newspaper published pieces that were harshly critical of the pamphlet's arguments. Among other things, the anonymous author was berated for making no distinctions between the colonies in different areas of North America. One critic insisted that the northern colonies (from New York northward) were in competition with Great Britain in the West Indian trade. He further charged that Americans engaged constantly in an illegal, clandestine trade with the French islands. Finally, the critic maintained that the prosperity of the northern colonies stemmed in large measure from British troops, who were stationed in those colonies during the war.[9] The controversy, set off mainly by Franklin's pamphlet, became intense, producing at least sixty-five pamphlets and countless newspaper articles and letters. Franklin's anonymity was short-lived. His identity as author of the Canada Pamphlet had already been divulged sometime before the agent wrote David Hall, his partner, on 27 June 1760, to say that the pamphlet had sold extremely well in England and that he had "gain'd some Reputation by it." Franklin hoped above all, he assured Hall, that the pamphlet would promote the cause of the colonies.[10]

Just how much support Franklin won in England for the American view is impossible to determine. Surely Dr. William Thomson of

---

[7]Ibid., 18, 24-25, 33.

[8]Ibid., 46-49.

[9]*Franklin Papers*, IX, 107-110.

[10]Ibid., IX, 179. The entire text of the Canada Pamphlet, along with helpful notes, can be found in the *Franklin Papers*, IX, 47-110. Insightful comments can also be found in Crane, *Letters to the Press*, 89-91.

Worcester, who wrote Franklin in November 1760 to praise the pamphlet, was only one of many readers swayed by the agent's arguments. Many purchased the pamphlet (at least several thousand), but how many readers were convinced by it could never be more than a matter of conjecture— even if the exact number of readers was known. Dr. Thomson certainly believed it and expressed the hope that powerful English officials would read the pamphlet and take heed. Franklin hoped for the same result, for that was his purpose in writing it. William Franklin, interestingly enough, was not altogether pleased with his father's handiwork. He approved of the pamphlet's purpose, but he disliked the fact that his father, in order to please "a Friend" (probably Richard Jackson), had directed a compliment toward Lord Halifax. William conceded that he would have to consider the gesture beneficial if it caused Halifax to view the colonies in a more favorable light; yet, at the same time, he hated the "Appearance of Flattery."[11]

A year after the Canada controversy reached its zenith, Benjamin Franklin was still attacking those who were willing to accept disadvantageous terms in return for a quick end to the war with France. Just prior to leaving for Holland in August 1761 the Pennsylvania agent-turned-propagandist, claiming support for his views from "all ranks and degrees," called for a "vigorous prosecution of the war, in preference to an unsafe, disadvantageous peace." He expressed his now well-worn sentiments under the pseudonym of "A Briton" in the 13 August issue of the *London Chronicle.*[12]

Simultaneously with playing the role of propagandist for the purpose of preventing an Anglo-French peace that would be detrimental to American interests, Franklin was battling the proprietors before British officials at Whitehall. At issue were nineteen laws passed by the Pennsylvania Assembly between 20 September 1758 and 19 October 1759, when Governor Denny had proved so cooperative. The proprietors objected to eleven of the laws. Two of them—the Supply Act, which taxed the proprietary estates, and the Agency Act, which placed Benjamin Franklin in charge of the funds from the Parliamentary grant—were, as previously noted, totally unacceptable to the Penns. Representing the proprietors in seeking the Crown's disallowance of the eleven undesirable laws was

---

[11]William Franklin to Joseph Galloway, 16 June 1760; William Thomson to Benjamin Franklin, 18 November 1760. *Franklin Papers*, IX, 123-24, 243-44.

[12]*Franklin Papers*, IX, 342-47; *London Chronicle*, 13 August 1761.

Ferdinand John Paris until his death on 16 December 1759. At that point the Penns turned to Henry Wilmot, whose efforts were supplemented by Attorney General Charles Pratt and Solicitor General Charles Yorke. The death of Paris caused the proprietors to delay in pressing the matter of disallowance until February 1760. Once the wheels of the bureaucracy finally began to turn, Franklin was occupied for seven straight months—until 2 September—with case preparations, various hearings, and waiting for a final decision.[13]

Presenting Pennsylvania's case before the Board of Trade, with Franklin and Robert Charles looking on, were William de Grey, Richard Jackson, and Francis Eyre, a highly respected barrister from Gloucestershire. Eyre prepared the case; De Grey and Jackson presented it to the Board. They argued that all nineteen laws were legally proper and necessary for the welfare of the colony. Hence, the Board should recommend their approval to the Privy Council. Counsel for the Penns, meanwhile, argued that eleven of the laws infringed on proprietary rights and privileges in some cases and on the royal prerogative in others. Eyre diligently urged the Board to consider the Agency Act separately from the other eighteen laws, as Franklin was eager to obtain the money allotted to the colony by the Parliamentary grant so that he could invest it to advantage at the earliest possible moment. Unfortunately, the attorney from Gloucestershire was unsuccessful in his plea.[14]

Although initial contact with the Board was made first by Eyre on 16 February 1760, and by Henry Wilmot on 13 March, the actual hearings were held on 21, 22, 23 May, and 3 June. Debate on the all-important Supply Act of 1759 took up most of the first two days, the other eighteen acts being discussed on 23 May and 3 June. On 5 June the Board deliberated on the laws and ordered a report, which was sent to the Privy Council on 24 June.[15] The report spent the first thirteen pages asserting the royal prerogative, which Charles Pratt had harped on at length throughout the debates. According to the attorney general, the Pennsylvania Assembly had ignored royal instructions and avowed democracy in its legislative actions. He even accused William Penn of setting a dangerous precedent earlier in the century when he had made allowances in the Charter of Privileges for a permanent assembly. Pratt argued that

---

[13]*Franklin Papers*, VIII, 178-83, 193-94, 264-76, 379-39, 432-33; IX, 131-73.
[14]Ibid., IX, 22-23, 125-28.
[15]Ibid., IX, 128-30.

this concession should now be repealed. The Board, convinced that Pratt was at least partly right, vigorously reaffirmed royal authority in colonial affairs. Even so, the report stopped short of recommending any reduction in the authority or privileges of the Pennsylvania Assembly. After its lengthy comments on the royal prerogative, the Board's report went on to furnish background information on the disputed Supply Act, pointing out that the proprietors were taxed retroactively by the act—on all "Supplies since 1755," not just the amount to be raised for 1759 and 1760. The report further noted that the proprietors were allowed credit for the £5,000 gift they had previously made toward the military effort. Members of the Board agreed with the proprietors that unlocated and unimproved proprietary lands should not be taxed and that the Penns should participate in choosing and instructing those who would assess the taxes. Since the Act of 1759 taxed *all* proprietary estates and gave the Assembly complete control over the assessors, the Board recommended disallowance of the statute on the ground that approval would result in "a Capital injustice" to the proprietors.[16]

With regard to the Agency Act, the other law of particular concern to the proprietors, the Board rejected the arguments of the Penns' counselors and recommended the statute's approval, asserting:

> . . . the interest, not only of the Province, but the Publick in General will be more effectually promoted by letting this Act be carried into execution, than by suffering the Money intended for the Encouragement of this Colony to lie useless in the Treasury, whereby the Publick Service may be retarded.[17]

As for the remaining seventeen laws, the Board recommended the disallowance of five and the approval of twelve. Although the Board's report indicated some victories for Franklin, particularly the recommendation regarding the Agency Act, its general tone should have caused the agent to exercise caution in pressing for royal government in Pennsylvania. Five men signed the report, which, in general, was more than a little critical of the Pennsylvania Assembly. One of the five was Lord Halifax, self-appointed champion of making the royal prerogative preeminent in colonial affairs. He and his four colleagues contended that

---

[16]Ibid., IX, 125-46.
[17]Ibid., IX, 165-67.

the Assembly had a consistent record of making serious encroachments against the prerogative and of making extraordinary claims to rights and privileges. The report noted that the proprietors, too, were culpable in the matter of the prerogative, for they had shown too little concern for protecting it until "their interests were affected as individuals." Finally, the report urged the Crown to take steps to "restrain the Powers of the Assembly" and "protect likewise the Rights of His Majesty."[18] Since the Board of Trade was tremendously influential in determining colonial policy and since, at this juncture at least, it was so prerogative-oriented, Franklin's unquenchable desire to oust the proprietors in favor of royal government was almost certainly rooted in his personal hatred for Thomas and Richard Penn—especially Thomas. After this report to the Privy Council from the Board of Trade, the incensed agent could hardly think that the Pennsylvania Assembly could expect any more consideration at Whitehall than it received from Spring Garden.

The Privy Council received the Board's report on 26 June, but not until 2 September did the King in Council render a verdict. In the nine-week interim Thomas Penn expressed his opinion of the report, as did Benjamin and William Franklin. Unfortunately the elder Franklin's letters to Isaac Norris on this matter have been lost, and so there is no direct evidence of his reactions. Yet, from William Franklin's comments in a letter to Joseph Galloway, one can ascertain the sentiments of the Pennsylvania agent with a reasonable degree of certainty. He obviously considered the Board's attitude a clear threat to Pennsylvania, for, according to William, Benjamin wrote William Pitt "imploring his protection for the Province." It is highly unlikely that the father disagreed with the son, who condemned the attorney general and the solicitor general for speaking on behalf of either side during the Board's hearings on the Pennsylvania laws. William pointed out that when the case finally reached the Crown, those two officials would be asked for their opinions. As advocates for the Penns, how could they give the Crown anything but a biased view? The younger Franklin saw this as a clear conflict of interest and labeled Pratt and Yorke a "Pack of d____d R____ls," who would favor the party offering the biggest bribe.[19]

Not surprisingly, Thomas Penn's reaction to the Board's report was more positive than negative, although he was irked by the accusation that

---

[18]Ibid., IX, 170-73.
[19]William Franklin to Joseph Galloway, 26 August 1760. Ibid., IX, 189.

he and his brother were not attentive enough to upholding the royal prerogative. He was pleased with the overall tone of the report, for it confirmed in no uncertain terms what he had earlier pointed out to Benjamin Franklin—namely, that the Pennsylvania Assembly claimed powers and privileges that were not granted in the charter the Crown had given to William Penn. Although the Board had endorsed the Agency Act, at least it had recommended disallowance of the Supply Act, in apparent agreement with the proprietors on the issue of taxing the proprietary estates. In the matter of proprietary powers and privileges—a matter no less dear to the Penns' hearts than the taxation of their estates —the Board had sided with the proprietors. Generally, Thomas Penn was pleased with the Board's recommendations.[20]

As the Franklins and Thomas Penn spoke their minds on the Board's report, they were already preparing for the next round. Since the Privy Council would have the final say, the fight was only half over. On 4 July 1760, Francis Eyre petitioned the King in Council for a hearing so that his clients could voice their objections to the Board of Trade's report. He then collaborated with De Grey and Jackson on a plan for presenting the case.[21]

Meanwhile, the Privy Council's Committee for Plantation Affairs had begun its review of the case. On 15 July the committee asked the attorney general and the solicitor general if the Crown could disallow objectionable clauses in acts without disallowing the entire statute and if such disallowance would take place immediately. The two royal legal advisers replied that standard procedure required approval or disallowance of the entire law, but exceptions were possible. Franklin was annoyed by the committee's raising the question of partial disallowance, and so were the proprietors. Yet it turned out to be a moot question, since the Privy Council took no such action.[22]

The final hearing on the Pennsylvania laws took place before the committee (not the whole Privy Council) on 27 and 28 August at the Council office in an area of Whitehall known as the Cockpit—a place that, nearly fourteen years later, would become indelibly stamped in Franklin's mind because of another hearing he would be required to

---

[20]*Franklin Papers*, IX, 130-31; Thomas Penn to James Hamilton, 5 June 1760, and 27 June 1760. Penn Papers, HSP.

[21]*Franklin Papers*, IX, 196-98.

[22]Ibid.

attend there. Representing the two sides were the same attorneys who had argued the case before the Board of Trade. Franklin claimed that Lord Mansfield, who had been a minister without portfolio in the Newcastle administration and was then chief justice of the Court of King's Bench, approached him when the hearing ended and that the two men worked out a compromise regarding the taxation of the proprietary estates.[23] Although some have doubted the accuracy of Franklin's story of the compromise, there is no compelling evidence for discounting the story entirely. Perhaps the agent oversimplified the train of events and remembered some of the details inaccurately, but in its essentials the account he gave is credible.

On the basis of the Board's report and the hearing before the Committee for Plantation Affairs, the King in Council issued the final order on 2 September 1760. Of the eleven acts opposed by the proprietors, six were disallowed. Thirteen of the nineteen statutes, including the all-important Supply Act of 1759 and the Agency Act, were allowed to stand. The Agency Act had already received the Board's endorsement and could not be disallowed anyway because the six-month limit within which the Privy Council was required to act had expired. Of some consolation to the proprietors was the fact that the order condemned the Supply Act as "fundamentally wrong and unjust" and allowed it only if six "Alterations and Amendments" were added. These included the compromise that, according to Franklin, was worked out by him and Lord Mansfield. The agreement was that Franklin and Robert Charles would persuade the Pennsylvania Assembly to pass an amending act incorporating the "Alterations" prescribed by the Privy Council and then sign with the Penns a statement to the effect that both sides would abide by the amended version of the Supply Act. The amending act required by the Order in Council was to: (1) define with precision all lands to be taxed so that unsurveyed waste lands would not be taxed, (2) assess the located uncultivated lands of the proprietors no higher "than the lowest Rates at which any located uncultivated Lands belonging to the Inhabitants shall be assessed," (3) designate all lands in towns and boroughs not granted by the proprietors as uncultivated and not as lots, (4) require the governor's approval of every issue and application of money raised under the Supply Act, (5) provide for commissioners to hear appeals from the

---

[23]Ibid.

inhabitants and the proprietors, and (6) insure that payments by tenants to the proprietors remain fixed according to the terms of the grants as if the Supply Act had never been passed.[24]

The "Alterations and Amendments" was supposed to bring final resolution to the dispute between the Pennsylvania Assembly and the proprietors over the taxation of proprietary property. But did it, in fact, resolve anything? Would the Assembly honor the pledge given by Franklin and Charles? The answer was: eventually "yes," immediately "no." The proprietors had come to realize during the Board hearing that their tax-dodging days were over, for on 12 April 1760, Governor James Hamilton, a man they could count on to defend their interests at almost all costs, had signed a Supply Act that included the taxation of the proprietary estates. Although Hamilton signed the bill with "Ill Grace," according to Isaac Norris, he did sign it. By doing so he foredoomed any further chance for the proprietors to evade paying taxes on their Pennsylvania property. Denny's succumbing to political pressure in 1759 was one thing; Hamilton's knuckling under less than a year after assuming the governorship was quite another. All the proprietors could do henceforth was work to keep the Assembly's tax bite from being too deep. The amendments required by the Privy Council indicated that their attorneys achieved that objective. Over the next several years the proprietary forces in Pennsylvania argued with opponents of the proprietors about the meaning of the amendments, especially amendment 2. Several land bills passed the Assembly, only to be rejected by the governor for not meeting the requirements laid down by the Privy Council. Not until 1764, when Benjamin Franklin was back in the province and serving as speaker of the Assembly, did the provincial legislature pass the amending act that he and Charles had promised in the summer of 1760 to recommend. Meanwhile, Thomas Penn's insistence that amendment 6 be strictly enforced turned many in Pennsylvania against him and played an important part in the Assembly's decision to support Franklin's quest for royal government.[25]

Historians have differed in their assessment of Franklin's efforts to defend Pennsylvania's nineteen laws at Whitehall. One has called the

---

[24]Ibid., IX, 198-202, 205-208; Randall, *A Little Revenge*, 164-65.

[25]Isaac Norris to Benjamin Franklin, 15 April 1760, and 28 July 1760. *Franklin Papers*, IX, 43-46, 181. Also see: IX, 198-202; Hutson, *Pennsylvania Politics*, 71-77, 87-92; Thomas Penn to James Hamilton, 30 August 1760, and September 1760. Penn Papers, HSP.

outcome a "shallow victory," while another has branded it a failure. Franklin himself considered it a partial victory, but certainly not a "shallow" one. In a letter to Lord Kames, the agent noted that the litigation had "at length ended, and in a great degree to our Satisfaction." To people in Pennsylvania he reported that Lord Mansfield had acted as a friend of the Assembly. Thomas Penn learned of this claim and strenuously denied it. He insisted that the chief justice sought to "do us justice" and extend "the King's prerogative at both ours and the Peoples cost by & by."[26] Franklin, however, was convinced that he and the Assembly had received more than a half loaf. After all, the proprietors would at last pay something in taxes, and, in spite of the limits that applied because of the compromise, the fact that they would have to share in the cost of defending the colony was a victory—even if the size of the victory was clearly debatable. Furthermore, thirteen of the nineteen laws—about two-thirds of them—were allowed to stand. Finally, the Privy Council's failure to disallow the Agency Act, so heartily despised by the Penns, was a victory of huge proportions for Franklin and the Assembly.

Although Thomas Penn had no desire to mend his relations with Franklin following the verdict of the Privy Council, the proprietor was fully aware, at last, that he was not dealing with some unlettered provincial who could be taken lightly. Consequently, Penn, through his new lawyer, Henry Wilmot, was soon asking favors of Franklin. He had Wilmot approach the Pennsylvania agent and ask him not to present to the Board of Trade any laws from the Assembly without first discussing the matter with the proprietors' attorney. When Wilmot sought Franklin out, he claimed that word had reached the Penns of a shift in the Assembly's attitude toward the proprietors, and they were eager to be accommodative. The Pennsylvania agent was favorably impressed with Wilmot (anybody was an improvement over Paris!), but he responded that he would follow the instructions of the Assembly in all matters. If it ordered him to present laws without prior discussion, he would do it. If, on the other hand, the matter was left to his discretion, Franklin said he would "try" to confer with Wilmot. Their meeting was held at Franklin's Craven

---

[26]Benjamin Franklin to Lord Kames, 27 September 1760. *Franklin Papers*, IX, 231; Hanna, *Franklin and Pennsylvania Politics*, 137, 145; Newcomb, *Franklin and Galloway*, 67;   Thomas Penn to James Hamilton, 12 December 1760. Penn Papers, HSP.

Street residence on 11 May 1761, and the agent regarded it as conciliatory.[27]

Why Franklin made the slightest effort to be conciliatory is a mystery in view of the fact that Thomas Penn was erecting every barrier he could to prevent the agent from receiving and investing Pennsylvania's money from the Parliamentary grant of 1759. At first glance it appeared that handling the Parliamentary grant would be a simple matter. Parliament appropriated £200,000 to be apportioned among the colonies to reimburse them for their expenditures in the colonial military campaign of 1758. What could be more simple than Pennsylvania receiving its share and then deciding how to use it? But simple it did not turn out to be, for the grant served to widen the political breach between the proprietors, who wanted some control over the money through the governor and his Council, and the Assembly, whose members insisted that the Assembly alone should spend or invest the funds. The stage was set almost immediately for still another bitter struggle, as the Assembly attempted to give control of the money to its agent in London, while the proprietors worked diligently to keep the money out of Franklin's hands. Not one but several agency acts had to be passed, and a second Parliamentary grant in 1761 (for the 1759 and 1760 campaigns) further blurred the political picture.

The grant of 1759 allotted Pennsylvania and Delaware (designated "the Lower Counties") money jointly for assistance to General James Abercromby's 1758 campaign. Pennsylvania's share was £29,902 and eight shillings for furnishing 2,446 men, while Delaware's was £3,090 and twelve shillings for supplying 281 men. In both cases certain fees had to be taken from the amounts to pay people at the British Exchequer. A member of the Barclay family—a well-known Quaker banking family of London—received and managed Delaware's share. Franklin, following a struggle with the Penns, finally obtained Pennsylvania's allotment and invested the funds—unwisely according to the proprietors in London and their supporters in Pennsylvania.[28]

---

[27]Henry Wilmot to Benjamin Franklin, 8 May 1761; Benjamin Franklin to Henry Wilmot, 9 May 1761. *Franklin Papers*, IX, 314-15, 318, 318 n. 7; Thomas Penn to Richard Peters, 13 June 1761. Penn Papers, HSP.

[28]Benjamin Franklin to Isaac Norris, 19 November 1760, and 22 November 1760; Isaac Norris to Benjamin Franklin, 27 February 1760. *Franklin Papers*, IX, 28, 28 n. 7, 241-42, 242 n. 11, 244-46, 245 n. 2, 335, 335 n. 2; Thomas Penn to Richard Peters, 8

Isaac Norris and the Pennsylvania Assembly prepared the way, or at least thought they did, for Franklin to receive the grant money when they passed the Agency Act in September 1759. Signed by Governor Denny, the statute instructed the Pennsylvania agent to deposit the money in the Bank of England and excluded the proprietors from having any part in the disposition of the funds. The Penns were furious, of course, and, as previously discussed, sought the act's disallowance. Immediately, Thomas Penn found out that the Bank of England would not receive the funds from Franklin and then allow the trustees of the Pennsylvania Loan Office to draw upon them according to the Agency Act's provisions. Hence, one of the proprietors' arguments for disallowance had been that the law could not be "complied with." The Board of Trade, of course, had agreed in part with the Penns, but with a view to the greater good of the province had endorsed the Agency Act. The Privy Council, as indicated earlier, had allowed the act to stand by taking no action on it within the time limits required. This meant that Franklin was free to receive the money after 2 September 1760. Yet he could not follow the Assembly's instructions because the Bank of England's rules prevented him from doing so. If he deposited the money there, he, and not the trustees of the Pennsylvania Loan Office, would have to draw upon it.[29]

When Franklin did receive the money on 4 November 1760, he deposited it in the Bank of England in his name and reported the situation to the Assembly. Several times the Assembly attempted to pass a new agency act with revised instructions. Governor Hamilton refused to sign the new bills. In the midst of this donnybrook over the Agency Act, Robert Charles resigned as Pennsylvania's regular agent, apparently because the Assembly had not commissioned him as co-manager of the money in the original act. Franklin offered half of his £60 commission to his fellow agent, only to have Charles reject the offer and ask the Assembly for a separate commission equal to Franklin's. The Assembly attempted to accommodate Charles, but Governor Hamilton insisted that any new agency bill give him and the proprietors a share in disposing of the grant. Charles, seemingly unhappy over being unable to obtain the

December 1759; Thomas Penn to James Hamilton, 8 and 12 December 1760, and 9 January 1761. Penn Papers, HSP.

[29]*Franklin Papers*, IX, 186 n. 4, 241-42, 242 n. 1, 244-46, 245 n. 2; Hutson, "The Parliamentary Grant for 1758," 582.

commission he thought was rightfully due him, wrote Isaac Norris on 16 October 1760, to say that he was resigning as agent.[30]

Since the Assembly could control the Parliamentary grant only under the Agency Act of 1759 and could obtain no new legislation to change its original instructions, control of the money, at least temporarily, rested with Franklin. Neither he nor the Assembly wanted the money sitting idly in the Bank of England, bearing no interest. The bills that Governor Hamilton refused to sign, and the resolutions adopted by the Assembly and sent to Franklin by Isaac Norris indicated to the agent that he and the Assembly were thinking along similar lines. Consequently, between December 1760 and August 1761 Franklin invested the funds. He purchased stock, which had a face value of £30,000 even, for the price of £26,900, nineteen shillings, and eight pence. His critics would soon accuse him of acting without legal authority and of mismanaging the money because, unfortunately for Franklin, his plunge into the murky waters of British financial markets resulted in a loss of several thousand pounds.[31]

Although the loss incurred through Franklin's investments seems to have been no fault of his, no one could make his detractors believe that. Actually the shortfall was caused by poor timing on the Assembly's part, along with the agent's inability to communicate quickly with that body's speaker. Following the investment of the funds, the Assembly empowered trustees Charles Norris, Thomas Leech, and Mahlon Kirkbride of the Pennsylvania Loan Office to issue bills of exchange against Franklin for money owed by the province. The value of the stock purchased by the agent plummeted in late 1761, when Britain broke off negotiations with France. Until that happened, it was assumed that the stock would soon rise to its face value of £30,000. In anticipation of that development, the Assembly had instructed the trustees to draw on Franklin for the entire amount. As soon as he learned of this, the agent hurriedly warned Charles Norris and Thomas Leech in a letter of 17 November 1761 that the stock

---

[30]Isaac Norris to Benjamin Franklin, 5 October 1760. *Franklin Papers*, IX, 175, 233-34, 332 n. 1; Hutson, "The Parliamentary Grant for 1758," 585-87; Kammen, *Rope of Sand*, 45; *Pennsylvania Colonial Records*, VII, 512-13; George Edward Reed, ed., *Pennsylvania Archives*, Volumes 1-12. Fourth Series. (Harrisburg: State of Pennsylvania, 1900–1902) III, 36-37.

[31]Isaac Norris to Benjamin Franklin, 22 October 1760. *Franklin Papers*, IX, 236-39, 236 n. 7, 335, 335 n. 2; Hutson, "The Parliamentary Grant for 1758," 583-85.

would bring only £23,837 and ten shillings, if it had to be sold before peace was made. Instead of the gain Franklin had expected, there would be a loss of more than £3,000. If the trustees did go ahead and draw on him, they should not, he warned, draw more than he was able to produce. The trustees did go ahead, and he was forced to sell the stock at an unpropitious time. He sold to the best advantage possible, but buyers were hard to find, and the drafts came faster than Franklin was able to find buyers. When the drafts totaled more money than the agent had at his disposal, he sought help from two banking houses—Sargent, Aufrere & Co. and John and David Barclay.[32]

By the time this disaster occurred, a second Parliamentary grant—the grant of 1761 for the 1759 and 1760 campaigns—had been announced. The Pennsylvania Assembly, following a compromise with Governor Hamilton, had named the two banking firms which had come to Franklin's rescue as the depositories for the new funds. Franklin proposed that the two banking houses cover the overdrafts made against him by the trustees and let the anticipated funds from the new grant serve as collateral for the loans made to him. The Barclays, under pressure from the Penns, refused to help the agent. Sargent, Aufrere & Co., however, came to Franklin's rescue again. Although John Sargent, one of the principal partners, chose not to follow the agent's suggested scheme, he did lend him the needed funds in Franklin's name with the expectation that the Assembly would stand behind its man in London. Not only did the firm lend Franklin the money he needed, but, because the partners were so impressed with him, they pledged gold medals each year to the Philadelphia Academy's two best scholars. Since the medals were the fruit of Franklin's efforts, William Smith, who had already approached the firm for a contribution, was suspicious of the bankers' motives. The Pennsylvania agent was deeply grateful to Sargent, Aufrere & Co. for the generous loans to him, as well as the gold medals pledged, and he promised to "express fully" his "Sentiments of it to our Friends" in Pennsylvania.[33]

Altogether Franklin's investments resulted in a net loss of £3,979, nine shillings, and eight pence. Justifiably, he blamed the loss on bad

---

[32]The long and involved correspondence concerning this matter is in the *Franklin Papers*, IX, 383-84; X, 3-6, 3 ns. 1 and 4, 4 n. 9, 5 n. 5, 7-10, 12-13, 27, 30, 143-45, 143 n. 8, 144 n. 9.

[33]Ibid (all sources cited).

timing: "A more unlucky Time could not have been pitch'd upon to draw Money out of the Stocks here, for it was in the midst of the Damp thrown upon them by the Breaking off the Negociations for Peace, the Resignation of Mr. Pitt, and the entring into a new War with Spain."[34]

For most of two years, 1761 and 1762, there was controversy in Pennsylvania over Franklin's handling of the Parliamentary grant. Yet Isaac Norris gave his approval to the agent's actions, expressing confidence in Franklin's abilities as an investor. At the end of September 1761 Norris informed Franklin that the Assembly, too, seemed well satisfied with the way he had managed the granted funds. Norris, himself, continued to send his own money for the agent to invest. Even so, because of the controversy surrounding the grant of 1759, the Assembly chose to handle the grant of 1761 differently. The compromise it worked out with Governor Hamilton provided that the funds would be deposited in two banks, one chosen by the Assembly and one by the proprietors. The Assembly picked Sargent, Aufrere & Co., while the proprietors selected John and David Barclay. As it turned out, "the Lords of the Treasury" did not release the money until the summer of 1762, just as Franklin was preparing to return to Philadelphia. William Allen, who sat gloating in Pennsylvania, boasted that keeping the controversial agent from laying hands on the grant of 1761 was "a matter to which I did not a little contribute."[35]

Obviously Franklin was extremely busy during the years 1760 to 1762 carrying out his duties as Pennsylvania's agent, but still he managed to become involved in countless other matters. The list is long and impressive. He became a member of Bray's Associates, an auxiliary organization of the Anglican Church founded by Thomas Bray to promote education and missionary work among Negroes and Indians in the British Empire. As a member, Franklin played an active role in planning for the establishment of three Negro schools in the mainland colonies. At the same time, he continued as an active member of the Royal Society. He also, as deputy postmaster general of the colonial post office, had to tend

---

[34]Benjamin Franklin to the Trustees of the Loan Office. 13 February 1762. *Franklin Papers*, X, 33-36, 34 n. 1; Hutson, "The Parliamentary Grant for 1758," 587-95.

[35]*The Burd Papers*. Extracts from Chief Justice William Allen's Letter Book. Selected and arranged by Lewis Burd Walker. (n. p., 1897) 49; see several letters from Isaac Norris to Benjamin Franklin. *Franklin Papers*, IX, 113-14, 114 n. 6, 310, 331-32, 331 n. 9, 357-62, 370-71; Thomas Penn to James Hamilton, 9 January 1762. Penn Papers, HSP.

to post office business from time to time. Upon the death in 1761 of William Hunter, Franklin's longtime co-director of the postal system, the Pennsylvania agent worked hard to prevent a replacement from being named to Hunter's post so that he could be *the* postmaster general. In this he failed, as Lord Bessborough, who directed postal affairs, accepted the recommendation of Lt. Governor Francis Fauquier of Virginia and named John Foxcroft, Fauquier's secretary, to replace Hunter. Franklin believed that the colonial post office was a model of efficiency because of the direction he had given it for twenty-four years, and he was not happy with Bessborough's decision. Even so, he made no outward protest, deciding to make the best of the situation.[36]

As Franklin worked on various projects he kept ever before him his objective of ousting the proprietors as rulers of Pennsylvania. Sometime in 1761 he met a young man named Springett Penn who happened to be the great-grandson of Pennsylvania's founder. Springett was descended from William Penn's first marriage; his great grandmother was Gulielma Maria Springett. Thomas Penn was Springett's great uncle, or, more accurately, his great half-uncle, since Thomas was William's son by his second wife, Hannah Callowhill. Springett seemed to believe that Uncle Thomas was trying to cheat him out of Springettsbury Manor, young Penn's estate in Yorke County, Pennsylvania. When Springett hinted at this to Franklin, the Pennsylvania agent had no trouble believing it and soon set out to prove that Springett, as a descendant of William Penn's first marriage, had a better claim to the proprietorship of Pennsylvania than did Thomas and Richard, who were *merely* sons of the second marriage. One wonders if the well-read agent got the idea from Louis XIV, who had made a similar claim in 1667 when asserting his wife's birthright to the Spanish Netherlands. Whatever the origin of the idea, Franklin kept toying with it and trying to promote it until Springett's death in 1766.[37]

[36]Ruth L. Baker, *Dr. Franklin, Postmaster General* (Garden City NY: Doubleday, Doran and Company, 1928), 69-71; *Franklin Papers* IX, 12-13, 20-21, 70-71, 363-364, 378-79; Maurice J. Quinlan, "Dr. Franklin Meets Dr. Johnson," *Pennsylvania Magazine of History and Biography* 73 (1949) 34-39; William A. Whitehead and others, eds. Volumes I-XLII. *New Jersey Archives* (Newark and other NJ cities: New Jersey Historical Society, 1880-1949) IX, 265-70.

[37]Benjamin Franklin to Edward Penington, 9 May 1761, and 12 January 1762. *Franklin Papers*, IX, 261-62, 315-17, 326; X, 6, 6 ns. 6, 9, and 11.

Besides business and business-related matters, Franklin found time to do things he enjoyed. For instance, he took time to "invent" the "armonica," a musical instrument which produced sounds from turning glasses touched by the moistened fingers of the musician. The great Mozart wrote compositions for the instrument, and professional concerts were given on the armonica. Franklin also continued his travels periodically, going to western England and Wales in the fall of 1760 and to the European continent in the summer of 1761. The latter trip he took in the company of his son William and his now close friend Richard Jackson. The three men left London around 15 August and, for about five weeks, toured Holland and what was then known as the Austrian Netherlands (now Belgium). Although the trip was enjoyable, there was reason to hurry back to London in September, for King George II had died the year before, and young George III's coronation was scheduled for 22 September. Franklin, aware that this would probably be the one chance in his lifetime to witness a coronation, was determined not to miss it. Hence, he was in the crowd that Tuesday in September when the procession began at the upper end of Westminster Hall and "continued through New Palace-yard, Parliament-street, and so round to the west door of the abbey to the choir, where his majesty was crowned." Someone gave Franklin an even better ticket than the one he had purchased, for he was able to see the "whole Ceremony in the Hall, and to walk in the Procession quite into the [Westminster] Abbey."[38] The experience was truly unforgettable for a colonial American who at that point in his life gloried in the British Empire.

In spite of his many activities, Franklin found time to write letters fairly regularly to people in Pennsylvania—his wife, David Hall, Joseph Galloway, and numerous others—to say that he would return soon. Finally, in the spring of 1762, following the fiasco brought on by the premature sale of the stock purchased with money from the Parliamentary grant, it was indeed time to go home. There were many preparations to be made for the return trip, but near the end of April Franklin took time out to go to Oxford University, where the American philosopher and scientist was awarded another honorary doctorate (Doctor of Civil Law). William Franklin, too, was favored with an honorary Master of Arts

---

[38]*The Annual Register, 1758-1790*, IV (1761) 215-42; *Franklin Papers*, IX, 211 n. 9, 231, 231 n. 7, 337, 348, 348 n. 3, 356, 364-65, 367-68; Randall, *A Little Revenge*, 166-67, 169.

degree. Young William's star was on the rise, as he would soon be installed as the royal governor of New Jersey and would wed Elizabeth Downes, a thirty-year-old aristocratic beauty who was the daughter of a Barbados sugar planter. The elder Franklin chose not to remain in England long enough to witness either event, since he was apparently miffed at William for not pursuing the hand of Polly Stevenson (sometimes called "Virgin Mary"). The Pennsylvania agent certainly had little to say about his son's appointment as governor, and Miss Downes was not first among those to whom he said farewell before sailing. As for William's appointment, it apparently came through his and his father's connection with Dr. John Pringle, who was chummy with the new king's mentor and confidant, Lord Bute. The post was secured after the surmounting of some obstacles associated with William's illegitimate birth.[39]

Whatever his reasons, Benjamin Franklin was not present to witness perhaps the two biggest events in his son's life. He was ready to leave England. Almost certain that he was leaving London "forever," he had many good-byes to say, but there would be no need for one to his old friend James Ralph, for Ralph had died on 24 January 1762. Some of his good-byes were highly emotional, especially the one to and from his "dear Polly," whom he had hoped would "become his own in the tender Relation of a Child"—a dream William had now shattered. The departing agent felt deeply about leaving his dear friend "Straney," and Strahan was no less moved at the thought of a separation that was "likely to be endless." As difficult as leaving was, Franklin had to go. Richard Jackson took charge of Pennsylvania's affairs, and near the end of August— William's wedding to Elizabeth Downes took place on 4 September!— Franklin ended his five-year stay in England, sailing home aboard the *Carolina*, commanded by Captain James Friend. On 1 November 1762, the *Carolina* docked at Philadelphia.[40] Franklin's mission was over.

---

[39]See Franklin's numerous letters to Deborah Franklin, David Hall, Joseph Galloway, and others, 1759–1761. *Franklin Papers*, VIII, 448-49; IX, 15-17, 37-40, 273-77, 401-402; X, 59, 76-78, 78 n. 2, 146-47, 147 n. 7, 151; Randall, *A Little Revenge*, 173, 178-79, 181; Skemp, *William Franklin*, 35-39.

[40]Benjamin Franklin to Mary Stevenson, 7 June 1762, and 11 August 1762; Benjamin Franklin to William Strahan, 20 July 1762; Mary Stevenson to Benjamin Franklin, 5 August 1762; William Strahan to David Hall, 10 August 1762. *Franklin Papers*, IX, 404, 404 n. 9; X, 102, 115-16, 115 n. 1, 132-33, 140-43; John B. Shipley, "Franklin Attends a Book Auction," *Pennsylvania Magazine of History and Biography* 80 (1956): 37-45.

Although a return to England to settle his account with Thomas Penn was certainly on Franklin's mind, he could not have known that the Assembly could be persuaded to go along with his plan. It would take two years to bring that body around to his way of thinking, but in 1764 the Assembly would send him on a second mission to London, where he would take up residence again at his home away from home on Craven Street.

Franklin's first mission came under intense scrutiny, first by contemporaries and subsequently by historians. Some of the latter have judged it a failure, while some of the former concluded that Franklin was much more attentive to his own interests than to those of Pennsylvania. Governor James Hamilton accused the agent of needlessly putting Pennsylvania to great expense and accomplishing nothing other than securing honorary degrees for himself and his son and landing a governor's post for William. Sarcastically the governor called these "no small acquisitions to the public and therefore well worth paying for." Wild rumors circulated—even in Boston—about what a ducal salary Franklin made as Pennsylvania's agent.[41]

In appraising Franklin's five-year mission in London, one is drawn first to what seems an obvious conclusion: the agent had his successes and failures. He surely failed to bring the Penns and the Assembly together through negotiations, but that was Thomas Penn's fault as much as Franklin's. With at least partial success he defended the Supply Act of 1759 before the officials at Whitehall and thus paved the way for the taxation of the proprietary estates—something that the proprietors had successfully resisted for years. Franklin also outmaneuvered the Penns on the issue of the Parliamentary grant of 1759, only to suffer financial losses because of the Pennsylvania Assembly's poor timing in demanding the funds. Although serving as a propagandist for the American colonies was not directly related to his mission, some of the views he expressed anonymously on various imperial issues, such as whether to retain Canada and to hold out for an advantageous peace, prevailed. What has been overlooked in assessing the mission is the fact that Franklin's work as agent revealed his devious nature. Because he came to despise Thomas Penn during their meetings, he committed himself to work for the overthrow of proprietary rule in favor of royal government. This he did

---

[41] Benjamin Franklin to Josiah Quincy, 8 April 1761; James Hamilton to Jared Ingersoll, 8 July 1762. *Franklin Papers*, IX, 298-300, 299 n. 1; X, 112-13.

knowing that a royal regime might well restrict Pennsylvania's freedom of action far more than proprietary rule did. Not one word did he utter to Pennsylvanians about the risks of royal government. Regardless of the risks to the province's liberty, the Penns had to be forced from power. Franklin had made up his mind, and he would say whatever he had to say and do whatever he had to do to achieve their ouster.

# 4. "Malice and Ill Nature": Franklin's Return to Philadelphia

Benjamin Franklin had been away in England for more than five years when he stepped from the ship at Philadelphia on 1 November 1762 to virtually a hero's welcome. People met the boat and cheered him; later a steady stream of Philadelphians flowed to his house to greet him. A month earlier he had been elected in absentia to a seat in the Pennsylvania Assembly. The excitement over his homecoming contradicted the reports that Franklin's bitter enemy, William Smith, had spread in England that all but a few of the agent's friends in his adopted home city had abandoned him. Perhaps Smith had engaged in some wishful thinking.

The returning agent reached home with two items heavy on his mind: returning to England as soon as he could arrange to do so, and persuading the Assembly to seek the replacement of the proprietors with a royal government. There can be little doubt that Franklin wanted to go back to London. Early in December—just over a month after returning home—he wrote William Strahan to say "let me find you well and happy when I come again to England; happy England."[1] He promised to have his affairs settled in such a way as to enable him to go in "two Years at farthest." Although he indicated that his moving to England depended upon convincing "the good Woman to cross the Seas," his tone leaves little doubt that he planned to go—with or without Deborah. Strahan was not the only one who was alerted to expect Franklin back. "Dear Polly" Stevenson wrote her teacher in August 1763 that he made many in London happy by "the hopes" he gave them of his "Return to England." She left posterity to wonder about her relationship with Franklin when she added, "I should be unfashionable if I did not wish for you here, but I have a nearer concern than most; all *esteem* you, it is only the favour'd few that can love you as I do."[2] One can readily understand how some historians have suggested the possibility that Franklin's relationship with

---

[1]Benjamin Franklin to Richard Jackson, 2 December 1762, and Benjamin Franklin to William Strahan, 2 and 7 December 1762. *Franklin Papers*, X, 160-62, 166-67.

[2]Benjamin Franklin to William Strahan, 7 December 1762; Mary Stevenson to Benjamin Franklin, 30 August 1763. Ibid., X, 169, 334-35.

Polly was not altogether platonic or merely a mentor-to-pupil one. To draw such a conclusion from the above quote alone, however, requires an overly active imagination.

Strahan continued to receive assurances that Franklin would return to London. On 28 March 1763, the former agent wrote to say he would see the London publisher before Strahan looked "much older." At home in Philadelphia, Franklin was devious about his plans for the future. To his family and friends he said nothing about returning to England. Deborah's aversion to sea travel and the fact that Franklin made plans to build a house when he had always rented previously convinced William Franklin that his father would never see England again. William, it appears, did not know his father as well as he thought he did, for the evidence strongly suggests that the elder Franklin was determined to return to England. The house he was planning to build on Market Street was for Deborah and Sally—and for him *only if* he decided to come back to Philadelphia again. He longed to be once more in the land where one neighborhood contained "more sensible, virtuous and elegant Minds" than one could find in America by "ranging 100 Leagues of our vast Forests." He went so far as to tell Strahan that he intended to put his affairs in such order that there would be no need for "another Return to America."[3] If Deborah and Sally would not accompany him (and Deborah was apparently adamant), they could be comfortable in a new house on Market Street, while he returned to Craven Street.

Before going back to England, however, Franklin had objectives to achieve, not the least of which was selling the idea of royal government to the Pennsylvania Assembly. So far he had expressed himself on the matter only to Isaac Norris and Joseph Galloway, neither of whom had responded enthusiastically. Clearly he had work to do, for his campaign in England against the Penns had produced few results, and there was certainly no groundswell of support for royal government in Pennsylvania during the closing months of 1762. Franklin would have to bide his time and wait for a propitious moment. Given the history of Pennsylvania politics, such a moment was bound to come, and, when it did, Franklin would be ready to seize the opportunity.

---

[3]Benjamin Franklin to Mary Stevenson, 25 March 1763; Benjamin Franklin to William Strahan, 28 March and 8 August 1763. Ibid., X, 232, 237, 237 n. 5, 320; XI, 453-56.

Meanwhile, Benjamin Franklin would occupy his seat in the Assembly and take care of his business as deputy postmaster general of the colonies. Upon returning to the Assembly he was faced with defending his reputation, for there were those in the legislative body who "industriously reported" that Franklin had lived extravagantly in England and squandered money from the Parliamentary grant for 1758. Such charges could scarcely be supported in view of the fact that the returning agent claimed only £714, ten shillings, and seven pence in expenses for the five years he resided in London. He returned what was left of the £1,500 that the Assembly had given him in 1757. Astonished at how little Franklin had spent, the Assembly refused to accept what he offered to return and paid him £2,214 and ten shillings—for a total of approximately £3,000 salary and £714 in expenses. Thus, just over £3,714 was the cost of his five-year mission.[4] Since regular agents were paid £100 to £200 per year, it would seem that Franklin was handsomely rewarded, but most agents were Englishmen who lived in England all the time and worked as agents only part-time. The printer-politician-turned-agent worked full-time and served far away from home for more than five years. Under the circumstances, Franklin being awarded more than ordinary remuneration does not seem so unreasonable.

The Assembly was highly pleased with Franklin's work as agent, thanking him for it and his many other services to Pennsylvania. He responded graciously. The Assembly's thanks, said Franklin, was "far above every other Kind of Recompence." Pleased that he had been fully exonerated of the charges of high living, he was convinced that the circulators of the report had been shown to be liars. Interestingly enough, one of the members of the Committee of Accounts was Chief Justice William Allen. He, along with the other members, signed the committee report that found Franklin's expense account to be just, but this did not keep him from resurrecting the charge of extravagance the following year. When Allen's inconsistency was pointed out, he pled forgetfulness, saying he forgot he had signed the report.[5]

With the matter of his expenses cleared up, Franklin could turn his attention to other business, although he remained quite active in the

---

[4]Franklin's Report to the Pennsylvania Assembly's Committee of Accounts, 9-19 February 1763; Benjamin Franklin to William Strahan, 28 March 1763. Ibid., X, 193-97, 206-207, 236, 238.

[5]Ibid.

Assembly. Feeling more kindly now toward son William and his new bride, both of whom arrived in Philadelphia on 19 February 1763, Franklin went with them to New Jersey to help William launch his career as royal governor. After seeing his son's inauguration, Franklin visited friends and relatives in New England and began to take care of his duties as deputy postmaster general. Post office business took him southward to Virginia and then to the middle colonies and New England in the company of John Foxcroft, successor to the deceased William Hunter. The two deputy postmasters general became close friends, and they worked well together.[6]

Upon his departure for England in 1764 Franklin would confidently leave management of the post office to Foxcroft, assisted by James Parker, who became "Comptroller." Parker's position eventually required him to move to New York City. With great reluctance he gave up his printing business in New Jersey, but Franklin's wish seemed to be Parker's command. There is no evidence that Franklin promised Parker the job of deputy postmaster general in America if the Pennsylvania agent successfully landed the important post office position in England for which he himself was angling. Parker might have known, however, that Franklin had urged the banker John Sargent to use his influence with Lord Egmont, the postmaster general in England, to help the Philadelphia philosopher secure the desired appointment. If Franklin had become deputy postmaster general in England, his logical successor in America would have been Parker. "The Doctor," as Franklin was more and more frequently being called, might well have imagined such a scenario. It was not to be, however, for Lord Egmont had already resigned as postmaster general to become first lord of the admiralty, even before Franklin asked Sargent to intervene on his behalf.[7] Parker was surely disappointed if he expected to replace Franklin, but this expectation or, perhaps, simple loyalty kept him doing Franklin's bidding for years.

Besides occupying himself with post office business in 1763, Franklin also devoted considerable thought and energy to speculation in land. In seeking a large grant of American land west of the Appalachians, the former Pennsylvania agent expected to work closely with John Sargent and Richard Jackson. The famed British attorney succeeded Franklin in

---

[6]Butler, *Franklin, Postmaster General*, 97, 125 127.

[7]Ibid.; John Sargent to Benjamin Franklin, 8 November 1763. *Franklin Papers*, X 362-65, 365 ns. 2 and 3. Also see: Ibid., X, 153-431, *passim.*

the spring of 1763 as Pennsylvania's "sole Agent" at a salary of £200 per annum—the combined salaries of former agents Richard Partridge and Robert Charles. Franklin and Jackson had discussed a colonization scheme before Franklin left England to return to Pennsylvania. Indeed, Franklin had dreamed of founding a western colony since 1754, and in 1756 he had invited evangelist George Whitefield to join him in the venture. Richard Jackson, now representing Weymouth in Parliament, could be very helpful, Franklin believed, in securing the land grant needed to make the philosopher's dream of a western colony a reality. With the French and Indian War over and the peace made in 1763, the former agent wrote Jackson to ask, "What think you now of asking for a Slice of Territory, to be settled in some manner like that I once propos'd?" He went on to say, "You know there was a Scheme between Mr. Sargent, Sir Matthew Featherstone, and myself, of obtaining a Grant in America, thro' some interest of theirs." Franklin wanted Jackson to have a share, and also Dr. John Pringle, but Pringle showed no interest in the scheme. There was an "unaccountable *Penchant* in all our People to migrate westward," Franklin reported—a strong hint that such a venture in colonization could not help but be profitable.[8]

After he returned to Pennsylvania late in 1762, Franklin's attention was first brought back to the matter of western land by Samuel Finley, president of the College of New Jersey. When a young man named James Lyon, a graduate of Finley's institution, approached the president early in 1763 with "a Scheme for a Settlement on the Mississippi," Finley sent him to Franklin, asking the latter to advise the young man, who was said to be of good character. Franklin soon became suspicious of Lyon and was convinced that someone else was really behind the scheme. He called Lyon's proposal "very crude" and labeled some of its details as "quite absurd." Lyon was eager to act quickly before someone else started the colony. After the initial contact and a letter from Lyon, Franklin apparently dropped the matter by ignoring the young man. Lyon himself

---

[8]Benjamin Franklin to Richard Jackson, 8 March and 11 April 1763. Ibid., X, 209, 214-15, 214 ns. 2 and 3, 246-47; David T. Morgan, "An Unlikely Friendship, Benjamin Franklin and George Whitefield," *The Historian* 47 (1985): 217-18, 218 n. 32.

gave up on the scheme and went off to Nova Scotia on another venture two years later.[9]

Disinterest in Lyon's "crude Scheme," which, according to Franklin, was suppressed by General Jeffrey Amherst, did not mean, of course, that the Doctor had lost interest in all western land schemes. He remained ever mindful that Americans seemed to have an irrepressible urge to move westward and that this could bring big profits to those who were there first with western land to sell. He noted that even Lyon's deficient scheme had "a great Number of Subscribers." He did see a problem, however, in trying to promote a colony west of the mountains and north of the Ohio River in 1763. Indians in the area had gone on the warpath, making any colonization effort there too risky for the time being. Hence, he temporarily shifted his interest toward what was then called the southwest and today is called the southeast—present-day Alabama and Mississippi.[10]

Franklin's interest in land schemes must have been widely known in Philadelphia, for the knowledge of it soon spread from there to London where none other than Thomas Penn talked about it. On 18 June 1763, the Penn brothers commissioned John Penn, Richard's son, as the new governor of Pennsylvania, to replace James Hamilton. A short while after that at "an Entertainment" in the new governor's honor, Thomas Penn took Franklin's friend Peter Collinson aside and said, "I hear Mr. Franklins comeing Over to Solicit a revival of Doctor Coxs Grant for Lands on the Mississippi. Do you know anything of it . . .?"[11] Penn was apparently anxious over the prospect of Franklin's return to England, and little wonder! In Pennsylvania the former agent was merely a bother, but in England he was a constant thorn in the proprietors' side, for he cost the Penns money to defend themselves at Whitehall.

What Penn had heard was both correct and incorrect—correct in that Franklin had taken an interest in the "Coxe Grant," but incorrect in the matter of Franklin's going to England to "Solicit a revival" of the grant. The former agent was counting on Richard Jackson to do that. The grant had to do with Dr. Daniel Coxe, court physician of William III, who

---

[9]Samuel Finley to Benjamin Franklin, 17 and 21 March 1763; Benjamin Franklin to Richard Jackson, 17 April 1763; James Lyon to Benjamin Franklin, April 1763. *Franklin Papers.* X, 224-25, 231, 256-57, 257 ns. 5-7.

[10]Benjamin Franklin to Richard Jackson, 10 and 27 June 1763. Ibid. X, 286, 297.

[11]Peter Collinson to Benjamin Franklin, 23 August 1763. Ibid. X, 331-32.

claimed in 1696 that he had acquired the rights to the Heath Grant—a huge land grant that Charles I had made to Sir Robert Heath in 1629. The area granted, first called "Carolana" and later "Carolina," included part of present-day North Carolina, all of South Carolina, and most of Georgia. Dr. Coxe, though claiming he had bought the rights to this vast territory, never journeyed to America, but his son, Colonel Daniel Coxe, did, and the colonel became a big landowner in New Jersey. He attempted unsuccessfully to win recognition of his family's claim to Carolina until his death in 1739. In 1763 the colonel's son and grandson approached Franklin for help in securing the Coxe grant, obviously promising him a share of the land. Franklin referred them to Richard Jackson and suggested that he and Jackson might purchase half a share each if the claim could be legally established. Franklin also planned to bring into the scheme his banker friend John Sargent and others.[12]

Jackson worked for several months in 1763 to establish the validity of the "Coxe Grant" but found "no Traces" of the "Grant from K. William." Before the year was out he concluded that the application would "prove very Uphill work," but he trudged on. During the spring of 1764 he was still in search of evidence to confirm the elusive grant. That Jackson and Franklin—especially Jackson because of his gargantuan reputation as a legal know-it-all—ever considered the Coxe claim to have any validity is astonishing. All and more of the land in question had been granted by Charles II in 1663 and 1665 to the eight Lords Proprietors of Carolina, and under their direction much of the land had long since been settled before 1696. The grant to the Lords Proprietors superseded all earlier grants. This had been made clear soon after the 1663 proprietary charter was issued, when claimants under the Heath Grant carried their claims to the Privy Council and were told that those claims were void. Dr. Coxe had not received a royal grant from William III, as his descendants led Richard Jackson and Benjamin Franklin to believe; instead, Dr. Coxe had bought the Heath Grant from private individuals. In other words, Coxe had been taken in by confidence men—just as Jackson and Franklin were bamboozled by his descendants. The Privy Council declared the claims of the Coxe family invalid in 1769, but for

---

[12]Benjamin Franklin to Richard Jackson, 8 and 22 March, 17 April, 22 September, and 19 December 1763; Richard Jackson to Benjamin Franklin, 12 November, 27 December 1763, and [13 April 1764]. Ibid. X 208-416, *passim.*, 212-13 n. 1; XI, 175-76.

some unknown reason compensated the Coxes with 100,000 acres of land in New York.[13]

In the spring of 1764, while Richard Jackson still searched for evidence that would prove the validity of the "Coxe Grant," he aroused Franklin's interest in a land speculation scheme in Nova Scotia. The former Pennsylvania agent committed himself to share in a project spearheaded by a Scotch-Irish Virginia adventurer named Alexander McNutt. Franklin's friend and political ally, John Hughes, also partici-pated. As one of the partners in the enterprise Franklin was ultimately entitled to 11,000 acres out of two 100,000 acre grants. This cost him a mere £53, which Deborah would pay to Anthony Wayne, later of Revolutionary War fame, sometime before 12 January 1766. At the time Wayne was paid the money, he was a surveyor and a partner in the Nova Scotia venture.[14] Franklin's keen interest in land speculation, which was heightened in 1763 and 1764 by Jackson's search to verify the "Coxe Grant" and his own commitment to the Nova Scotia scheme, would soar to even greater heights upon his return to England.

Franklin's preoccupation with land speculation schemes and his need to catch up on post office business in 1763 may have contributed to his silence on royal government for Pennsylvania. More than likely, however, he was waiting for the right moment—a moment when a serious issue would once more precipitate public dissatisfaction with the proprietors. He bided his time, and the moment for which he waited came. The way was prepared for him to launch his campaign for royal government late in 1763 by two events: (1) John Penn's arrival on 30 October to assume the governorship, and (2) the Paxton Boys' attack on the Conestoga Indians during the last two weeks in December. John Penn, determined to protect the Penn family's rights and property, soon caused another round of political battles between the Assembly and the proprietors, and the turmoil created by the Paxton Boys, a mob from Donegal and Paxton on the Pennsylvania frontier, prompted Franklin to contend publicly that proprietary government was not up to the job of maintaining law and order in Pennsylvania.

When John Penn took over as governor in the fall of 1763, Franklin announced his intention of trying to get along with the young man. On

---

[13]Ibid (all sources cited).

[14]Montagu Wilmot to Alexander McNutt and Associates: Two Land Grants. Ibid., XII, 345-50, 348 n. 8.

19 December 1763, he noted his impressions of the new governor in a letter to Peter Collinson, but he also indicated that he was still holding a grudge against Thomas Penn. The Doctor wrote:

> He is civil, and I endeavour to fail in no Point of Respect; so I think we shall have no personal Difference, at least I will give no Occasion. For though I cordially dislike and despise the Uncle, for demeaning himself so far as to back bite and abuse me to Friends and to Strangers, as you well know he does, I shall keep that Account open with him only, and some time or other we might have a Settlement; if that never happens, I can forgive the Debt. . . . He can sleep in Peace at present. I am not coming over as he has heard, to solicit anything about Dr. Coxe's Grant.[15]

Franklin's opportunity to press for that settlement was nearer at hand than he realized, and in less than three months whatever cordial feelings he had toward young John Penn would vanish forever.

When the Paxtons Boys committed their various acts of violence, local authorities in the Lancaster area made no effort to bring them to justice. Nor did the new governor. Convinced that the provincial government intended to take no effective steps to protect people on the frontier from Indian attacks and that only a show of force would produce results, the Paxtoneers put together a mob of five hundred to six hundred men and marched toward Philadelphia. They meant to intimidate the governor and the Assembly and make them provide protection for the frontier. Upon learning of the mob's approach, Governor Penn rushed to Franklin at midnight for help and for a time used Franklin's house as headquarters to deal with the emergency. Anxiety saturated the air in Philadelphia as this crisis unfolded during the first week of February 1764. The governor sent a delegation to Germantown to talk to the Paxtoneers. Franklin was a member of it. When the Paxton Boys were promised that the Assembly would consider all their grievances, they turned back.

Franklin was convinced that he had helped rescue young Penn from a tight spot and that the Assembly had shown every sign of cooperation with the governor. Then, "without the least Provocation," Penn accused the Assembly of "Disloyalty and with making *an infringement on the King's prerogative*" because it had named a minor official to a post

---

[15]Benjamin Franklin to Peter Collinson, 19 December 1763. Ibid. X, 401.

without consulting him. This gave Franklin his chance to challenge proprietary rule and advocate once more royal rule for Pennsylvania. He seized the opportunity. In a letter of 14 March 1764, he told John Fothergill, ". . . all Hopes of Happiness under a Proprietary Government are at an End." He claimed that the government was unable to keep the peace and that the people, because of Governor Penn's attitude, would not rally to his support if another mob came. Pennsylvania was moving toward anarchy and confusion, Franklin contended, and he warned that only a royal takeover could prevent the colony from ending up with no government.[16]

Several historians have rightly observed that the Paxton Boys crisis had widespread political repercussions, the most significant of which was the push for royal government. Although Franklin fell out with John Penn over the governor's alleged ingratitude and pettiness toward the Assembly, the former agent *emphasized* the larger issue of the proprietary government's ineffectiveness in maintaining law and order. Furthermore, the Paxton Boys affair led to a realignment of political forces in the colony. The Franklin-led moderate Quakers, who dominated the Assembly, wanted the rioters punished. They were irked by Penn's seeming forbearance toward the Paxton Boys. Imaginations ran wild. Some Quakers were convinced that there was a conspiracy behind the defiance of the rioters in Lancaster County. Instead of doing the right thing and punishing the murderers of peaceful Indians, Penn and the proprietary party, some believed, intended to use the Paxton Boys to intimidate the Assembly. Because the Paxtoneers were mostly Presbyterians, the Quakers condemned all Presbyterians as rioters, and this caused the Presbyterians to unite against the Quaker-controlled Assembly. Warring Indians and rioting frontiersmen caused ordinarily calm Pennsylvanians of all parties to lose their grasp on sound judgment. Overreaction was commonplace in Pennsylvania in 1764.[17]

Benjamin Franklin was an old hand at managing crises. During King George's War he had come to the fore, offering solutions to complex political and defense problems. Also, during the French and Indian War

---

[16]Benjamin Franklin to Richard Jackson, 11 February 1764; Benjamin Franklin to Francis Bernard, 21 February 1764; Benjamin Franklin to John Fothergill, 14 March 1764. Ibid. XI, 76-78, 87, 101-105. Also see: Ibid., XI, 69-75.

[17]Benjamin Franklin to Richard Jackson, 14 March 1764. Ibid., XI, 69-75, 107; Hutson, *Pennsylvania Politics*, 98-105; Newcomb, *Franklin and Galloway*, 74.

he had pushed Governor Robert Hunter Morris aside at a critical time and seized the initiative. A crisis was his call to action, and the threat the Paxton Boys and the Delaware Indians posed to Pennsylvania in 1764 provided the signal he was waiting for to launch his campaign for royal rule. His plan of attack was simple. He would persuade the Assembly to petition the Crown for a royal takeover, and John Penn had certainly put most of the Assembly members in a mood to approve of the idea. At the same time, Franklin would encourage Springett Penn to press his "Claim" as the rightful proprietor of Pennsylvania. The Doctor was sure that if Springett could secure title to the province, he would willingly sell his governmental rights to the Crown. Franklin considered every possible angle, for he was determined to rid Pennsylvania of government by the Penns. At the end of March, the former agent was certain that a petition seeking royal government would soon be sent to the king. To Richard Jackson, he wrote:

> Be assured that we all think it impossible to go on any longer under a Proprietary Government. By the Resolves [just proposed by the Assembly] you will see, that [there] never was greater Unanimity in any Assembly. . . . You will endear yourself to us forever, if you can get this Change of Government completed.[18]

Besides John Penn's attitude toward the Paxton Boys and his pettiness in defending the prerogatives of the proprietors and the Crown, the Assembly had already entered the lists against the governor again over a new supply bill and the old issue of taxing the proprietary estates. Because of the Indian restlessness associated with Pontiac's rebellion in the Ohio Valley, the Assembly on 22 December 1763 moved to honor a request by General Jeffrey Amherst for 1,000 men to help fight the Indians. Two weeks later, on 6 January 1764, the Assembly voted to raise £55,000 to supply those troops. A bill containing provisions for this appropriation passed on 24 February. Penn rejected the bill, and the Assembly offered him a new bill, again appropriating £55,000 on 14 March. The governor refused to sign that bill, too, until 30 May 1764, following several changes upon which he insisted. During the time between his first receiving the bill and his finally signing it—over two

---

[18]Benjamin Franklin to Richard Jackson, 29 and 31 March 1764; [Springett Penn] to Benjamin Franklin, 22 December 1764. *Franklin Papers*, IX, 260-62; XI, 148, 150-52.

months—political war raged in Pennsylvania. An unbridgeable chasm soon opened between the governor and the Assembly. In fact, by the time Penn signed the bill, the Assembly had already adopted a petition to the king asking him to send a *royal* governor to take over the province.[19]

Once again the discontent was rooted in the taxation of the proprietary estates. Franklin pointed out that the bill that passed on 14 March "comply's with four of the [six] Stipulations made at the Council Board" in 1760. The Assembly, however, viewed as too "unjust" the provisions that the proprietors' located uncultivated lands should be taxed no higher than the worst land of others and that proprietary town lots be exempted altogether. Several times the Assembly attempted to amend the bill to satisfy Governor Penn. This led to bitter quarrels between the governor and the Assembly over the compromise Benjamin Franklin and Robert Charles had worked out at the Privy Council hearing four years before. Neither the governor nor the Assembly was persuaded by the other's interpretation. Finally, the Assembly gave ground, and near the end of May, after Franklin had replaced Isaac Norris as speaker, the governor was offered a bill with wording he could accept. Even so, the Assembly steadfastly refused to yield to Penn's demand that the body go back and formally amend the Supply Acts of 1759 and 1760 to conform to the Privy Council's order of 1760. On 30 May 1764, the governor signed into law the Supply Act of 1764, but by that time he had alienated almost the entire Assembly. This was made clear by the message the Assembly sent the governor under Franklin's signature on the same day. The members fired a parting shot by calling for a more "equitable Government," which they hoped was "not far distant."[20]

Ultimately, John Penn had fought the family fight in vain, for his uncle and father had decided to accept the Assembly's interpretation of the Privy Council's order regarding the taxation of the proprietors' uncultivated lands. Acting on the advice of Henry Wilmot, Thomas and Richard Penn informed their governor of this in a letter dated 1 June 1764. They were doing it, they claimed, because they saw "some equity" in the Assembly's position and not because the Assembly was ready to

---

[19]Benjamin Franklin to Richard Jackson, 8 March and 1 June 1764. Ibid. XI, 95-97, 217-18. Also see: Ibid., X, 405-406, n. 2; XI 7-18, 111-47, 203-213.

[20]Ibid (all sources cited).

apply for royal government.[21] In spite of their disclaimer, it seems more than merely coincidental that the Penn brothers saw no merit in the Assembly's interpretation until that body was about to petition for a royal takeover.

Although Governor Penn was aware of the proprietors' decision by mid-August, he made no official announcement of it for months. After consulting with James Hamilton and Benjamin Chew, Penn decided it was in the best political interests of the family to withhold the announcement until after the election in October. William Allen apparently divulged the new policy soon after the election, as rumors spread through the province that the Penns had yielded on amendment 2, but the governor offered no official statement until 15 January 1765. At that time he instructed the county commissioners and local assessors to interpret the Supply Act in accordance with the Assembly's version of the previous March. The Philadelphia commissioners refused, insisting on following the law he had signed, thus igniting another dispute. Tempers were so short by this time that no accord could be reached concerning the assessment and taxation of proprietary lands.[22]

Meanwhile, the campaign for royal government had been initiated, and it resulted in additional heated controversy. Franklin, the ringleader, started on 24 March 1764 to rally support for the cause. He wrote and circulated for signatures the "Petition of the Pennsylvania Freeholders and Inhabitants to the King." One German translation of the "Petition" was printed. Other petitions, besides Franklin's, were also passed around. Hundreds of signatures were collected, and the various petitions went to the Assembly with requests that they be passed on to the Crown.[23]

In April Franklin expanded his propaganda efforts in favor of royal government by publishing a pamphlet called "Cool Thoughts on the Present Situation of our Public Affairs, In a Letter to a Friend in the Country." In it the Doctor explained the advantages of royal government and assured doubters that Pennsylvanians would retain all the rights and privileges they already enjoyed. His assertions were soon attacked in rebuttal pamphlets known as *The Plain Dealer, Nos. II and III*. As the controversy raged, John Penn wrote his Uncle Thomas to blame all the

---

[21]Ibid. XI, 203-214, 213-14 n. 9; Hutson, *Pennsylvania Politics*. 122-26, 169-70; Thomas and Richard Penn to John Penn, 1 June 1764. Penn Papers, HSP.

[22]*Franklin Papers*. XI, 213-14 n. 9.

[23]Ibid. XI, 145-47.

commotion on Benjamin Franklin. He said there had been "at least an appearance of Peace and Quietness" until the proprietors' nemesis returned from his travels through the colonies. Then had come the "old Sparks" and "more violence than ever." Franklin, the governor contended, was bent on mischief because "Malice and Ill Nature" were "so deeply implanted in his own black heart."[24] Whether or not John Penn was accurate about the color of Franklin's heart, he was absolutely right about the principal source of contention in Pennsylvania.

Responding to the numerous petitions for royal government, the Pennsylvania Assembly on 23 May, by a "great Majority," named a committee to draft a petition to the king. Franklin was on that committee, as was his close ally, Joseph Galloway. The Doctor had already written a petition by the time the committee met. Ultimately the Assembly adopted it. There were deliberations on the afternoon of 24 May. John Dickinson, able lawyer and large landowner, spoke against it, arguing that royal rule might result in a loss of political and religious privileges enjoyed by Pennsylvanians under the proprietary government. Galloway offered a rebuttal. Isaac Norris, Franklin's old political ally and confidant, fearing that Quaker religious privileges might be placed in jeopardy by royal rule, reversed his position and apparently spoke against the petition the next morning. After the debate, which ended on 25 May, several changes were made in Franklin's petition before a "great Majority" agreed to it and ordered it "to be transcribed."[25]

When the Assembly convened on Saturday morning, 25 May, Isaac Norris sent word that the two previous days had overtaxed his "Constitution" and that he could not attend. Not knowing when he might be able to return, he asked the Assembly to choose a new speaker. Franklin was unanimously elected to replace Norris, and John Penn confirmed the new speaker. That afternoon the Doctor signed the final version of the petition so that it could be forwarded to England. To calm the fears of some who had spoken out against the petition, a provision had been added, asking the Crown to continue "those Civil and Religious Privileges" that had made Pennsylvania attractive to so many settlers for so many years. Only three members of the Assembly—the "Noble Few" as William Smith would call them later—voted against the petition. They

---

[24]Ibid. XI, 153-73; John Penn to Thomas Penn, 5 May 1764. Penn Papers, HSP.

[25]*Franklin Papers*. XI, 193-200, 217-18; Hutson, *Pennsylvania Politics*, 122-26; *Pennsylvania Colonial Records*, IX, 182.

were John Dickinson of Philadelphia County, Isaac Saunders of Lancaster County, and John Montgomery of Cumberland County.[26]

Even before the petition was adopted, some members of the Assembly spoke of sending Franklin "home" with it to assist Richard Jackson in pressing the application for royal government. The devious Dr. Franklin feigned disinterest in the suggestion, asserting that Jackson was perfectly capable of handling the matter alone. He told Jackson that he would love to see England and his friends there, but that he hoped his going would be unnecessary, since he did not wish to put the public to the expense of sending him. Yet, in a letter written to William Strahan on 30 March, Franklin had indicated that the only thing holding him back was that, if he went on another mission for the Assembly, he might not be able to remain in England as long as he desired. One suspects that the soon-to-be new speaker of the Assembly was being more forthright with Strahan than with Jackson, perhaps because the latter would have been offended if the Doctor had not expressed complete confidence in the regular agent to press the petition alone. Franklin went on to say in his letter to Jackson that he was displeased by the compromise the Assembly had been compelled to make with John Penn in the Supply Bill of 1764 because of amendment 2. What, Speaker Franklin asked, was Jackson's recollection of the intention of that amendment's wording? Ironically, on the same day Franklin was writing to Jackson about amendment 2, the proprietors were writing to John Penn, instructing him to accept the Assembly's interpretation of the ambiguous amendment.[27]

Franklin had delayed launching his campaign for royal government until he was sure he had enough support to win. He had been ever on the alert for an issue he could exploit. The crisis precipitated by the Paxton Boys and John Penn's response to it had opened the door a crack for him; then the governor's insistence on minimal taxation of proprietary property in accordance with the pro-Penn interpretation of the Privy Council's directives flung the door wide open for the opportunistic Franklin. As early as 14 March he was sure that the colony would soon be ready to accept his solution to Pennsylvania's problems. After noting the asperity that had arisen between "the Presbyterians and Quakers," the

---

[26]Ibid (all sources cited).

[27]Benjamin Franklin to William Strahan, 30 March 1764; Benjamin Franklin to Richard Jackson, 1 June 1764. *Franklin Papers.* X, 149, 218-20; Thomas and Richard Penn to John Penn, 1 June 1764. Penn Papers, HSP.

Doctor, with optimism dripping from his pen, told Richard Jackson, "All Parties begin now to wish for a King's Government." A fortnight later he wrote Jackson that "we think it impossible to go on any longer under Proprietary Government."[28] Franklin probably thought the matter was settled at the end of May, when the Assembly adopted the petition for a new government with only three dissenting votes. If he did indeed think that, he was soon in for a huge surprise.

Actually the Presbyterians in Pennsylvania never favored royal government, viewing it as a diversionary tactic by the Quakers to enable them to retain control of the colony's Assembly. They saw themselves as the intended victims of a Quaker plot, and they soon started a movement to have the petition for royal government rescinded. The proprietary party, because its leaders were out of pocket in the spring of 1764, did nothing except wait for the "executioner's knife." Richard Peters, James Hamilton, William Smith, and William Allen were away. John Penn, who was young, inexperienced, and lazy, knew not what to do. The picture changed dramatically in the summer of 1764 when William Smith and William Allen returned from England. Smith soon managed to bring the opponents of royal government together in a fragile coalition that included the proprietary party, the Presbyterians, the Germans, and John Dickinson who had defected from the Quaker ranks. The coalition was shaky because the Presbyterians hated Smith, while John Dickinson hated the proprietary party leader Benjamin Chew, whom some called the "Prime Minister" to the governor. Even so, these unlikely elements soon worked together against royal government as part of Smith's "Confederation." Their efforts were given impetus in mid-August when William Allen returned to Philadelphia. The chief justice spread the word that Richard Jackson had asserted a change in government would cost £100,000 sterling and that "Parliament will oblige us to pay, and saddle us besides with a Salary to be paid by us to a King's Governor of £5,000 sterling per Annum more." Allen claimed that Lord Halifax, former president of the Board of Trade, had condemned the royal government movement, calling it tantamount to rebellion. The chief justice asserted

---

[28]Benjamin Franklin to Richard Jackson, 14 and 29 March 1764. *Franklin Papers*. XI, 107, 148.

further that royal government would lead to more, not less, external control.[29]

Even before Allen arrived on the scene Franklin was aware that there was more anti-royal sentiment in Pennsylvania than he had first imagined or wanted to believe. On 12 July he wrote to Richard Jackson, "The Proprietary Party are endeavouring to stir up the Presbyterians to join in a Petition against a Change in Government: what that [Endea]vour will produce I cannot say." In another letter to the Pennsylvania agent on 9 August, Franklin expressed some concern over the counter petition the proprietary party was circulating, for Smith's campaign, which was grounded in the claim that the province's privileges would be "demolish'd by the Change," was gaining momentum. Soon the "Confederation" leaders boasted of supporters in "great Numbers," and Franklin predicted that the matter would be decided by the election in October. Great numbers indeed! The "Confederation" ultimately collected upwards of fifteen thousand signatures, about three times more than the proponents of royal government ever had.[30] Franklin was in for a hard fight, and he knew it.

With the return of William Allen on 13 August the anti-royal campaign picked up added emotional intensity. His story about the huge cost of achieving and maintaining royal government no doubt scared many Pennsylvanians, since it came, according to Allen, from the colony's own agent, "Omniscient" Jackson. Franklin strongly doubted that Jackson had said anything of the kind, and he wrote the agent to ask him. By the time Jackson responded, Pennsylvania's 1764 election was over, and the Doctor, who had been voted out of the Assembly, was on his way to England to assist the province's regular agent in carrying out a new mission for the Assembly. Too late, Jackson's 18 November letter arrived to say he never mentioned the specific figure of £100,000. Nor had he

---

[29]*Burd Papers*, 57-58; Benjamin Franklin to Richard Jackson, 1 September 1764. *Franklin Papers*. XI, 327-28; Hutson, *Pennsylvania Politics*, 165-66.

[30]Benjamin Franklin to Richard Jackson, 12 July and 9 August 1764. *Franklin Papers*. XI, 256, 264; Hutson, *Pennsylvania Politics*, 133-34, 167-68; G. B. Warden, "The Proprietary Group in Pennsylvania, 1754–1764," *The William and Mary Quarterly* 21 (1964): 388.

said, as Allen deceptively reported, that the Crown would "unconstitutionally strip the Province of its Privileges."[31]

The Pennsylvania agent's attitude toward the petition for royal government was actually somewhat ambiguous. He favored royal government; that much is certain. He did not hesitate to tell William Allen—and Thomas Penn, too—that the proprietors could bear a great deal more in taxes than those imposed by the Supply Act of 1764 without suffering any hardship. What he was uncertain about was the timing of the petition. While he thought that the summer of 1764 was a good time to present the petition, he was not sure it was the best time. Once again, the proprietors had shown reluctance to be taxed to support a defense measure, but "if the Proprietary is disposed to give way; it may be better, 'till future Misconduct on his part makes it necessary, to delay presenting the Petition." Although there is no direct evidence that Jackson knew of the proprietors' decision to reverse themselves on amendment 2, he could have known, or he might have sensed through his contacts with Allen and with Thomas Penn, that a concession was likely. What seems obvious is that Jackson wanted to hold off pursuing the application for royal government until he was confident the effort would succeed. In the summer and fall of 1764 he lacked that confidence. If Franklin ever mentioned Jackson's hesitancy to anyone in Pennsylvania, there is no evidence of it.[32]

When Franklin wrote Jackson on 1 September to inquire about William Allen's assertions, the Doctor predicted that the approaching election would be a "warm one." Still he expressed confidence that "a Majority of the old Members will continue" and that the application for royal government would be pursued. He noted that he had been attacked in "five scurrilous Pamphlets, and three Copperplate Prints" before responding to accusations against him. The royal government issue, Franklin informed Jackson, would soon be decided at the polls, and vials of verbal abuse were poured on the leaders of both sides right down to the first of October. The attacks went beyond the issue to the persons who championed each side of the question. John Penn, William Allen, William Smith, and some Presbyterian preachers were lambasted by the

---

[31]Benjamin Franklin to Richard Jackson, 1 September 1764; Richard Jackson to Benjamin Franklin, 11 August and 18 November 1764. *Franklin Papers.* XI, 312-13, 327-28, 462-65.

[32]Ibid (all sources cited).

pro-royal forces, while Franklin and his chief lieutenant, Joseph Gallo-way, took most of the battering from the anti-royal camp. Franklin was right in believing that nobody received more abuse than he did. According to the proprietary group, he was angling to be the first royal governor of Pennsylvania, he had lived lavishly off the public during his recent mission to England, he had misused the Parliamentary grant for 1758, he had once called the German settlers of the colony "Palatine Boors," and he had fathered an illegitimate son, who happened to be the incumbent royal governor of New Jersey.[33]

The vitriol flowed until time for the election of 1764, which was held on 1 October in the counties and on 2 October in the Philadelphia. Franklin was a candidate in both the city and the county. The "Old Ticket," Franklin's Quaker coalition, which stood for the shift to royal government, was pitted against the "New Ticket," which was composed of the various elements of the "Confederation" that, of course, stood for retaining proprietary rule. Isaac Norris, who had spoken against royal government but was not part of the "Confederation," was a candidate on both tickets. The "New Ticket" gained some seats in the Assembly, but not nearly enough to prevent the petition for royal government from being pursued. The "Confederation's" biggest victory in the election was that it caused the personal defeat of Benjamin Franklin and Joseph Galloway, as neither man was reelected. A little over a week after losing his place in the Assembly, the leader of the "Old Ticket" wrote Richard Jackson, ". . . I am no longer in the Assembly. The Proprietary Party by great industry against great Security carried the Election of this County and City by about 26 votes against me and Mr. Galloway." He further lamented that his opponents had taken "1000 Dutch from me." Gloatingly Franklin added, "But the Majority of the last Assembly remain" and its members would still seek royal government.[34]

The Doctor was right. When the new Assembly convened on 15 October, two proposals were presented concerning the petition for royal government—one to recall it and the other to have Jackson sit on it until

---

[33]Benjamin Franklin to Richard Jackson, 1 September 1764. Ibid. XI, 327-29. Also see: Ibid. XI, 369-90; J. Philip Gleason, "A Scurrilous Colonial Election and Franklin's Reputation," *The William and Mary Quarterly* 18 (1961): 73-79; Hutson, *Pennsylvania Politics*, 142-43.

[34]Benjamin Franklin to Richard Jackson, 11 October 1764. *Franklin Papers*, XI, 397. Also see: Ibid., XI, 390-94; Hutson, *Pennsylvania Politics*, 169-76.

he received further instructions. The first was defeated twenty-two to ten, while the second fell by a vote of twenty to twelve. A third proposal ordering Jackson to proceed with caution and to seek further instructions if he saw any danger of the colony's losing its "Privileges civil and religious," carried twenty to twelve. Isaac Norris, who had once more been elected speaker, fell ill again and asked to be replaced. He was succeeded by Joseph Fox, who had been elected on the "Old Ticket" but who had bipartisan support. Since Governor Penn was not in town to confirm the new speaker, the proprietary party attempted to postpone any further action by the Assembly. The attempt failed. Fox, though not yet confirmed by the governor, kept the Assembly in session. That body's Committee of Correspondence soon wrote Jackson, in accordance with the Assembly's resolution, to desist in pressing the royal government petition and to seek new instructions if he sensed that Pennsylvania's political and religious privileges would be jeopardized in any way by the change in government.[35]

Less than two weeks after the new Assembly took action on the royal government petition, it took another step that confirmed William Allen's worst fears. The body voted nineteen to eleven to send Benjamin Franklin back to England as co-agent to help Richard Jackson promote the petition. John Dickinson led the eleven who voted against the move. This anti-Franklin group soon published a protest, giving the reasons for its negative vote. Its members offered as objections: (1) Franklin had been repudiated at the polls after serving fourteen years in the Assembly, (2) he was a sworn enemy of the proprietors and would totally disrupt communications between them and the colony, (3) he would create perpetual turmoil in the province by pressing relentlessly for royal government, and (4) he had mishandled public money.[36]

*The Protest* offered by the eleven anti-Franklin assemblymen upset Franklin. He felt compelled to respond. On November 5, two days before he left for England, he answered it with *Remarks on a Late Protest*. He defended his appointment as agent and savagely denounced his critics. He was outraged at the charge that he had mishandled public money, and he made a strong case in his defense. He then accused his opponents of

---

[35]*Franklin Papers*, XI, 402-412, 422-26; Merrill Jensen, *The Founding of a Nation* (New York: Oxford University Press, 1968) 90.

[36]William Allen to David Barclay & Sons, 24 October 1764. *Burd Papers*, 62, 82-85, 87-88; William Allen to Thomas Penn, 21 October 1764. Penn Papers, HSP.

loyalty to the proprietors and disloyalty to the Crown. After all, William Allen had been heard to say that "the King's little Finger" would be "heavier than the Proprietor's whole Loins." As for being defeated at the polls, he noted that he had lost by only a handful of votes out of 4,000 cast. And what about his detractors and their repeated repudiation at the polls? They had been rejected for "almost twice 14 Years" and could not win election in their own county or city, but had to gain a seat by running in one of the "out Counties, the remotest of the Province!" In the fourteen elections he had won, claimed Franklin, he had never declared his candidacy. Others had entered his name. Without ever soliciting a vote he had won fourteen elections—six of them while absent in England. When he did lose, he lost because his critics lied about him and cheated in the elections with "double Tickets" and "whole Boxes of forged Votes." He also accused the proprietary party of withholding news about the proprietors' decision to yield in their interpretation of amendment 2, hoping that the election would change the composition of the Assembly. Then the new Assembly could withdraw the petition for royal government and be subservient to whatever the proprietors wanted. Franklin no doubt stretched the truth beyond believable limits when he denied any "personal" difference with the proprietors and claimed he opposed them only on the "public Account."[37] That the Doctor despised Thomas Penn is unquestionable.

The *Remarks* was the newly appointed co-agent's parting shot at his enemies. Somewhat hypocritically he professed forgiveness toward them, as he left the "Country I love"—perhaps for the last time, he said, implying that at his age he might die before he could return. On 7 November he sailed for England, and on the same day he wrote Richard Jackson to say that he was on his way over for a year to help Jackson carry out the policies of the Assembly and possibly "be of some Use in our general American Affairs." Three hundred friends accompanied Franklin to Chester, where he boarded the *King of Prussia*, captained by James Robinson. He departed with great fanfare, as was usually the case when he left Philadelphia or returned to it. In spite of all Franklin said to people in England and America to downplay his interest in going back to England, he could not have been happier about it. In a letter of 12 July

---

[37]*Burd Papers*, 90-91; Benjamin Franklin's *Remarks on a Late Protest* in the *Franklin Papers*, XI, 429-41. Also see: William Allen to Thomas Penn, 13 December 1764. Penn Papers, HSP.

to Jackson, he had tried to bait the regular agent into encouraging his return. He asked for Jackson's sentiments on the petition for royal government and the need for Franklin to help pursue it in London. He implied that a call from Jackson would take him back to England "to spend the Remainder" of his days.[38] Ostensibly he was going for one year, but, as he had done during his first mission, he would find compelling reasons for staying year after year.

What did the election of 1764 mean in Pennsylvania? Franklin had predicted that it would resolve the issue of whether or not to pursue a change in government. Apparently he was right. Although he and Galloway suffered personal defeat—probably because the "New Ticket's" heaviest assault was directed at them, the anti-proprietary forces retained control of the Assembly. Not only did the petition for royal government proceed, but Franklin's allies in the Assembly retained enough votes to send him to England to shepherd the petition over the imperial bureaucratic hurdles at Whitehall. One historian has argued that the royal government movement really suffered defeat at the polls in 1764, that Franklin did not actually control the Assembly behind the scenes, that the Assembly voted not to recall the royal government petition in order to keep the pressure on Thomas Penn, and that sending Franklin to England was merely a bluff. In a word, the Assembly's decision to keep the royal government petition alive was really a calculated effort to retain proprietary government, for the new Assembly viewed the petition only as a rod to hold over Penn's head to force him into extensive reforms.[39] This is surely creative and imaginative use of the evidence—too creative and imaginative. It is based mainly on a statement by William Allen in a letter to Thomas Penn. The Pennsylvania chief justice told the proprietor that the Assembly never really intended to have the petition presented to the Crown.[40]

The question is: Did Allen know what he was talking about? Probably not. After all the other side controlled the Assembly, and after his highly partisan activities in the recent election, it is extremely doubtful that the anti-proprietary members of the Assembly would have

---

[38]Benjamin Franklin to Richard Jackson, 12 July and 7 November 1764. *Franklin Papers*, XI, 256, 446-49. Also see: Ibid., XI, 441.

[39]Hutson, *Pennsylvania Politics*, 179-80. For a contrary view, see: Hanna, *Franklin and Pennsylvania Politics*, 167.

[40]William Allen to Thomas Penn, 11 March 1765. Penn Papers, HSP.

disclosed their intentions to a leader of the proprietary faction. The facts are clear: Franklin's allies controlled the Assembly, although he was no longer in it. Furthermore, his chief lieutenant, Joseph Galloway, would return to the Assembly the following year and, in 1766 would become the body's speaker. For the next few years Franklin's influence would be felt in the Assembly through Galloway. Franklin had lost a minor battle, not the war. From England he would continue his fight in the Assembly through his allies, although ultimately he would drop the struggle for royal government because he realized from his vantage point in London that it was futile. By the time he did so, he became involved in a new and greater cause, while Joseph Galloway continued to champion the lost cause of royal government long after all hope of achieving it was gone.

# 5. "The Madness of the Populace":
## The Futile Quest for Royal Government and the Furor over the Stamp Act

When Benjamin Franklin returned to England near the end of 1764 to carry out his second mission for the Pennsylvania Assembly, he was actually on two missions. One of them was official and a matter of common knowledge. He was to persuade British authorities to honor an Assembly petition that called upon the Crown to turn Pennsylvania into a royal colony. The other mission was known only to Franklin, it seems, for there is no evidence that he confided it even to his closest political allies. With him he carried a currency-revenue scheme that he hoped to offer quietly to George Grenville, the current chief minister, as a substitute measure for the Stamp Act Grenville had proposed earlier in 1764. Franklin's public mission was almost sure to fail, and he should have known it. As for his personal secret mission, he had no chance at all to convince Grenville to forsake his stamp tax in favor of the Pennsylvania agent's alternative plan. Franklin could not have known that, however, until he returned to London.

Upon reaching the imperial capital and stirring around Whitehall for a month or two, the Doctor could see which way the political winds were blowing, and they were not blowing in the direction he preferred. Still, he pushed on with his financial plan until Grenville rejected it. Even after that he persisted in trying to promote it until he discovered it would be most unpopular in America. At the same time he unsuccessfully worked for his currency scheme, he played a controversial role in the passage and abortive implementation of the Stamp Act. Franklin's part in that statute, which was so odious to Americans, remains enshrouded in controversy. His Pennsylvania political enemies during 1765 convinced enough people that Franklin favored the act, or even sponsored it, so that his reputation in that province and other parts of America was temporarily ruined. Quickly sensing his miscalculation and possible political destruction as a result of acquiescing in the Stamp Act's passage, the Doctor worked to counteract the charges against him and managed not only to exonerate himself in the eyes of most colonists, but also to turn himself into a hero.

On 10 December 1764, Franklin returned, unannounced to his home away from home on Craven Street. Margaret Stevenson was out when he arrived, and she was "a good deal surpriz'd" upon walking into "her Parlour" and finding the Doctor waiting for her. One of the first things Franklin did in the next few days was write a brief note to Polly Stevenson to inform her of his return to London. Then, before much time passed, he brought his grandson Temple to live with him on Craven Street, in addition to young Sally Franklin, the daughter of an English cousin, Thomas Franklin of Lutterworth. In 1767 Temple would go off to Kensington to a boarding school run by James Elphinton, William Strahan's brother-in-law. William Franklin's young son would remain at the school until he left for America with his grandfather in 1775.[1]

News of Franklin's safe arrival in London did not reach Philadelphia until 14 March 1765. When it did, it evoked a night of joyous celebration. Bells "rung almost all night," and people "ran about like mad men," shaking hands over "this great event" when they "met in the street." They "drank the Wine" and poured "Libations" for Franklin's "Health, success and every other happiness."[2] A few months later a Philadelphia mob, convinced that Franklin had promoted the Stamp Act, would threaten to tear down his house. Popularity can be a fickle and fleeting mistress.

Once settled again on Craven Street, the Doctor fell easily into the way of life that he had come to enjoy before his departure from England in 1762. He made regular stops at the Pennsylvania Coffee House to talk to people just arriving from the province and to read Pennsylvania newspapers. He also became active again in the proceedings of the Royal Society and attended meetings of Bray's Associates. Within a few months of his arrival he renewed his correspondence with some of his Scottish friends—Lord Kames, Alexander Dick, and William Robertson. He informed Kames that he had reconciled with William, giving his "Consent and Approbation" to his son's marriage to Elizabeth Downes "soon after I left England." The best Franklin could say for his daughter-in-law was that she was "a very agreeable West India Lady." Undoubtedly he

---

[1] Benjamin Franklin to Mary Stevenson, [12-16 December 1764]. *Franklin Papers*, XI, 521. Also see: Ibid., XIII, 443-44, and Nolan, *Franklin in Scotland and Ireland*, 105-106.

[2] Cadwalader Evans to Benjamin Franklin, 15 March 1765. *Franklin Papers*, XII, 82-84; John Penn to Thomas Penn, 16 March 1765. Penn Papers, HSP.

thought Elizabeth was no Polly Stevenson, but at least the animosity between father and son over the marriage had passed.[3]

The Pennsylvania agent also wrote to a host of friends and confidants back in Philadelphia, but to none more frequently than his printing-business partner, David Hall, and his political partner, Joseph Galloway. To Deborah he resumed writing the same kind of letters he had written during his first mission. He informed her that his friends in London had given him a warm welcome, although many were in the country because Parliament was in recess until 10 January. He reported that a "violent Cold" had worried him "extremely" for ten or twelve days. Almost immediately he told her that he hoped to be home again "about the End of Summer." Doubt must have filled her heart and mind as she read those words, since her husband had made numerous similar promises between 1757 and 1762. If Deborah did not greet his hints of a quick return with skepticism in the spring of 1765, she surely must have been filled with doubt a year later. She heard several times about his health, his gouty foot, his waiting for Parliament to adjourn so that he could go to Bath, his speaking to members of Parliament "abroad," and his having people visit him on Craven Street to discuss "our American Affairs." Consistently Franklin wrote of his health and busy schedule, throwing in occasional empty promises that he would return home soon. Meanwhile, Deborah worried about the safety of their daughter Sally, as well as her own, and feared having their house torn down around her. Before long she pined away, hoping against hope that her husband would return before she died and continuing to write him pathetic letters revealing her terrible loneliness and her atrocious spelling.[4] Mrs. Franklin did not know, but perhaps suspected, that she had laid eyes on Benjamin Franklin for the last time in November 1764.

Regardless of how much Franklin enjoyed being back in England or how much his wife of nearly thirty-five years suffered at home in Philadelphia during his absence, his primary interest was in accomplish-

---

[3]Benjamin Franklin to David Hall, 12 January 1765; Benjamin Franklin to Lord Kames, 2 June 1765; Benjamin Franklin to Charles Morton, 29 October 1765; Alexander Dick to Benjamin Franklin, 5 July 1765. *Franklin Papers*, XII, 19, 19 n. 7, 159-65, 197-98, 341-42.

[4]Benjamin Franklin to Deborah Franklin, 27 December 1764; 9 February, 11 May 1765, and 22 February 1766; Deborah Franklin to Benjamin Franklin, 21 February, 7-12 April, and 22 September 1765. Ibid., XI, 534; XII, 42, 46, 102, 127, 165-66, 270-74; Randall, *A Little Revenge*, 197-203.

ing his mission. He knew that the British ministry was in a taxing mood, for George Grenville had pushed the Sugar Act through Parliament in 1764 and had dangled before Americans the probability of a burdensome stamp tax. Franklin, through his correspondence with Richard Jackson, was fully cognizant of Grenville's plans. He knew that the colonists in general and Pennsylvanians in particular were not receptive to any new taxes. Jackson had sent his first warnings late in 1763, writing, "I fear something relating to America will be done very much against my Opinion, but I shall endeavour to prevent it by all the means in my Power both in the House and out of House." He was firmly opposed to "Inland Duties," or internal taxes, although he could not oppose all duties since Parliament was faced with raising, he said, £200,000 to pay for garrisoning 10,000 troops in America.[5] The following month Jackson wrote Franklin again of his apprehension that Parliament would impose direct taxes. "I dread internal Taxes," he told the Doctor.[6] By 1 June 1764 it was known in Pennsylvania that the Stamp Act had been postponed, and Jackson's constituents there credited him with "deferring" it. The Pennsylvania agent was quick to deny credit, saying he had "very little Weight" or influence in Great Britain.[7]

While Franklin expressed the hope that the Stamp Act would never pass, he took the Sugar Act of 1764 in stride—this in spite of the fact that in Philadelphia it had made "a great Stir among our Merchants." He thought the merchants overreacted, and he advocated a wait-and-see attitude. Perhaps, he suggested, the hurtful effects would be less severe than anticipated. If so, he claimed, "we shall grow contented with it." (He would soon adopt a similar stance with regard to the Stamp Act—to his great regret.) The Doctor was convinced that ill effects from the Sugar Act in Pennsylvania, if there proved to be any, would ultimately produce similar effects in Great Britain and thus cause the law to be repealed. Franklin could propose a better plan by far than either a stamp tax or the duties associated with the Sugar Act, he told Jackson, if the two men "were together to talk it over."[8] The plan Franklin had in mind, of course,

---

[5]Richard Jackson to Benjamin Franklin, 12 November 1763. *Franklin Papers*, X, 371-72.

[6]Ibid., X, 415.

[7]Benjamin Franklin to Richard Jackson, 1 June 1764; Richard Jackson to Benjamin Franklin, 11 August 1764. Ibid., XI, 215, 313-14.

[8]Benjamin Franklin to Richard Jackson, 25 June 1764. Ibid., XI, 234-37.

was the currency-revenue scheme he would soon propose to Grenville in February 1765.

Over and over Franklin expressed his opinion in letters to people in England that British taxes that hurt America would ultimately hurt the mother country, too. Yet, fully cognizant of American opposition to new taxes to finance a British garrison for which colonials saw no need, the Doctor did not often share his views on taxation with his fellow citizens in Philadelphia. His first reaction to the threat of new taxes had been, "If you choose to tax us, give us Members in your Legislature, and let us be one People." He soon thought better of this proposal, however, probably because the Pennsylvania Assembly made it clear to Richard Jackson that he should work for the repeal of the Sugar Act and stand firm against a stamp duty and all other intended taxes "repugnant to our Rights and Privileges as Freemen and British Subjects." The Assembly emphasized the right of the colonists to tax themselves and expressed the view that colonial representation in Parliament was impractical. Fully aware of most Pennsylvanians' intransigence to new taxes, Franklin worked on his currency-revenue scheme, which, he believed, would serve the dual purpose of expanding the American currency supply *and* raising a revenue for the imperial treasury. He knew how expensive the French and Indian War had been, and he conceded that Britain needed additional revenues. If the currency aspect of his scheme proved acceptable to Americans and the revenue aspect pleased the British ministry, he would ingratiate himself to people on both sides of the Atlantic. Knowing how sensitive the tax issue was, however, Franklin intended to test the political waters before revealing his plan. When he left for England, even Joseph Galloway and Franklin's other Pennsylvania allies knew nothing of the Doctor's currency-revenue project.[9]

Franklin must have thought that he could expedite the royalization of Pennsylvania, if he could propose a revenue scheme acceptable to both the ministry and the colonies. He was obsessed with ousting the Penns and was prepared to go to almost any lengths to do it. Still he had to know that he was in for a mighty struggle with little prospect of success. His efforts to sway British officials toward royal government in 1761 had

---

[9]Crane, *Letters to the Press*, 25-30; Benjamin Franklin to Richard Jackson, 16 January, 1 May, and 22 September 1764; Benjamin Franklin to Peter Collinson, 30 April 1764. *Franklin Papers*, XI, 19-20, 181-83, 186, 347-51; Newcomb, *Franklin and Galloway*, 108-109.

been met, for the most part, by indifference. How could he have expected any change of attitude in 1764? To be sure he had influenced a majority in the Pennsylvania Assembly to petition for royalization, but the ministry, Parliament, the Board of Trade, and the Privy Council had shown little favoritism toward the Assembly during his first mission. Would the Privy Council, which in 1760 had shown great reluctance to take any damaging action against the proprietors, now take away the Penns' right to rule Pennsylvania? The Doctor was either too optimistic, considerably unrealistic, or was overly impressed with his powers of persuasion.

Even so, he once more opened the campaign to end proprietary government in Pennsylvania and pursued it enthusiastically through most of 1765. He and his Pennsylvania allies were convinced that they had the necessary support of the people in the province, that their cause was just, and that they would prevail. Joseph Galloway wrote on 23 January to say, "The Majority, you left at your Departure in Assembly, continue firm in their Desires to get rid of a Proprietary Government." Clearly defeated, the anti-royalization minority had stopped offering measures against the change, and the people were "every day growing more unanimous" in support of a royal government. Franklin was sure that all Quakers would fall in line on the issue out of fear that the Presbyterians would seize control of the government unless the proprietors were ousted.[10]

Besides the presumed growing popular support for royalization throughout the province, the Franklin forces were encouraged by the continuing political chaos in Pennsylvania and the proprietary government's weakness in the face of it. Surely, they believed, such developments would sway British officials to support their petition. John Ross, a Philadelphia lawyer and a Franklin cohort in the Assembly, wrote the Doctor that Pennsylvania had the "form without the Powers of Government," for rioting had been ignored. "Even his Majesty's troops" had been "attack'd and fired upon." Without a royal takeover Ross knew not how "such proceedings of a Lawless Mob" would end. Another Franklin ally, Samuel Wharton, wrote to the agent about riots and Indian massacres in the frontier counties. When Wharton's mercantile firm had sent supplies to the king's troops, the supplies had been destroyed "by a Number of Irish Presbyterians." Governor John Penn had done nothing

---

[10]Joseph Galloway to Benjamin Franklin, 23 January 1765; Benjamin Franklin to John Ross, 14 February 1765. *Franklin Papers,* XII, 25-26, 67-68.

about the incident, according to Wharton, and the grand jury would not indict the culprits, in spite of the presentation of "plain and positive Proofs." The "Grand Jurors were relatives of the Robbers," Wharton asserted. Reports of such outrageous conduct by mobs in Pennsylvania further convinced Franklin that a switch to royal government could certainly be achieved. To Samuel Rhoads, a former assemblyman and in 1765 the man in charge of building Franklin's house in Philadelphia, the Doctor wrote, "The Change so much wish'd for and now become so necessary must sooner or later take Place, and I think it Near at hand, whatever may be given out to the Contrary." Matters were not progressing faster, Franklin informed Cadwalader Evans, another of his Pennsylvania supporters, because of the unsettled state of the British ministry.[11]

After returning to Pennsylvania at the end of his first mission, Franklin had convinced his supporters that he had influence with powerful British politicians. His son's appointment as royal governor of New Jersey had appeared to confirm the claim. The Doctor's allies remained convinced of it right up to and beyond the provincial election in October 1765. Out of the thirty-six assemblymen chosen in that election, twenty-eight, according to Joseph Galloway, were in favor of royal government. Half of those who had signed the "Protest" against Franklin on the eve of his 1764 departure for England were voted out. This meant that Franklin and Jackson would be continued as agents to pursue the change in government on the same terms as had been declared by the previous Assembly. By mid-November Galloway expressed apprehension with regard to "Occurrences" that might retard royalization, but he was confident that the colony's two agents would continue the struggle to bring it about. He claimed that 90 percent of Pennsylvanians had come to favor the change. The "Occurrences" of which Galloway wrote were the disturbances caused by the passage of the Stamp Act. Deploring the violent opposition of the colonists to the stamp tax, Galloway reasoned that such actions could only damage the province's case at Whitehall.[12]

---

[11]Benjamin Franklin to Samuel Rhoads, 8 July 1765; Benjamin Franklin to Charles Thomson, 11 July 1765; Benjamin Franklin to Cadwalader Evans, 13 July 1765; John Ross to Benjamin Franklin, 20 May 1765; [Samuel Wharton] to Benjamin Franklin, 27 May 1765. Ibid., XII, 138-39, 142-43, 205-210.

[12]Joseph Galloway to Benjamin Franklin, [8-13 October 1765] and 18 November 1765; Pennsylvania Assembly's Committee of Correspondence to Richard Jackson and Benjamin Franklin, 16 October 1765. Ibid., XII, 305-306, 321-23, 378.

In spite of all the turmoil, the Franklin forces remained hopeful and thought that events were moving in a direction favorable to their cause. The proprietary forces thought the same thing! Thomas Penn had long been confident that his governmental rights were secure, and even Franklin's return to England to promote royal government did little to shake that confidence. In the spring of 1765 rumor had it in Philadelphia that William Allen had a letter from Penn stating that Lord Pomfret, Lord of the Bedchamber and also Thomas Penn's brother-in-law, had received assurance from the king himself that the proprietors would not be asked to yield their right to govern Pennsylvania. A few months later, in the fall of 1765, Allen went to the London Coffee House at Front and Market streets in Philadelphia and announced that any chance for a royal government had passed because of recent changes in the British ministry. The ministers with whom Franklin might have had some influence, Allen declared, had been replaced with men who were friends of the Penns.[13]

The supporters of proprietary government were right in this instance. Not only had all danger to the Penns passed, there is little evidence that the proprietors were ever in jeopardy of losing governmental control of Pennsylvania. In November 1765 the Privy Council deferred action on the Pennsylvania Assembly's petition for royal government. Franklin chose to regard the postponement as temporary, while Thomas Penn believed— correctly—that the royal government issue was dead. He wrote that the petition had been postponed "sine die," which, to him, meant "for ever and ever." While Richard Jackson did not dare say so openly, he was afraid that Penn was right. About two years earlier he had warned Franklin that a petition to oust the Penns would meet formidable obstacles, and he had demonstrated little enthusiasm for pursuing it at the time Franklin returned to England. The Doctor, who was never short on ego, chose to believe that he could surmount all obstacles. Even after the setback at the Privy Council he continued to believe, or at least said he did, that royal government could still be won for Pennsylvania. Gradually, though, he lost hope, while letting Joseph Galloway and other allies back home think for years that royal government might somehow be effected. Not long after the Privy Council's action, Galloway wrote that he was irate. Thomas Wharton used the word "upset," but in June 1766 Galloway wrote, "It greatly revives the People here to find by your letter to the

---

[13]Thomas Wharton to Benjamin Franklin, 13 October 1765. Ibid., XII, 115, 315-17.

Committee of Correspondence that our Petition for a Royal Government will be proceeded on, as soon as the general Affairs of the Colonies are Settled."[14] Franklin, devious man that he was, sent assurances for several more years of eventual success, knowing full well that royal government for Pennsylvania was a lost cause. If he had told the truth, there would have been no excuse for him to remain in London.

Failure to secure a favorable response from the Privy Council was not Franklin's only serious problem by the autumn of 1765. Not only had he miscalculated on the willingness of British politicians to approve a royal government for Pennsylvania, he had also underestimated the hostility that Pennsylvanians and other Americans felt toward new imperial taxes —particularly the stamp tax. It was his fear that trouble over taxation might become a barrier to royalization that prompted Franklin to draw up a revenue scheme that would satisfy people on both sides of the Atlantic. He must have believed that he could persuade George Grenville to adopt his plan and drop the Stamp Act. It was soon obvious to him, however, that Grenville was committed to the act. Hence, the Doctor submitted to the inevitable. Once the Stamp Act passed in Parliament, Franklin decided that there could be no harm in taking practical advantage of the new law. Consequently, he recommended his good friend John Hughes for the post of stamp agent in Pennsylvania. This was a huge mistake, one which brought threats of violence to his family and property in Philadelphia. Moreover, his popularity plummeted in Pennsylvania and other American colonies. Franklin's handling of the Stamp Act very nearly ruined him politically throughout America.

The Doctor had mentioned to Richard Jackson in 1764 that he had a plan. As indicated earlier, he said nothing about it to Galloway or other allies in Pennsylvania. Nor did he take the agents who represented other colonies into his confidence when he reached England. Instead he conferred with Thomas Pownall, former governor of Massachusetts, and the two of them worked on the plan with the idea of showing it to Grenville in February 1765—before Parliament could enact the Stamp

---

[14]*Acts of the Privy Council*, IV, 741; Benjamin Franklin to Cadwalader Evans, 9 May 1766; Joseph Galloway to Benjamin Franklin, 27 February 176[6] and 16 June 1766; Thomas Wharton to Benjamin Franklin, 12 March 1766. *Franklin Papers*, XIII, 179-80, 190-92, 268-69, 317; Hanna, *Franklin and Pennsylvania Politics*, 198-200; Hutson, *Pennsylvania Politics*, 205-207; Thomas Penn to John Penn, 30 November 1765. Penn Papers, HSP.

Act. The scheme called for Parliament's authorization of a legal-tender paper currency that would be administered through loan offices to be established throughout the colonies. The loan offices would lend bills of credit to borrowers at 6% interest on the security of real estate mortgages. The bills would circulate as legal tender, thus expanding the currency supply in the colonies. Net proceeds from the interest would go to the Crown in lieu of direct taxes. Furthermore, the plan included provisions for systematic repayment of the loans and safeguards to prevent depreciation and inflation. Everyone would benefit, and there would be no serious quarrels over sensitive constitutional issues. A major flaw in the scheme was that revenue could be expected to decline precipitously during depression years.[15]

Before Franklin and Pownall could put the finishing touches on the currency-revenue scheme and make contact with Grenville to present it to him, the Doctor was chosen as one of four agents to see Grenville and offer an alternative to the Stamp Act. At the meeting, which was held on 2 February 1765, the Pennsylvania agent said nothing about his plan to his colleagues or to Grenville. Instead he went along with the three other agents in proposing the traditional requisition system, whereby each colony responded to particular requests from the Crown when there was a need for men or supplies. If Grenville had accepted this proposal, Franklin planned to abandon his revenue scheme, for the requisition system was clearly the method favored by most Americans for contributing to imperial needs. Grenville rejected the agents' proposal out of hand, after receiving a negative reply upon asking if they could agree on the proportion each colony should pay.[16]

Still hoping to forestall the Stamp Act, Franklin and Pownall sent the recently arrived agent's currency-revenue scheme in writing to Grenville on 12 February. The minister, who, according to Franklin, was "besotted

---

[15]Verner W. Crane, "Benjamin Franklin and the Stamp Act," *Colonial Society of Massachusetts, Transactions* 32 (1937): 57-59; Crane, *Franklin: Englishman and American*, 96-101; Crane, *Letters to the Press*, 25-30; Joseph Albert Ernst, *Money and Politics in America, 1755-1775* (Chapel Hill: University of North Carolina Press, 1973) 96-100, 104-105; *Franklin Papers*, XII, 47-61; Kammen, *Rope of Sand*, 146; Newcomb, *Franklin and Galloway*, 108-110, 112.

Franklin's first involvement in developing a currency scheme and arguing for it was 1729. He was a staunch opponent of tight-money policies and an ardent advocate of an abundant medium of exchange. See: *Franklin Papers*, I, 140-41, 147, 149, 153.

[16]*Franklin Papers*, XII, 30, 30 ns. 3-5, 47-61; Kammen, *Rope of Sand*, 112-13.

with his Stamp-Scheme," gave the plan little, if any, consideration and pushed ahead with the Stamp Act. By 14 February the Doctor knew that the Stamp Act, in spite of strong American opposition, would soon be passed by Parliament. And so it was—on 21 February in the House of Commons and 8 March in the House of Lords. Agent Jackson, as a member of the House of Commons, had spoken forcefully against the act on the floor of the Commons on 6 February. He had argued that while Parliament possessed the right to pass the act, it should refrain from doing so. The view he expressed came to be reiterated again and again in America during the next decade. A direct tax imposed on Americans by a body in which they were not represented, Jackson asserted, would threaten their liberties and the liberties of all Englishmen.[17]

In the months that followed, when the Stamp Act's passage caused an unprecedented uproar in the colonies and considerable second guessing in England, Franklin once again tried to promote his currency scheme as an acceptable substitute for the stamp tax. He was delighted in December 1765 when some members of the new Rockingham ministry showed an interest in the plan, but the Grenville faction killed it with indifference and half-hearted support. Ironically, this worked to Franklin's advantage, since the scheme was lambasted in America when word of it circulated throughout the colonies in 1766. Once the Doctor learned of the American opposition to his plan—Americans were not aware that Franklin was the author of it—he quickly dropped it and did everything he could to disassociate his name from it. Henceforth, he became an ardent champion of the old requisition system, a politically safe position for a colonial agent who wished to retain his popularity in the colonies.[18]

Trying to prevent the Stamp Act's passage by offering a substitute measure for it was not the only political effort Franklin made in the spring of 1765. Few colonists paid attention to the work he did to keep British soldiers out of American homes. When the Quartering Act of 1765 was first proposed, it provided for billeting His Majesty's troops in private colonial dwellings if the need arose. Franklin and his fellow colonial agents argued that Americans should not have to billet soldiers

---

[17]*Franklin Papers*, XII, 37-40, 47-61, 65-66, 65 n. 2, 66 ns. 3 and 4.

[18]Crane, *Franklin: Englishman and American*, 102; Benjamin Franklin to William Franklin, 9 November 1765; Benjamin Franklin to Joseph Galloway, 11 October 1766. *Franklin Papers*. XII, 361-65, 447-50; Kammen, *Rope of Sand*, 129. Also see: *Franklin Papers*, XII, 47-61.

under conditions any different from those in England, where billeting in private homes had been made illegal in 1628. With the help of Thomas Pownall, Franklin succeeded in securing a word change that excluded billeting in private homes. As finally enacted, the statute required colonial governors to rent vacant buildings for use as barracks.[19] Franklin was proud of making this contribution to the preservation of American rights. Any hope he had of being applauded for it was dashed, however, when Pennsylvanians and other colonists became convinced that he had betrayed them in the matter of the stamp tax. At best he had cooperated with Grenville; at worst he had encouraged the hated tax in order to win royal support in his battle to royalize Pennsylvania. That was how it looked to many Americans, and the agent's enemies did their best to keep the scenario alive.

News of the Stamp Act's enactment reached Pennsylvania in mid-June. Just before it did, in late May, two of Franklin's political allies, Samuel Wharton and Hugh Roberts, wrote the Doctor that the criticism of him—so savage during the election of 1764—was subsiding. "We do not hear a sentence transpire against you," wrote Wharton. Roberts noted that Franklin's enemies were in decline, saying, "the Flame is expired."[20] Little did the two men realize that Franklin was about to be engulfed by a new wave of invective; the barbs that had been hurled at him over the royal government issue the year before would seem mild by comparison to what was impending because of Franklin's presumed role in the Stamp Act. On 19 June a Philadelphia merchant, probably Charles Thomson, wrote Franklin that the city was greatly alarmed over the Stamp Act, which the merchant called "a new Tax . . . enforced by ways subversive to English liberty." A few days later Franklin's business partner, David Hall, informed the Pennsylvania agent that nothing was talked about in Philadelphia but the Stamp Act, with which the people were "much displeased."[21]

---

[19]Benjamin Franklin to Deborah Franklin, 18 April 1765; Benjamin Franklin to Samuel Rhoads, 8 July 1765. *Franklin Papers*, XII, 106-107, 205. Also see: Ibid., XII, 118-20.

[20]Hugh Roberts to Benjamin Franklin, 20 May 1765; [Samuel Wharton] to Benjamin Franklin, 27 May 1765. Ibid., XII, 136, 142.

[21]Philadelphia Merchants to Benjamin Franklin, 19 June 1765; David Hall to Benjamin Franklin, 20 and 22 June 1765. Ibid., XII, 183-88, 189-90; *London Chronicle*, 17-20 August 1765.

Before Thomson and Hall's letters could reach Franklin and make him aware of the hostile reaction back home, he wrote an unfortunate and oft-quoted letter to Charles Thomson on 11 July. The contents of the letter provide strong support for the charge that the Pennsylvania agent, at the very least, accepted the Stamp Act as a law that, no matter how distasteful, had to be obeyed by all law-abiding Englishmen throughout the empire. He made it clear to Thomson that he did everything he could to prevent the law's passage and that his efforts were like trying to keep the sun from setting. Now, he told Thomson, there was only one course to follow, and that was to make "as good a Night of it" as possible. "We may still light Candles," he told his merchant friend. If Franklin thought Thomson would join him in this obviously acquiescent attitude, he was badly mistaken. The merchant's response to the letter condemned the Stamp Act and the government that had passed it, calling it taxation without representation and a denial to Americans of their rights under the British Constitution. Instead of lighting candles, Thomson warned the Pennsylvania agent, the people would soon begin "the works of darkness."[22]

In the public mind, confirmation of Franklin's acquiescence or, per-haps, even support of the Stamp Act was reinforced by his recommen-dation of John Hughes, the agent's close friend, as stamp agent for Pennsylvania. Thomas Penn had also been asked to recommend someone, but the proprietor showed considerable political acumen by declining, for he rightly perceived that "the People might suppose we were consenting to the laying this load upon them." Through the summer of 1765 Franklin remained oblivious to the damage he had done himself by philosophically accepting the Stamp Act and securing the appointment of John Hughes as a provincial stamp agent. His letters during those months indicated that he did not expect the act to be repealed and that he intended to take as much practical advantage of it as he could. He said he would work for repeal, but he saw little likelihood of success. To John Hughes he wrote:

> As to the Stamp-Act, tho' we purpose doing our Endeavour to get it repeal'd, in which I am sure you would concur with us, yet the success is uncertain. If it continues, your undertaking to execute it may make you unpopular for a Time, but your Acting with Coolness and

---

[22]Benjamin Franklin to Charles Thomson, 11 July 1765; Charles Thomson to Benjamin Franklin [24 September 1765]. *Franklin Papers*, XII, 206-208, 279.

Steadiness and with every Circumstance in your Power of favour to the
People, will by degrees reconcile them. In the meantime, a firm Loyalty
to the Crown and faithful adherence to the Government of this Nation
. . . will always be the wisest Course for you and I to take whatever
may be the Madness of the Populace or their blind Leaders . . .

This letter demonstrates beyond doubt that Franklin was not yet aware of
America's deep hostility toward the Stamp Act. He did not know that his
friend Martin Howard, Jr., of Rhode Island would be hanged in effigy by
a Newport mob merely because he asked Franklin to help him secure the
appointment as stamp agent for Rhode Island. Nor did he know that
David Hall was losing numerous subscribers to the *Pennsylvania Gazette*
because he advocated obeying the law and refused to print attacks against
the Stamp Act. The Pennsylvania agent was yet unaware that his life
might have been in danger if he had ventured home in the late summer
of 1765. Hall wrote on 6 September that he would be afraid for
Franklin's "Safety, as the Spirit of the People is so violent against every
One they think has the least concern with the Stamp Law," and they had
"imbibed the Notion that you had a Hand in the framing of it, which has
occasioned you many Enemies." Finally, Franklin had no idea in the
summer of 1765 that John Hughes had been put dangerously in harm's
way, as on three occasions mobs threatened to pull down his house.[23]

Still oblivious to the huge number of new enemies he had made, the
Doctor was defending his position on the Stamp Act as late as 14 September 1765. He told David Hall that he had done everything he could
to prevent the law's passage and asserted that the "Abettors of Proprietary
injustice" would continue attacking him even if he had been successful
in his opposition to the stamp tax. He approved, he said, of Hall's policy
not to print inflammatory pieces attacking the statute. By this time
William Franklin, whose attitude toward the Stamp Act was essentially
the same as his father's, was doing everything he could to defend the
elder Franklin. He had argued in July that the Pennsylvania agent had

---

[23]Paul W. Conner, *Poor Richard's Politics: Benjamin Franklin and His New American
Order* (New York: Oxford University Press, 1965) 144; Benjamin Franklin to David Hall,
20 August 1765; Benjamin Franklin to John Hughes, 9 August 1765; David Hall to
Benjamin Franklin, 6 September 1765; Martin Howard, Jr. to Benjamin Franklin, 14 May
1765; Extracts of Letters from John Hughes [8-17 September 1765]. *Franklin Papers*, XII,
130, 130 n. 3, 234-35, 241-42, 255-59; Thomas Penn to William Allen, 13 July 1765.
Penn Papers, HSP.

opposed the Stamp Act and would work for its repeal, but William made it clear that his father expected to fail in the attempt. As for himself, the New Jersey governor felt caught in the middle, trying not to offend the people of his province or the British ministry. William disliked the Stamp Act, but, as his father did, he accepted it and intended to enforce it in New Jersey. He condemned mob action and commended John Hughes for his determination not to be intimidated into resigning as stamp agent of Pennsylvania.[24]

By the time Benjamin Franklin realized the depth of the bitterness toward him and the Stamp Act, the danger to his family and property had passed, and the hotly contested election of 1765 in Pennsylvania was over. Deborah Franklin wrote her husband on 22 September to tell him that she had sent Sally to New Jersey for her safety and had persuaded Cousin Josiah Davenport to "fech a gun or two." This occurred at the height of the election campaign of 1765, when a mob threatened to level the houses of Joseph Galloway, John Hughes, and Samuel Wharton, as well as Franklin's house. It was alleged that the Pennsylvania agent "had obtained the Stamp Act" and that his friends "were warm Advocates for carrying it into Execution." Members of the Quaker party managed to raise a force of 800 White Oaks (as Franklin's mechanic supporters were called) to stand against the mob, which ultimately disbanded without resorting to violence.[25]

The commotion in Philadelphia was precipitated mainly by the proprietary party's efforts to pin the Stamp Act on Franklin and his allies. With appreciable success the party spokesmen argued that the Stamp Act was a prime example of royal government and that all who favored royalization must be supporters, if not promoters, of the despicable statute. When the Franklin forces retaliated by accusing the proprietary party of disloyalty to the king, the party leaders, fearful that any further assaults on the Stamp Act by them might aid the cause of the royal government advocates, became less outspoken. Thus was the proprietary party unable to capitalize on the Stamp Act issue to the extent it desired. Nor could the Quaker party capitalize on it. In order to win support in

---

[24]Benjamin Franklin to David Hall, 14 September 1765; William Franklin to Benjamin Franklin [26 July 1765], 7 September and 13 November 1765. *Franklin Papers*, XII, 222, 260-62, 267-68, 367.

[25]Deborah Franklin to Benjamin Franklin, 22 September 1765. Ibid., XII, 312-14, 312 n. 5.

England for their royal government petition, party leaders felt compelled to soft-pedal the explosive issue. The Franklin-Galloway forces, despite the popular furor over the Stamp Act, won the election of 1765 rather handily, as Quaker moderation prevailed. This did not mean that Franklin's personal reputation escaped major damage. Many who supported Quaker moderation in 1765 and refused to join the mobs believed the Stamp Act was wrong and assigned Franklin a role in its enactment. Galloway made it clear that opposition to the stamp tax and to Franklin for his part in it cut across party lines. When he wrote to William Franklin on 14 November 1765, Galloway admitted, "Too many of our friends were inclined to unite with these wretches" in mob action.[26]

By 9 November 1765, the Doctor had received sufficient information from home to know that his political reputation was in shambles in Pennsylvania and other parts of America. Even Jane Mecom, his favorite sister, who lived in Boston, was perplexed by her famous brother's actions, especially his recommendation of John Hughes to be a stamp agent. She tried to make herself believe that Franklin had a good purpose, which, as yet, had not been revealed to the public. Although her brother was now fully aware of how serious his problem was in the colonies, he remained calm. He merely wrote to David Hall and William Franklin and flatly denied the charge that he had framed or promoted the Stamp Act. He informed them that he was working with the new ministers of the Rockingham cabinet, especially Lord Dartmouth, to secure the immediate suspension and ultimate repeal of the controversial act. He counted on his partner and his son to spread his side of the story. This marked the first step in a public-relations campaign by the Pennsylvania agent to restore his pro-American image in the minds of the people back home. He would devote much energy to this end during 1766. The campaign included public praise for the old requisition system as the ideal way of providing American contributions to the imperial coffers. Privately the Doctor

---

[26]Joseph Galloway to Benjamin Franklin, 18 [July] 1765, and [8-13 October 1765]; Joseph Galloway to William Franklin, 14 November 1765; [Samuel Wharton] to Benjamin Franklin, 13 October 1765. Ibid., XII, 216-19, 270-74, 372-75; Hutson, *Pennsylvania Politics*, 193-98, 201-202; Newcomb, *Franklin and Galloway*, 121-24, 142-43; Benjamin H. Newcomb, "Effects of the Stamp Act on Colonial Pennsylvania Politics," *William and Mary Quarterly* 23 (1966): 260-269, 271.

continued to promote his currency scheme, until he found out that it, too, was likely to be politically ruinous.[27]

As part of his campaign to redeem himself politically, Franklin wrote letters to key supporters (in addition to his partner and son) to explain his position. He also called on people in England, who had influence in America, to send letters portraying him as one who had opposed the Stamp Act in the first place and was now working hard for its repeal. For example, Dr. John Fothergill, the London physician well known to many Philadelphia Quakers, wrote James Pemberton, a leading Pennsylvania Quaker political figure, in February 1766, to say, "I can safely aver that Benjamin Franklin did all in his power to prevent the Stamp Act from passing" and "he asserted the rights and privileges of America with the utmost firmness, resolution, and capacity." This statement, which was published in the *Pennsylvania Gazette* on 8 May 1766, helped restore Franklin's reputation in Pennsylvania. Another declaration, a public statement by evangelist George Whitefield, to the effect that the Pennsylvania agent was most instrumental in securing the repeal of the Stamp Act, was probably helpful to Franklin throughout the colonies. No minister was more widely known all over America than the eloquent evangelist, according to whom, the *entire* credit for repeal was due Franklin and two London merchants, Barlow Trecothick and Capel Hanbury.[28] Whitefield exaggerated, of course, but, then, he was frequently given to extravagant language.

Letters and statements by Franklin and his friends in England to people in the colonies doubtlessly helped the agent in his public-relations campaign. Nothing he did, though, was more beneficial than his public examination before the House of Commons. During hearings on the Stamp Act and the uproar it had caused, the Rockingham Whigs

---

[27]Benjamin Franklin to David Hall, 9 November 1765; Benjamin Franklin to William Franklin, 9 November 1765; Jane Mecom to Benjamin Franklin, 30 December 1765; Benjamin Franklin to Joseph Galloway, 11 October 1766. *Franklin Papers*, XII, 361-65, 366, 417; XIII, 447-50.

[28]John Fothergill to James Pemberton, 27 February 1766. Corner and Booth, *Letters of Dr. John Fothergill*, 256; Casper Kribble to David Deshler, John Wister, and Richard Wister, 21 October 1765; Benjamin Franklin to [Thomas Crowley?], [6 January 1766]; Benjamin Franklin to [Hugh Roberts], 27 February 1766; Benjamin Franklin to Jonathan Williams, 28 April 1766; Benjamin Franklin to Daniel Wister, 27 September 1766; William Franklin to Benjamin Franklin, 30 April 1766. *Franklin Papers*, XII, 328-30, 328 n. 8, 329 n. 3; XIII, 23-26, 176 n. 4, 177-78, 253-56, 255 n. 8, 429.

questioned various people in the House of Commons, which sat as Committee of the Whole during the proceedings. On 13 February 1766, Franklin was queried for four hours. Most of the questions asked by proponents of repeal had been given to the agent in advance so that he could respond with prepared answers. Some questions, however, were asked by opponents of repeal and had to be answered spontaneously. In his responses, the Doctor said everything that most Americans and the Rockingham ministry wanted to hear. Americans, asserted the Pennsylvania agent, paid "many and very heavy taxes"—real estate, personal, poll, and excise taxes. They had consistently supported His Majesty's wars with men and supplies, claimed Franklin, and they should not be taxed by a body in which they had no representatives. He conceded that Parliament possessed the right to levy duties on American trade, but contended that it had no right to impose internal taxes on the colonists. "The people will pay no internal tax," the agent insisted. Thus, he made a sharp distinction between internal taxes and trade duties, which were regarded as "external" taxes. He believed that Americans would pay their fair share of imperial expenses if they were *asked* and not forced. He went on to predict that the American boycott of British goods, already implemented by the colonies, would be effective and would hurt Britain as much as America, if the Stamp Act were not repealed.[29]

What a performance! The Pennsylvania agent who had been teetering on the precipice of political disaster for months was saved, in large measure, by this staged performance in the House of Commons. More than saved, in fact. In a few months, when the news spread across the Atlantic and through the colonies, Franklin became a genuine American hero, for in March 1766 the Rockingham Whigs secured the repeal of the hated Stamp Act. Thanks to a superb public-relations campaign, the Doctor received most of the credit in America for that accomplishment. So elated were Americans over the rescission that they took no notice of the Declaratory Act's passage. That ominous statute became law on the same day of the Stamp Act's repeal, and it claimed for Parliament the authority to legislate for the colonies "in all cases whatsoever."

---

[29] *The Examination of Doctor Benjamin Franklin, before an August Assembly relating to the Repeal of the Stamp Act, &C* (Philadelphia: Hall & Sellers, 1766) 3-6, 8, 12-13, 15. Located in the John Carter Brown Library, Brown University; *Franklin Papers*, XIII, 124-62, *passim.*; Kammen, *Rope of Sand*, 121.

Franklin's intimate friend William Strahan obtained a transcript of the Doctor's examination and sent it to David Hall, who printed and sold it. Surpassing even George Whitefield's hyperbole, Strahan argued that his friend's testimony, more than anything else, was responsible for the *"speedy* and *total* Repeal of this odious Law." Franklin's sensible answers, so Strahan claimed, completely convinced Lord Rockingham that repeal was essential to a restoration of harmonious relations between the mother country and her American colonies. The examination received a great deal of publicity in 1766 and 1767, both in England and America. As late as July 1767 the editor of *The Gentleman's Magazine* commented favorably upon it and published select questions and answers from it. Near the end of 1767 the *Georgia Gazette* in Savannah gave Franklin's performance in the House of Commons very high praise. By this time, though, the tide had long since turned in the Doctor's favor. As early as 20 May 1766, Charles Thomson wrote him to say, "Your Enemies at last began to be ashamed of their base insinuations and to acknowledge that the Colonies are under obligation to you." Three days later Joseph Galloway wrote in the same vein, noting that repeal had "open'd the Eyes of Many who entertained a Contrary Opinion of you, from the wicked Calumnies of your Enemies." Proprietary party leaders, however, continued to heap abuse upon the Doctor—especially William Allen who steadfastly maintained that Franklin was the "greatest Enemy to the Repeal of the Stamp Act of all the Men in England."[30]

Still clinging to a shred of hope that he might yet effect royalization for Pennsylvania, Franklin never spoke ill of the British government during his campaign to rescue his reputation. Instead, he consistently spoke disapprovingly of mob violence. He praised the Rockingham Whigs and expressed confidence that Parliament would not allow its mistakes to go unrectified for very long. He advised Pennsylvanians not to gloat over the repeal of the detested stamp tax, but instead to express appreciation to friendly British merchants who had helped, to cooperative British officials, and to the Crown. Franklin's suggestion prompted the Pennsylvania Assembly to adopt an address to the king expressing gratitude for repeal. Through Lord Shelburne, the agent was able to have the address

---

[30]Charles Thomson to Benjamin Franklin, 20 May 1766; Joseph Galloway to Benjamin Franklin, 23 May and 7 June 1766. *Franklin Papers*, XIII, 278, 285-86, 295. Also see: Ibid., XIII, 124-62; *The Gentleman's Magazine* 37 (1767): 368-69; *Georgia* (Savannah) *Gazette*, 2 December 1767.

presented to His Majesty. The Doctor was disappointed that more Americans did not emulate the provincial Assembly he served and thank the king for approving repeal.[31]

Seventeen sixty-five and 1766 were two of the busiest and hardest years Franklin spent in England—and not altogether because of the Stamp Act. Sometimes the Pennsylvania Assembly could be demanding at inopportune times. In October 1765, right in the middle of the Stamp Act crisis, the Assembly asked its two agents to secure a copy of the royal confirmation of a Pennsylvania election law which had been passed in 1706. The agents did as instructed, and Franklin sent the results to the Assembly's Committee of Correspondence on 11 January 1766. By that time the Assembly had heard about the Currency Act of 1764 and had decided to request its repeal. On 14 January 1766, the Assembly, believing that the act would throttle the Pennsylvania economy, approved a petition calling upon Parliament to rescind the Currency Act. Upon receiving the petition Franklin drafted a bill that provided for the repeal of the objectionable statute and for the establishment of a new system of colonial currency. His plan resembled the scheme he and Pownall had presented to Grenville the year before, but it called for using the interest income in America to pay service costs, instead of sending the proceeds to England as a tax substitute.[32] At least one historian has argued that the colonies needed little relief from the Currency Act of 1764, because it only prohibited *new* legal tender laws in the colonies and required Americans to retire on schedule all legal tender issues then current. Besides, he contends, Maryland had proved that currency could circulate without making it legal tender. This argument fails to consider the act in the context of Britain's perennial tight-money policy, which often kept the colonies strapped for an adequate medium of exchange. The Pennsylvania

---

[31]Benjamin Franklin to Joseph Fox, 24 February 1766; Benjamin Franklin to David Hall, 24 February 1766; Pennsylvania Assembly's Committee of Correspondence to Richard Jackson and Benjamin Franklin, 6 June 1766. *Franklin Papers*, XIII, 168-70, 290-91; Hutson, *Pennsylvania Politics*, 215; Kammen, *Rope of Sand*, 187.

[32]Ernst, *Money and Politics*, 101-104, 359-60; Benjamin Franklin to the Pennsylvania Assembly's Committee of Correspondence, 11 January 1766. *Franklin Papers*, XIII, 28-29, 28 n. 2. Also see: Ibid., XIII, 204-207 ns. 3-9.

Assembly was right to seek the law's repeal, and it is unfortunate that Franklin's efforts failed in 1766.[33]

The Assembly members were not always satisfied with their agents during 1766. Some apparently came to believe that only three men were privy to the colony's business in England. They were Benjamin Franklin, Joseph Galloway, and, to a lesser extent, Richard Jackson. Thomas Wharton informed the two agents in the spring of 1766 that they were being criticized for always writing to Galloway instead of the Assembly's Committee of Correspondence, as their instructions required. When the Committee wrote in May and sent the agents all the laws the Assembly had passed in January, along with instructions to work for their approval, its members included an order for the agents to send all letters pertaining to the public business to "the Speaker [Joseph Fox] and Committee of Correspondence." Franklin seems to have gotten the message, for he soon began sending monthly reports, some of which were quite lengthy, to *the Committee*. In June he wrote that all American business at Whitehall had come to a standstill because of unsettled conditions in the ministry. The Duke of Grafton, Secretary of State for the Northern Department, had resigned, and there was talk of reorganizing colonial affairs. Since little business was being transacted, Franklin had decided to take a six-to-eight-week vacation. He asked for permission to return home the following spring. He took his vacation (traveling as usual with Dr. John Pringle) in Holland and the German states, taking the waters at Bad Pyrmont in western Germany and visiting the Royal Library in Hanover. The two men left London on 15 June and returned on 16 August.[34]

While Franklin was on the Continent, the Rockingham ministry collapsed and was replaced on 30 July by the Pitt-Grafton ministry. On 22 August, less than a week after he returned to London, the Doctor wrote the Committee of Correspondence in Philadelphia to report on the ministerial changes and to assure Pennsylvanians that most of the new

---

[33]Jack Sosin makes this argument in "Imperial Regulations of Colonial Paper Money, 1764–1773," *Pennsylvania Magazine of History and Biography* 88 (1964): 185, 188.

For Franklin's unsuccessful efforts to bring about repeal, see: Ernst, *Money and Politics*, 103-104, and *Franklin Papers*, XIII, 205.

[34]Thomas Wharton to Benjamin Franklin, 2 March 1766; the Pennsylvania Assembly's Committee of Correspondence to Richard Jackson and Benjamin Franklin, 8 May 1766; Benjamin Franklin to the Pennsylvania Assembly's Committee of Correspondence, 12 April and 10 June 1766; Benjamin Franklin to Deborah Franklin, 13 June 1766. *Franklin Papers*, XIII, 190-92, 236-40, 267-68, 297-99, 314-16.

ministers were friendly toward America. He was especially complimentary of Lord Shelburne, the new Secretary of State for the Southern
Department—this in spite of the fact that the new secretary was married
to the niece of Thomas Penn's wife. At the time Franklin wrote this
report, which included comments on his vacation as well as remarks on
ministerial changes, the Assembly was in no mood to receive the
information gladly. Its members were angry with their two agents for
allowing a trade bill to slip through Parliament with a provision cutting
off Pennsylvania's trade with Ireland. The Committee of Correspondence
admonished the agents to pay "particular attention" to details when such
bills were before Parliament in order to prevent grievances from arising.
Actually, the bill had inadvertently been wrongly worded, and the mistake
was soon corrected as a result of Franklin's efforts.[35]

The Pennsylvania Assembly's displeasure with Franklin in 1766 could
have been related to the political rivalry between Joseph Fox and the
Doctor's chief lieutenant, Joseph Galloway. It is certain that it had
nothing to do with the Stamp Act, since the Assembly and the agent had
been in mutual agreement that, as far as that issue was concerned,
moderation was the best policy. If indeed the unhappiness with Franklin
was promoted by Speaker Fox and his supporters, better times were on
the way. The 1766 provincial election again left the Quaker party in
control of the Assembly and brought a new speaker to the chair—Joseph
Galloway. He had been able to retain his seat in the Assembly in spite of
a determined campaign by the proprietary party to oust him. John Penn
and William Allen, who were either politically naive or could not bear to
give Thomas Penn any bad news, wrote the proprietors to say that Franklin was losing ground in Pennsylvania and that the Assembly elected in
1766 was more moderate. Such a report flew in the face of the fact that
the new Assembly proceeded to reappoint Franklin and Jackson as agents

---

[35]Benjamin Franklin to the Speaker and Committee of Correspondence of the
Pennsylvania Assembly, 22 August and 8 November 1766; Pennsylvania Assembly's
Committee of Correspondence to Richard Jackson and Benjamin Franklin, 20 September
1766. Ibid., XIII, 383-84, 419-21, 420 n. 1, 486-87; Hutson, *Pennsylvania Politics*, 217-
18.

and to tell them that its members, like the members of the three previous assemblies, believed it was "necessary" to seek royal government.[36]

Although Galloway was pleased with the outcome of the 1766 election and his ascendance to the speakership, he was anxious about the obstacles in the way of obtaining royal government, primarily because Chief Justice Allen constantly assured everyone who would listen that the Penns were now quite secure in their proprietary right to govern. Allen pointed out that Lord Shelburne was closely connected to the Penns by both marriage and friendship. Had the chief justice assumed too much from the fact that the proprietors were well-connected with the key figures currently in power at Whitehall? It must have seemed so to Galloway, when he soon received a letter from Franklin, assuring the new speaker that Shelburne supported Pennsylvania's petition for royal government and that his lordship had told Thomas Penn that the Penns should relinquish their proprietorship voluntarily. Franklin promised to push the matter vigorously when the new "Season of Business" began in London.[37] Thus, 1766 ended with the Pennsylvania agent promising to press on with his mission, while the seeds of doubt regarding its success were being sown back home.

Besides trying to convince his cohorts in Pennsylvania that royal government was still a possibility, Franklin encountered another problem —a personal *and* political one—as 1766 drew to its close. William Franklin, Joseph Galloway, and Thomas Wharton, all Franklin spokesmen, fell out with the Doctor's longtime partner in the printing business. The younger Franklin became convinced that David Hall favored William Allen over the Pennsylvania agent. Hall, William claimed, was a greater enemy to his father than William Smith, because Smith was open in his

---

[36]Pennsylvania Assembly's Committee of Correspondence to Richard Jackson and Benjamin Franklin, [18 October 1766]; Joseph Galloway to Benjamin Franklin, 28 October 1766. *Franklin Papers*, XIII, 447 n. 6, 465-67, 478-81; Newcomb, "Effects of the Stamp Act," 271-72; Newcomb, *Franklin and Galloway*, 144-45; Thomas Penn to John Penn, 8 November 1767. Penn Papers, HSP.

[37]Benjamin Franklin to Joseph Galloway, 11 October and 13 December 1766; Joseph Galloway to Benjamin Franklin, 28 October 1766. *Franklin Papers*, XIII, 447-50, 478-81, 520-23.

In the spring of 1766 Franklin apparently did very little about promoting the royal government petition, probably because he was too busy rescuing his reputation from the damage it had sustained during the Stamp Act crisis. See: Thomas Penn to John Penn, 10 May 1766; Thomas Penn to William Allen, 6 June 1766. Penn Papers, HSP.

opposition while Hall was sneaky—"a meer Snake in the Grass." Consequently, Galloway and Wharton had backed one William Goddard, a protege of James Parker, in establishing the *Pennsylvania Chronicle* to present the views of the Franklin forces. Using James Parker's old press and Franklin's house on Market Street, steps which William Franklin authorized, the Franklin proponents launched the newspaper in January 1767.[38] The Doctor, who still trusted Hall, was not altogether pleased with this move, for it soon caused him some problems.

In spite of the many matters that claimed Franklin's attention in 1765 and 1766, he found time to revive his interest in land speculation and his longtime dream of establishing a colony west of the Appalachian Mountains. With his interest piqued once more, Franklin enthusiastically gave himself to the work of effecting his plan, continuing to promote it for as long as he was in England and even after he left. Ever since he and William had led forces into western Pennsylvania in 1755, both of them had dreamed of securing land in the west and turning it into a fortune. Even before that, the elder Franklin had talked about a new colony or two in the transmontane region. He also continued his interest in Nova Scotia. In 1766 he sought to add to his holdings there by applying for an additional grant of 20,000 acres, and in 1767 he received that grant. By this time his son had already urged Franklin to set his sights on a much bigger land venture. On 17 December 1765, the New Jersey governor had written his father about a land scheme concerning the Illinois Country. George Croghan, an Irishman who had long been involved in the Indian trade, had negotiated a peace that included some land cessions from the Indians in that area. William proposed that his father work to have the land, conceded by the Indians to the Crown, turned over to the "Sufferers," who were Croghan, another Indian trader named William Trent, and the Philadelphia firm known as Baynton, Wharton, and Morgan. The Crown could then charge quit rents on the land, while leaving it up to the "Sufferers" to compensate the Indians. The "Sufferers," also called the "Suffering Traders," claimed to have suffered losses during the French and Indian War while serving the king. At first they sought monetary indemnification for their losses, but they later decided to drop their pleas for money and instead ask to be indemnified through land grants.

---

[38]William Franklin to Benjamin Franklin, 13 November 1766. *Franklin Papers*, XIII, 498-502.

Eventually the "Suffering Traders" expanded their membership to include the two Franklins, John Hughes, Joseph Galloway, and Sir William Johnson, His Majesty's superintendent of Indian affairs for the area north of the Ohio River. Their plan was to obtain a royal grant of 1,200,000 acres and establish a colony in the Illinois Country. All that was necessary for the success of their scheme was to persuade the British ministry to confirm the boundaries that Croghan, representing Sir William Johnson, had negotiated with the Indians. The matter was complicated by conflicting claims to the western territory made by the colonies of New York, Pennsylvania, and Virginia. The Doctor's job was to win support at Whitehall for the colony, for the boundaries agreed upon by the Indians, and for the land grant itself. He was hard at work on the project by the fall of 1766. In discussing it with some of the ministers, Franklin won the support of Lord Shelburne, who liked the plan but feared the Treasury would object to it as too costly a venture. The Pennsylvania agent soon found that Lord Hillsborough, president of the Board of Trade, opposed the scheme out of fear that a new colony in the American west would lure Irish workingmen away from their homeland. Franklin continued to lobby Shelburne while simultaneously persuading Phineas Lyman, colonial agent for Connecticut, to merge a proposed grant of his with the Illinois grant and to join the Illinois scheme. The Doctor also enlisted the support of Maurice Morgann, Shelburne's undersecretary of state for the Southern Department. The long-dreamed-of project took a considerable amount of Franklin's time. Though it took many curious twists and turns over nearly ten years, the Pennsylvania agent remained committed to this grandiose land scheme that would never be brought to fruition.[39]

How Franklin found time for so many projects and activities during 1765 and 1766, especially while the Stamp Act crisis raged, is amazing. Not only did he undertake the promotion of a western colony, he again, as he had done during his first mission, wielded the propagandist pen

---

[39]Thomas P. Abernethy, *Western Lands and the American Revolution* (New York: Russell and Russell, 1959) 15, 22-25, 28-36, 99; *Acts of the Privy Council*, IV, 817; *Franklin Papers*, XII, 395-400, 403-406; XIII, 123, 171-173, 330, 389, 414-16, 424-25, 430, 446-47, 486; Articles of Agreement for the Illinois Company. Ohio Company [William Trent] Papers, Etting Collection. Historical Society of Pennsylvania; Randall, *A Little Revenge*, 96-97, 203-210, 214-16; Jack Sosin, *Whitehall and the Wilderness* (Lincoln: University of Nebraska Pres, 1961) 142-43.

under a variety of pseudonyms—"A Traveller," "F. B.," "N. N.," "A Virginian," and "Pacificus Secundus." He also wrote satire under his own name, as he did when he lampooned a bill before Parliament in the spring of 1766, a bill providing for the transportation of felons to the American colonies. Richard Jackson circulated the piece among his fellow members of Parliament. It provoked some laughter, but it failed to prevent passage of the bill. Everything that Franklin wrote at this time was clearly pro-American—hence his care, at least in most cases, to conceal his identity with pseudonyms. He defended the American attitude toward the Stamp Act and lauded the colonists' contributions to the successful prosecution of the French and Indian War. He attacked the idea of "virtual representation" championed by some Englishmen and condemned taxation without representation. Writing as "A Virginian," he insisted that Americans, in their opposition to the Stamp Act, were merely exercising their rights as Englishmen. Moreover, he denied the "imagined" charges that Americans were on the verge of pressing for independence.[40]

There were still other activities. Along with John Foxcroft, he continued as deputy postmaster general of the colonies, and he was compelled to devote some attention to the duties of that office. There was also his printing business, which his partner David Hall had run since 1748. The agreement they had made called for dissolving the partnership in April 1765. Before leaving for England, Franklin had given his power of attorney to James Parker so that Parker could settle all accounts with Hall. However, Parker's final report proved unsatisfactory to Franklin, for it indicated that the Doctor owed Hall £993, eleven shillings, and six pence. The Pennsylvania agent drafted some "Observations" about some of the entries in Hall's books and promised to send them to him, but Franklin never did. When Hall died six years later in 1772, the accounts remained unsettled. Hall's sons would later attempt a settlement with the Doctor, but there is no record of a final settlement ever taking place.[41]

[40]Verner W. Crane, "Certain Writings of Benjamin Franklin on the British Empire and the American Colonies," *The Papers of the Bibliographical Society*, XXVII, part I, 1934, 2-3, 3 n. 19; Crane, *Letters to the Press*, xxvii, 30-31; *Franklin Papers*, XII, 132-35, 240-42, 245-46, 253-55, 406-407, 410-16; XIII, 4-6, 18-22, 63-72; Kammen, *Rope of Sand*, 85-89.

[41]Anthony Todd to Benjamin Franklin, 2 January 1765. *Franklin Papers*, XII, 12. Also see: Ibid., XII, 110, 280-82, and XIII, 87-116.

Along more personal lines, Franklin continued, on occasion, to write letters and send presents to friends and relatives. To his cousin, Mrs. Keziah Coffin, he sent a pair of candlesticks in 1765, and to another "kinsman," Jonathan Folger, he gave "a little Book of English History." Through Deborah's letters and his responses to them he maintained a keen interest in his new house in Philadelphia. He was distracted, too, by his poor relations in Boston—Jane Mecom and her children, who were in need because of the death of Jane's husband in 1765. Franklin did all he could for Jane and also tried to help her ne'er-do-well son Benny, who was the Doctor's namesake. With Franklin's assistance, Benny Mecom had gone into business, but in 1765 the young man went bankrupt. Financial disaster would follow Benny to the grave. Franklin family grief continued into 1766, when Benjamin's brother Peter, postmaster of Philadelphia, died on 1 July. In addition to dealing with family matters, the Pennsylvania agent received the usual requests from acquaintances for assistance in landing them government jobs and from young men and their parents for letters of recommendation that would help the young men secure admission to the University of Edinburgh.[42]

As Franklin dealt with matters public and private during 1765 and 1766, the somewhat bizarre case of Springett Penn came up again near the end of 1765, at the time when Franklin was feeling the pressure of the Stamp Act crisis most keenly. Edward Penington wrote Franklin to say that he feared Springett would sell Pennsbury Manor to Thomas Penn for half what it was worth and knock Penington out of a commission. Four years earlier, when he would have received a commission, Penington, on Franklin's recommendation, had advised Springett not to sell. Now that Penington faced the prospect of losing his commission, he was not happy about listening to Franklin earlier. The entire situation changed when Springett died of tuberculosis in November 1766, before he could dispose of the manor. Pennsbury then passed to Springett's mother, Ann Penn. Franklin, perhaps still hoping to keep Springett's (now his mother's) claim to Pennsylvania alive for use as possible leverage against Thomas Penn, sent Ann Penn a letter of condolence. She, too, intended to sell Pennsbury, but she died a few months later. The estate then passed into the hands of the man Ann Penn had recently married, a

---

[42]See numerous letters to and from Benjamin Franklin in Ibid., XII, 247-48, 251-52, 292-99, 417, 419, 419 n. 7; XIII, 60, 84-86, 86 n. 8, 388, 530-32.

Dublin, Ireland, attorney named Alexander Durden.[43] Any chance of getting at Thomas Penn through Springett Penn's claim to Pennsylvania—if indeed there had ever been much of a chance—was gone forever.

The Pennsylvania agent must have felt genuine relief when the furor over the Stamp Act died down and life returned to normal by late 1766. His political reputation was somewhat battered, but still intact. He had come face to face with political ruin, and he knew it. A herculean public-relations campaign had helped the Doctor survive, and for years he remained highly sensitive to charges that he had favored the Stamp Act or had attempted to profit from it. As late as 1774 he became embroiled in a battle through correspondence with the Reverend Josiah Tucker, dean of Gloucester, who made such charges in a pamphlet. Franklin backed Tucker down, making the Anglican churchman admit that Franklin had appealed to George Grenville on behalf of a friend and not himself. On the other hand, the Doctor admitted that he would never have recommended John Hughes for stamp agent of Pennsylvania if he had foreseen that the deed would be interpreted as advocacy of the Stamp Act. In 1776—two years after the Franklin-Tucker fray—when Franklin had left England, Tucker got in the last word by asserting that Franklin and his fellow colonial agents had at least acquiesced in the Stamp Act, even if they had not approved of it.[44]

Franklin's part in the Stamp Act was clearly controversial among his contemporaries, and historians, too, have had little success in reaching a consensus on that question. According to Verner Crane, the Doctor was a determined opponent of the hated act from the outset, while Bernard Fay has portrayed Franklin as a thoroughgoing pragmatist who took the act in stride and intended to use it to advantage for himself and his friends. William S. Hanna has asserted that Franklin was willing to accept the Stamp Act as the price for securing royal government for Pennsylvania, and Theodore Thayer has argued that Franklin was willing to accept the Stamp Act if he could get away with it politically. Blending several of these arguments, Thomas Wendel has insisted that the Penn-

---

[43]Edward Penington to Benjamin Franklin, 14 November 1765; William Franklin to Benjamin Franklin, [13 July 1766]; Benjamin Franklin to Ann Penn, 20 November 1766. Ibid., XII, 370-71, 370 n. 2; XIII, 333, 506-507, 506 n. 3, 507 n. 7; Hutson, *Pennsylvania Politics*, 56-58.

[44]See the several letters that were exchanged by Benjamin Franklin and Josiah Tucker in February 1774. *Franklin Papers*, XXI, 83-85, 123-28, 126 n. 4.

sylvania agent was trying to be all things to both the colonies and the mother country in order to help himself and the colonies.

Like historians, many of Franklin's contemporaries were convinced that the Doctor was above all else a political being, but not all agreed on whose interests he put first—his or the colonies. One might take lightly the comments of Massachusetts agent Dennys DeBerdt and his peevish friends, who claimed that Franklin remained neutral on the Stamp Act until he saw "which way the cause would be carried, and then broke out fiercely on the American side," because those people heartily disliked the Pennsylvania agent.[45] On the other hand, it is more difficult to disregard the observations of the honest and intelligent Ezra Stiles, who was on good terms with Franklin and benefited from the Doctor's friendship. During the 1760s Franklin used his influence with Principal William Robertson to secure honorary Doctor of Divinity degrees from the University of Edinburgh for several American ministers. Stiles was one of them. The Doctor went to work early in 1765 on behalf of Stiles, who was a Yale graduate and pastor of the Second Congregational Church in Newport, Rhode Island. A little over a month after Franklin contacted Principal Robertson, the Rhode Island minister was awarded the honorary doctorate.

Four years later, in May 1769, Stiles drew some conclusions about Franklin's efforts in favor of Stiles himself, the Reverend John Rogers (a friend of George Whitefield) of New York, and the Reverend Samuel Cooper of Boston. Stiles's considered opinion was that Franklin played politics at all times. "His real idea has been coalition of all parties, being true friend to America, and gaining honour from all: till he conceived the Scheme of dethroning the proprietary Gov[ernment] in Pennsylvania," asserted the Congregational minister. Continuing his scenario, Stiles noted that the royal government scheme caused the Doctor trouble with Pennsylvania's Presbyterians and Germans. He then schemed with "Crown officers" to royalize all colonies. Since Franklin could not kill Penn "singly," he thus courted royal support for the task. When the Pennsylvania agent failed in his effort to oust Penn, he gave some consideration to spending his last years in New England. Hence his interest in obtaining

---

[45]Crane, *Benjamin Franklin: Englishman and American*, 68-69; Bernard Fay, *Franklin, The Apostle of Modern Times* (Boston: Little, Brown and Company, 1929) 315-23; Hanna, *Franklin and Pennsylvania Politics*, 173-84; Kammen, *Rope of Sand*, 149; Thayer, *Pennsylvania Politics*, 112-17; Wendel, *Politics of Liberty*, 133.

honors for New England ministers. By securing John Hughes's appointment as stamp agent, Franklin damaged his reputation in America, but,
thanks to his examination before the House of Commons, he "retrieved
his Char[acter] with us." Securing doctorates for prominent American
ministers, asserted Stiles, was just one more political move to win
additional American support.[46]

Stiles, it appears, knew Franklin rather well. His "Conjecture" does
not have about it the air of someone with an ax to grind. Instead, it has
all the earmarks of an honest and informed man who tried to make a fair
assessment of another man. It is probably a valid judgment of Franklin's
political motives and activities. In sum it says that the Doctor was
basically pro-American, but he was willing to work closely with royal
officials if doing so would bring about the ouster of the hated Thomas
Penn. He was even willing to accept the Stamp Act and take practical
advantage of it for his friend John Hughes, until he discovered that such
a position had all but ruined him in America. Always resilient upon
realizing a damaging mistake, the devious Dr. Franklin took calculated
steps—his examination before the House of Commons, securing honorary
doctorates for respected American ministers, and other steps—to undo the
damage he had done. From Stiles's "Conjecture" and other evidence, it
is obvious that in politics, the Doctor was ever the calculator—and the
rebounder when he found that he had miscalculated. Politics was his
game, and he was a shrewd player. What he was really thinking was
never easy to discern.

---

[46]Benjamin Franklin to William Robertson, 4 March 1765, and 12 December 1768;
Benjamin Franklin to [George Whitefield], 6 December 1768; William Robertson to
William Strahan, 18 February 1765; William Robertson to Benjamin Franklin, 1 April
1765; Ezra Stiles' Memoir and Conjecture, 1 May 1769. *Franklin Papers*, XII, 69-70, 80-
81, 98-99; XV, 290; XVI, 122-25.

# 6. "Too Much of an American": Another Crisis, Another Agency

The Stamp Act crisis, which gave Benjamin Franklin the biggest scare of his political career, made him realize that his ultimate loyalty lay with the American colonies. Although he angled for years to land a political position in the mother country, he never abandoned the American cause. Secretly, he continued to be a fervent advocate of the colonies, but in public he did not go—at least until the eve of the Revolution—far enough to put himself at risk in England. If he thought his political tightrope walking was over when the Stamp Act was repealed, he was again mistaken, for the years 1767 and 1768 brought a new crisis caused by the passage of the Townshend Duty Act and a new responsibility, as he became the colony of Georgia's agent. The Doctor's holding two agencies caused British officials to identify him more closely with American discontent and made his appointment to a lucrative and prestigious post in the British government less likely. By the time he received word of his appointment as Georgia agent, he was, in fact, entertaining some mildly radical ideas about American rights and the place of the colonies in the British Empire. Before Franklin could bask long in the glory he gained as the American most influential in bringing about the repeal of the Stamp Act, the Townshend Duty crisis closed in on him and caused him to define and refine further his views of the British Constitution and the rights, privileges, and obligations of Americans under its provisions.

If Pennsylvania's royal government petition was dead by 1767, as Thomas Penn believed it was, there was really no valid reason for Franklin to remain in England. He could easily have returned to Philadelphia, leaving Pennsylvania's regular agent, Richard Jackson, to handle the colony's business at Whitehall. Yet, while there was no official need of Franklin's remaining, he had his own reasons for wanting to stay longer. His continuing quest for a post in the British government and the need for him to promote the Illinois land scheme were two of the foremost. In order to stay, he continued to hold out to Joseph Galloway and the Assembly the possibility of reviving the royal government petition, although he was not very hopeful or encouraging during 1767. While royal government advocates like Galloway, Thomas Livezey, and Thomas Wharton waited hopefully for good news from the Doctor,

Franklin blamed his failure to make progress on the instability of the Pitt-Grafton ministry. Wharton wrote on 14 January 1767 that he hoped the new year would bring the change "in our Government from Proprietary to Royal." In October 1767 the Assembly's Committee of Correspondence, when advising Franklin and Jackson of their reappointment as agents, noted that the Assembly still wanted a royal government. Livezey, a member of that committee, wrote his own letter to Franklin to say that he did not yet despair of achieving royalization, in spite of the fact that some avowed it could never happen while Thomas Penn lived. This prompted Livezey to joke that he did not wish the proprietor dead, but he would like to see "how he would look when he was Dead." He further remarked that he did not want Penn "to Die against his will, but if he Could be prevail'd on to Die for the Good of the People, it might make his Name as Immortal as Samsons Death Did his."[1]

Throughout 1767 Franklin painted for the Pennsylvania Assembly the picture of a shaky ministry and the lack of a propitious opportunity to revive the colony's petition for royal government. In April he sent this message to Joseph Galloway, along with news that the titular head of the ministry, William Pitt, who had recently been elevated to the peerage as the earl of Chatham, was almost "totally disabled by perpetual Gout and for some time past with Fevers." By the time Franklin wrote Galloway again, telling him of rumored ministerial changes, another stumbling block to royal government had appeared—"the general Rage against America artfully work'd up by the Grenville Faction." New York's refusal to comply with the Quartering Act had produced a serious adverse reaction against all the colonies among British political leaders. In June the Pennsylvania agent wrote that the continuing turmoil in the British government would likely prevent a presentation of the Pennsylvania petition in the summer of 1767 and make it necessary for Franklin to stay "another Winter." From a letter the Doctor wrote to Galloway on 8 August, the Pennsylvania speaker should have guessed that the agent had given up on the petition. Blaming his failure to revive the petition on unavoidable and unforeseen difficulties, Franklin suggested that the Assembly might decline to reappoint him as agent if its members were

---

[1]Thomas Wharton to Benjamin Franklin, 14 January 1767; Pennsylvania Assembly's Committee of Correspondence to Benjamin Franklin and Richard Jackson, 17 October 1767; Thomas Livezey to Benjamin Franklin, 18 November 1767. *Franklin Papers*, XIV, 7-8, 285-88, 310.

discouraged and tired of paying him to pursue the matter. He offered to serve the province for as long as he remained in England, even if he was not reappointed. Claiming he had been asked to remain (probably by Dr. John Fothergill and the promoters of the Illinois scheme), Franklin stated that he intended to do so in order to take care of some personal business.[2] The personal business almost surely had to do with promoting the Illinois colony.

Franklin's blaming ministerial instability for his failure to press the Pennsylvania petition for royal government must have puzzled Galloway and his colleagues in the Assembly. Was not William Petty, second earl of Shelburne, Secretary of State for the Southern Department at that time and were not he and Franklin, according to the Doctor's own claim, very good friends? Shelburne's office was the one through which such a petition could most likely be promoted, and Franklin had assured the Assembly the previous year that his lordship favored royal government for Pennsylvania. While it is true that the Pitt-Grafton ministry was distinguished for neither its harmony nor its energetic leadership—thanks in part to Pitt's poor health—it did manage to carry on the business of the government. And Shelburne, no matter how much he thought Thomas Penn should give up his right to govern Pennsylvania, was never prepared to force the proprietor's hand. Penn made this quite clear in a letter to Richard Peters on 18 May 1767. He wrote:

Lord Shelburne and every other Minister no doubt wish to persuade us to resign our Government, and would agree to give us terms very different from those offered to our Father, but he has no thought of forcing us or [holds the opinion] that it can be done, if they could, why should they give hints of ten times the money. I think it is quite impossible that Mr. Franklin's accounts can have any foundation, as for myself I am determined not to yield to any offer that will be made to me, and have told the Ministers I am not to be frightened into compliance by Mr. Franklin or any of his tools.[3]

On the next day after writing to Peters, Penn expressed similar sentiments in a letter to William Allen, assuring the Pennsylvania chief

---

[2]Benjamin Franklin to Joseph Galloway, 14 April, 20 May, 13 June, 8 August, and 1 December 1767. Ibid., XIV, 124-25, 163-65, 184, 228-32, 329-33.

[3]Thomas Penn to Reverend Mr. [Richard] Peters, 18 May 1767. Penn papers, HSP. Also see: *Franklin Papers* x, 348, n2.

justice that the proprietors would never be forced to give up their governmental rights. Penn admitted to having been informed that if he *chose* to give up those rights, he would receive "a very valuable consideration" for doing so. He assured Allen that he would never choose to relinquish his power to govern, especially as long as Benjamin Franklin was active in promoting a royal government for Pennsylvania. The senior proprietor wondered why the Assembly kept the Doctor in London on an impossible mission. He also wondered what Franklin could possibly be doing with his time, since, according to Lord Shelburne, the agent seldom visited the secretary's office. Penn was convinced that Franklin would "very soon run the length of his tether."[4]

The year 1767 slipped away with Thomas Penn's remaining convinced that Franklin was on a fool's errand and with the Doctor's grumbling about ministerial instability. Late in 1767 and early in 1768 a political realignment did occur at Whitehall. The new post of Secretary of State for the American Department was created. Lord Shelburne turned down the new office, choosing to stay on as Secretary of State for the Southern Department until October 1768. Wills Hill, the earl of Hillsborough, accepted the post and thus became the first man to head the new department, moving into the office on 20 January 1768. There were other changes, but the appointment of Hillsborough to the American Department and Lord Sandwich's appointment as Postmaster General were the ones that directly affected Franklin. At first the Pennsylvania agent was not alarmed by the changes. He reported them very matter-of-factly to William Franklin and Joseph Galloway, and, writing as "Old England, in its senses," he attacked a writer styling himself "Old England" for criticizing the reorganization. According to "Old England," the governmental changes only added to the bureaucracy and gave the Crown more power. Franklin lashed out at "Old England" for suspecting "plots and deep designs where none exist." While the Doctor did not consider Hillsborough a "general enemy," he did note that his lordship was strongly opposed to paper money issues. Franklin reported to son William that there was talk of making the Pennsylvania agent Hillsborough's undersecretary! Giving no hint that he would turn down the job, if it were offered, Franklin

---

[4]Thomas Penn to William Allen, 19 May and 31 July 1767; Thomas Penn to Benjamin Chew, 31 July 1767. Penn Papers, HSP.

stated that there was little chance that it would happen because of the perception in England that he was "too much of an American."[5]

While Franklin adopted a wait-and-see attitude toward Hillsborough, Thomas Penn expressed some regret, but not alarm, that American affairs had passed from Shelburne to Hillsborough. Of Wills Hill, the Pennsylvania proprietor remarked that he was a man of honor and "good capacity," but added that he had "no intimacy with him, as . . . with the former." Still, Penn was convinced that Hillsborough would do the proprietors no injury, unless his official responsibility required it. Thomas was also sure that the ministry was too occupied with the trouble-making political maverick John Wilkes (an outlawed member of Parliament from Middlesex who had returned to England from exile) to pay any attention to Franklin.[6]

For several months the Pennsylvania agent could not discern Hillsborough's attitude toward the colony's petition for a royal government, but he wrote encouraging words to royal government advocates back home. The devious Dr. Franklin went so far as to tell Thomas Livezey that "Anxiety and uneasiness" were painted on the proprietor's brow, when it was highly unlikely that he had even seen Thomas Penn. Meanwhile, in Pennsylvania, Joseph Galloway had fallen ill and had grown discouraged and impatient. He bemoaned the mess in the colony, where violence was committed with impunity—all because the proprietary government was weak and ineffective. Galloway hoped that the "Distracted and distressed Situation" would grab the king's attention and cause him "to take the Government under his immediate Directions." While the speaker of the Assembly was losing heart in Philadelphia, Franklin was becoming ever more disgusted in London with the political corruption there and the inability of authorities in the mother country to control the disturbances provoked by the fiery John Wilkes. In writing about British elections, Franklin commented on "drunken Electors," "Confusion and Disorder," and "Profusion of Money." To son William he remarked that on election day Britain would be sold "for about Two Millions" and that

---

[5]Benjamin Franklin to William Franklin, 9 January 1768; Benjamin Franklin to Joseph Galloway, 9 January 1768. *Franklin Papers*, XV, 14-17. Also see: Ibid., XV, 17-19; Sosin, *Whitehall and the Wilderness*, 167.

[6]Thomas Penn to John Penn, 7 January and 7 May 1768; Thomas Penn to Dr. [Thomas] Gra[e]me, 10 March 1768. Penn Papers, HSP.

the devil himself could buy it by offering another half million.[7] By this time Franklin was facing the prospect of admitting to the Pennsylvania Assembly that his mission could not be accomplished. It is altogether possible that he was crafting his excuse for the failure he would soon have to confess. If royal government in England was steeped in corruption and had no more success in dealing with disturbers of the peace than did proprietary government in Pennsylvania, Franklin could argue that the rejection of the colony's petition had turned out to be a blessing in disguise.

As the Doctor waited for the final "no" on the royal government petition, hoping against hope that Hillsborough would somehow see the matter Pennsylvania's way, Franklin continued to push for the repeal of the Currency Act of 1764, but to no avail. He discussed repeal with Hillsborough in February 1768, and the secretary indicated that he would support repeal for New Jersey, New York, and Pennsylvania only. Hillsborough expressed doubt, however, that Parliament would agree even to limited repeal. While Franklin had Hillsborough's ear, he asked his lordship to support the royal takeover of Pennsylvania's government, and the secretary promised to investigate the matter. It was not until August that Hillsborough gave his final answer to the Pennsylvania agent. After investigating, as he had promised he would, the secretary sided with the proprietors. Franklin concluded that Hillsborough had "a stronger Partiality for Mr. Penn than any of his Predecessors," and he saw no need to pursue the matter again until there was another change in the ministry. For all practical purposes, the agent's mission was over, but with friends encouraging him not to leave England, he decided to stay a while longer to see "what Turn American Affairs" would take. For seven more years he would continue this pattern of waiting around for a favorable political change, until he felt compelled by his legal troubles in England and Deborah's death in Philadelphia to return home. After 1768, though, he would forget the royal government petition altogether. By 1769 Galloway and the other royal government advocates in the Assembly seemed to have given up, too, although Franklin and Jackson's reappointment as

[7]Benjamin Franklin to Joseph Galloway, 13 March and 14 May 1768; Benjamin Franklin to Thomas Livezey, 20 February 1768; Benjamin Franklin to William Franklin, 13 March 1768; Joseph Galloway to Benjamin Franklin, 10 March 1768. *Franklin Papers*, XV, 54, 71-73, 78-79, 129-30.

agents in October 1768 carried with it the instructions of previous years—including the order to secure royal government for the province.[8]

Franklin could not afford to let his Pennsylvania allies know that he was losing interest in the petition for royal government during 1767 and 1768, for securing its approval was what they were paying him to do in England. Once he admitted final defeat on the matter, there would be no reason for him to remain in London as Pennsylvania's agent. A bigger issue had emerged, one that diverted Franklin's attention because it affected *all* the colonies, but the Pennsylvania Assembly might not agree that it was more important than royal government for a single colony. Actually, the issue was the same old issue of Parliament's right to tax the colonies and legislate for them. This time, however, it appeared in a tricky form. The recently appointed Chancellor of the Exchequer, Charles Townshend, persuaded Parliament to levy new trade duties on the colonies by passing the Townshend Duty Act on 29 June 1767. During his examination before the House of Commons in 1766, Franklin had conceded Parliament's right to levy such duties. Yet he quietly opposed the Townshend duties at the time they were proposed. He took no public stand, however. Determined not to repeat the mistakes of 1765, he waited for the reaction of Pennsylvania and the other colonies before announcing his position. When word reached him that Boston was in an uproar over the Townshend duties and especially over the Board of Customs Commissioners that had been established there under the same act, the Doctor expressed disapproval of Boston's intemperate response. Although Franklin ultimately took the offensive against the duties, he consistently refused to endorse violent resistance.[9]

The Townshend duties never created as much tension between Britain and her colonies as had the stamp tax. Still, feelings were strong enough. As early as 25 February 1767, Franklin himself was growing tired of British claims that the colonies had been founded at Parliament's expense and that this gave Parliament the right to tax them. The Pennsylvania

---

[8]Benjamin Franklin to Joseph Galloway, 17 February, 2 July, and 20 August 1768; Pennsylvania Assembly's Committee of Correspondence to Benjamin Franklin and Richard Jackson, 15 October 1768; Joseph Galloway to Benjamin Franklin, 17 October 1768; Ibid., XV, 48-50, 174-86, 189-90, 228-32; Hutson, *Pennsylvania Politics*, 223-27, 229; Kammen, *Rope of Sand*, 255; Newcomb, *Franklin and Galloway*, 180-81.

[9]Benjamin Franklin to William Franklin, 25 November 1767; *Franklin Papers*, XIV, 323-24; Newcomb, *Franklin and Galloway*, 180-81.

agent denied that Parliament had paid for the founding of the colonies. Private adventurers, asserted Franklin, had paid for settlement and had conquered the new country without aid from king or Parliament. Moreover, he warned those in England who would listen that America might soon become great and powerful, and then a union between the colonies and the mother country might become more advantageous to England than America.[10]

As the Doctor listened to British arguments in favor of taxing the colonies, and, as he heard reports of American reactions followed by British determination to show Americans their place, he became more and more pro-American and less and less pleased with the British government. Perhaps he even wondered how he could ever have wanted royal government for Pennsylvania in the first place, but, of course, what he had *really* wanted was to oust Thomas Penn as proprietor; royal government was merely a means to that end. Poor Joseph Galloway, who could only see what he regarded as chaos unchecked in Pennsylvania, remained totally oblivious to the strain in the relationship between Britain and her colonies. Incredibly, when Galloway heard about the Townshend Duty Act, he thought it would help bring on the change to royal government in Pennsylvania, since some of the proceeds from the duties were to be used to pay royal officials. This meant that the salary of Pennsylvania's royal governor, in the event royal government was achieved, might be paid by the Crown, and that would remove the objections of those Pennsylvanians who thought royal government would be too expensive. Galloway did not like "the Scheme" and wished it "had never been thought of," but since it was the law, he was ready to use it to advantage.[11] The speaker had obviously learned nothing from the Stamp Act crisis, but Franklin had learned to oppose unpopular acts, not use them.

Although the Doctor moved steadily toward outright rejection of any taxes imposed on the colonies by a body in which Americans were not represented, his public utterances, except for the ones he published under pseudonyms in the press, were always moderate in tone. He did go so far, however, as to submit his old political enemy John Dickinson's "Letters from a Farmer in Pennsylvania" to the British press, and Dickinson's views were not considered moderate by British officials. This series of letters, which began appearing on 5 November 1767 in the *Pennsylvania*

[10]Benjamin Franklin to Lord Kames, 25 February 1767. *Franklin Papers*, XIV, 67-70.
[11]Joseph Galloway to Benjamin Franklin, 9 October 1767. Ibid., XIV, 276-77.

*Chronicle*, argued that there had been no taxation for revenue in America before the Stamp Act and that the Townshend Duty Act was designed to raise a revenue and only incidentally to regulate trade. Therefore, the duties it imposed were no more acceptable than the stamp tax had been. Dickinson stated that he could accept true regulatory duties, but not taxes levied to raise an imperial revenue. William Franklin and Joseph Galloway had condemned Dickinson's effort, and Galloway, calling the letters radical and provocative, used them against Dickinson in the election of 1768. The Doctor, on the other hand, chose to be fair minded and approved of Dickinson's letters, viewing them as an example of peaceful resistance. Still, Franklin did not agree with Dickinson entirely, for the Pennsylvania agent had about reached the conclusion that there could be no middle ground on Parliament's right to legislate for the colonies. It could legislate for the colonies on *all* matters or *none*, and, in his secret convictions, he had decided in favor of none. Thus, Franklin was ready to deny to Parliament even the regulatory duties that Dickinson declared he could accept. Even so, the agent remained convinced that the "Farmer's Letters" had been very influential in "spiriting the People up against the late [Townshend] Duties."[12]

In addition to using Dickinson's arguments against the Townshend Duty Act, the Pennsylvania agent expressed his own views, usually in the press under one pseudonym or another. His "Causes of the American Discontents before 1768" appeared in the 5–7 January 1768 issue of the *London Chronicle*. The piece was signed "F & S," and in it Franklin lauded the traditional requisition system, contending that it had worked well and that abandoning it in favor of the new tax policies had been a mistake. The Doctor called for an American boycott (under the cover of his pseudonym, of course) against goods taxed by the Townshend Duty Act and urged Americans to live frugally and manufacture what they could for themselves. He warned that the "new system of politics" could cause disunion. The agent complained to his son William that Griffith Jones, editor of the *London Chronicle*, had softened some of the stronger language in the piece so that the article could "neither scratch nor bite." Franklin was not sure whether Jones was a supporter of George Grenville

---

[12]Benjamin Franklin to William Franklin, 13 March 1768; Benjamin Franklin to Jean-Baptiste Le Roy, 21 September 1768; William Franklin to Benjamin Franklin, 22 August 1767. Ibid., XIV, 237-38; XV, 74-78, 206. Also see: Ibid., XV 110-12, 111 n. 3 and Newcomb, *Franklin and Galloway*, 185, 196.

or just a very cautious man. William Goddard picked up "Causes of the American Discontents before 1768" through William Franklin and published it in the *Pennsylvania Chronicle*. According to the younger Franklin, the piece was "much admired."[13]

The Doctor offered similar arguments in another article that appeared during 1768 in *The Gentleman's Magazine*. In this piece Franklin signed himself "A. B." and asserted that Americans should give up their money by their consent *only*. He compared America to the German state of Hanover, both of which were under the British king's jurisdiction. Hanover, however, was not taxed by Britain. Franklin refuted the idea that the colonists should accept taxes out of gratitude for British protection or because the money was needed for defense. Americans, he reiterated, had "the right of Englishmen to give their own money with their own consent." "A. B." argued that Americans had gladly complied with requests for money under the requisition system, but that right had been taken away "by the mistaken *policy of one man*."[14] That man, of course, was George Grenville, chief architect of the Sugar and Stamp acts. Franklin seems to have suspected Grenville of somehow being involved in designing the Townshend Duty Act. The Doctor made it quite clear many times that he blamed Grenville, more than anyone else, for the new imperial policy.

Franklin's more forthright pro-American stance eventually brought him into conflict with his longtime friend William Strahan. The London publisher, and now member of Parliament, believed that Parliament had every right to tax the colonies. He had regarded the Stamp Act as inexpedient and had worked with Franklin to secure its repeal, but he could not accept Franklin's new position—that Parliament could impose *no* taxes on the colonies. Partial repeal of the Townshend duties was as far as Strahan was ever willing to go, while the Pennsylvania agent came to insist that total repeal alone was acceptable.[15]

Except for Joseph Galloway, the Pennsylvania Assembly and Franklin were thinking along the same lines, as far as the Townshend duties were concerned. In February 1768 the Assembly's Committee of Corre-

<hr>

[13]Crane, *Letters to the Press*, 106-107, 151-52 n. 1, 268; Benjamin Franklin to William Franklin, 9 January 1768; William Franklin to Benjamin Franklin, 10 May 1768. *Franklin Papers*, XIV, 101-116, 129-34; XV, 4-5, 11-12, 16, 121; XVI, 7-8.

[14]*"Subjects of Subjects," Ibid., XV, 36-38.*

[15]*Franklin Papers*, XIX, 407.

spondence instructed Pennsylvania's two agents to join other colonial agents in seeking repeal of the Townshend Duty Act on the ground that it was injurious to the rights of the American people and to American commerce. Some months later, on 22 September, the committee again criticized the Townshend Duty Act and asked the province's agents to petition the Crown for its repeal. The committee members argued that Parliament had no right to tax Pennsylvanians and that the Townshend Duty Act was "bad Policy" for two reasons: (1) it restricted American commerce and drained specie from the colony by requiring payment in silver, and (2) it made provincial officers independent of the legislature by providing money for their salaries. If the law was not repealed, asserted the committee, the colonists themselves would manufacture the taxed articles and thus bring about "a virtual, if not an actual Repeal of the Statute."[16]

Franklin did as instructed regarding the petition for repeal, but it took months to have the petition considered. Meanwhile, the Pennsylvania agent kept up the fight in ways he thought best, mainly through a stream of propaganda in the press. He wrote articles asking why Parliament had repealed the Stamp Act on the ground that it was improper and then turned around and enacted the Townshend Duty Act, which had the same effect. He challenged the widespread notion that British troops should be sent to America to put the colonists in their place and wondered if brave English officers and soldiers would want to "shed English blood to stifle the British spirit of liberty now rising in the Colonies." Franklin hoped there would be one wise and good man in England who would push for conciliation and prevent civil war, but he feared there was not. He even expressed the view that the colonists were subjects of "the King of Great Britain" and were exempt from the jurisdiction of Parliament. In so many words, the Doctor said that Americans, because they were not represented in Parliament, were not bound by any of Parliament's laws. He further argued that the money raised by the Townshend duties helped neither Britain nor her colonies, since the proceeds paid useless government officials who were merely holders of sinecures. Because Americans felt strongly enough against the Townshend duties to boycott British trade, the mother country's economy was bound to suffer, Franklin warned. It was just not smart, he asserted, to insist on the right to tax if doing so

---

[16]Pennsylvania Assembly's Committee of Correspondence to Benjamin Franklin and Richard Jackson, 22 September 1768. Ibid., XV, 210-14.

interrupted a thriving trade. The Pennsylvania agent even tried to argue that Britain's trade with the mainland North American colonies was more beneficial to the mother country than her trade with the West Indian colonies.[17] As usual, Franklin concealed his identity by employing a variety of pseudonyms.

While the Doctor chipped away with his pen at what he viewed as an unwise policy, he gradually reached the same conclusion that many people in America had reached much earlier—that the new imperial policy was not just unwise; it was unconstitutional. Franklin's old and dear friend James Parker, now living in New York, wrote to condemn the new trade policies and the Townshend duties that reflected them. Parker was particularly angry over the Board of Customs Commissioners that had been established in Boston under the authority of the Townshend Duty Act. Like Parker, more and more Americans were becoming angry, and they were disturbed enough to take drastic action. Late in 1768, the Pennsylvania agent was informed that Philadelphia merchants intended to stop importing British goods, unless English merchants could put enough pressure on Parliament to repeal the Townshend Duty Act, the Currency Act of 1764, and the Sugar Act. The ministry and Parliament proved unsympathetic to American demands for repeal. In December 1768 British officials rejected Pennsylvania's petition for repeal. Because no support could be mustered for it among the leaders who commanded a majority of the votes in Parliament, it was taken off the floor before a vote could be called. Still, Franklin hoped the dispute over the Townshend duties could be "amicably and equitably settled." His hope of somehow restoring harmony must have been dashed on 15 December 1768, when Lord Hillsborough introduced eight resolutions in Parliament condemning American riots and protests and hinting that leaders of the disturbances in Boston might be tried for treason. Because British officials rejected American demands for repeal, Philadelphia merchants implemented a policy of non-importation of British goods in March 1769.[18]

---

[17]Most of Franklin's propaganda pieces appeared in the *London Chronicle* and the *Public Advertiser* and are published in the *Franklin Papers*. See XV, 187-89, 191-93, 206-210, 220-22, 233-42, 251-55, 280-82.

[18]Thomas Wharton to Benjamin Franklin, 7 November 1768; Philadelphia Merchants to Benjamin Franklin, 10 November 1768; James Parker to Benjamin Franklin, 22 November 1768; Benjamin Franklin to an Unknown Correspondent, 28 November 1768. Ibid., XV, 264-70, 272-73, 286-88; XVI, 14-15. Also see: Arthur M. Schlesinger, Sr., *The Colonial Merchants and the American Revolution, 1763-1776* (New York: Atheneum,

Franklin's drift toward radicalism during the crisis over the Townshend duties began to put a strain on his political partnership with Joseph Galloway. While the two men remained friends, the Doctor moved closer to the views of Charles Thomson and John Dickinson. Ultimately the agent identified with a new party, which was led by former Franklin opponents who represented the ordinary rural and urban elements of Pennsylvania society. Thomson, who became Franklin's new chief ally, was a bitter enemy of Galloway. The Pennsylvania speaker advised Franklin to be leery of Thomson's friendship, but the Doctor ignored Galloway, just as he had ignored his son's warnings about David Hall.[19]

Until 1768 Franklin had to keep the Assembly's hopes for royal government alive in order to remain in England in some official capacity. That changed during the Townshend Duty crisis, when he became colonial agent for a second colony—Georgia. Just who promoted Franklin for the Georgia agency and how that person settled upon the Doctor is not known. What is known, however, is that somebody (possibly Franklin himself or, perhaps, Peter Timothy, who published the *South Carolina Gazette*) made sure that the Doctor's name appeared periodically in the *Georgia Gazette*, published in Savannah. In December 1764, just after Franklin had left for England on his second mission for Pennsylvania, the *Georgia Gazette* reported that he was very popular as Pennsylvania's agent. The death of Peter Franklin was mentioned in the Savannah newspaper on 20 August 1766, because he was the agent's brother. A letter sent from London praised Franklin's efforts to secure repeal of the Stamp Act and was published in the *Gazette* on 2 July 1766. No less than three times in 1767 the *Gazette* reported on Franklin's activities in England, and in January 1768 the paper printed a story about the agent's visit to Paris, along with a glowing account of his renowned experiments in electricity. Franklin was thus well known to literate Georgians long before he was proposed as agent. His image in that province was that of a great scientist and a defender of American rights.[20] In all likelihood,

---

1968, originally published in 1918) 125-29.

[19]*Hutson, Pennsylvania Politics*, 234-41; Newcomb, *Franklin and Galloway*, 206-207; John J. Zimmerman, "Charles Thomson, 'The Sam Adams of Philadelphia,'" *Mississippi Valley Historical Review* 45 (1958): 479-80.

[20]Georgia Gazette, 6 December 1764; 2 July and 20 August 1766; 15 July, 2 and 9 December 1767; 6 January and 28 December 1768. Also see: David T. Morgan, "A New Look at Benjamin Franklin as Georgia's Colonial Agent," *Georgia Historical Quarterly*

Franklin played some part, either directly or indirectly, in creating the flattering image.

The Doctor was appointed Georgia agent in the spring of 1768 as a compromise selection, in the hope that his appointment would end a two-year feud between the two houses of the Georgia legislature. For two years the lower house had attempted to appoint Charles Garth, who was already serving as South Carolina's agent. The upper house consistently refused to concur in the appointment of Garth, and Governor James Wright had backed the upper house by persuading officials in London not to receive Garth as Georgia's agent. Hoping to end the political stalemate, Wright responded positively in the early months of 1768 when the lower house proposed Franklin for the agency. Although the upper house exhibited little enthusiasm for the Doctor, its members went along.[21]

The ordinance making Benjamin Franklin agent for Georgia was signed by "Alex Wylly, Speaker" of the lower house, and Noble Jones for the upper house and assented to by Governor Wright on 11 April 1768. Thus, for the first time since William Knox had been dismissed as agent in November 1765 for favoring the Stamp Act, Georgia had an official agent to represent the colony in London. Actually there was a second agent, a Crown agent who kept an eye on Georgia affairs for the Crown. Paid from the royal coffers, the Crown agent was Dr. John Campbell, an English writer of some note. Campbell served in this capacity from 1765 to 1775, but there was little, if any, contact between him and Franklin.

---

68 (1984): 223-24.

It is interesting that William Franklin probably knew of his father's appointment as Georgia agent before he did. William wrote his father on 10 May, less than a month after the appointment, saying he had seen it reported in the *South Carolina Gazette*. It seems altogether possible that Peter Timothy passed his news along to the *Georgia Gazette* and vice versa. See: William Franklin to Benjamin Franklin, 10 May, 1768. *Franklin Papers*, XV, 125.

[21]*William W. Abbot, The Royal Governors of Georgia, 1754-1775* (Chapel Hill: University of North Carolina Press, 1959) 109, 136, 142-44, 160; Allen D. Candler and Lucian L. Knight, eds., *The Colonial Records of the State of Georgia*, 25 volumes. (Atlanta: State of Georgia, 1904–1916 [Volumes I-XXVI except XX and typescript volumes XXVII-XXXIX except XXVII and XXVIII, parts 1 and 2, 1937], XIV, 567, 575-576, 579, 581; XVII, 433, 437, 439, 449; XIX, part 1, 12-14.; Kenneth Coleman and Milton Ready, eds., *The Colonial Records of the State of Georgia*, Volumes XX, XXVII and XXVIII, parts 1 and 2 (Athens: University of Georgia Press, 1977-1979) XXVIII, part 2, 253; *Franklin Papers*, XV, 94-97; Morgan, "Franklin as Georgia's Colonial Agent," 222-23.

The effective date of Franklin's appointment was 1 June 1768, and the ordinance by which it was made, called upon the new agent to "follow and pursue all such instructions, as he shall from time to time receive from the General Assembly" or from the Assembly's Committee of Correspondence, which was to consist of nine men from the lower house and five from the upper house. Seven members of the committee constituted a quorum and could send instructions, as long as at least two members from the upper house were present when the committee met. The new agent's salary was to be £100 per year over and above expenses.[22]

Assuming that Franklin would accept the Georgia agency, the committee wrote him on 19 May 1768 and asked him to investigate the disallowance by the Crown of two Georgia laws. One, called "An Act for the better Ordering and Governing Negroes and other slaves in this Province," was needed, according to the committee, to keep enough labor for Georgia to produce a sufficient supply of "Staple Commodities" to "Subsist." The other law aimed at providing some financial relief from Britain's tight money policies and at encouraging "Settlers to come into the Province." The committee encouraged Franklin to accept the agency and "generally promote our interest and appear and solicit against" anything he thought might be harmful to Georgia's trade and future prosperity. He was further asked to report to the committee and told that he would receive additional instructions from it.[23]

The arrangement by which Franklin was to receive instructions and make reports did not work out in practice, at least not much of the time. Instead of hearing from and reporting to the committee, the agent was soon up to his old ways. He directed most of his correspondence to Noble Wimberly Jones, who became speaker of the lower house not long after Franklin's appointment. This practice had already caused him to be rebuked by the Pennsylvania Assembly, and it would eventually cause him serious trouble with the Georgia upper house. Only occasionally did Franklin correspond with the committee instead of with Jones. The letters the agent received from Jones tended to be filled with admonitions, like the one to keep up the good fight against those acts of Parliament that were "so Grievous to His Majesty's Loyal Subjects." Jones also encour-

[22]*Georgia Colonial Records*, XIX, part 1, 12-14; Morgan, "Franklin as Georgia's Colonial Agent," 222-23, 223 n. 3.

[23]*Georgia Colonial Records*, XIV, 559-85; XVII, 419-48; XVIII, 102-44, 648-88, 743-48; *Franklin Papers*, XV, 94-97; Morgan, "Franklin as Georgia's Colonial Agent," 224.

aged Franklin to work for a restoration of the harmony that was presumed to have existed between Britain and her colonies in a bygone day.[24] Over the following six years the two men exchanged numerous letters.

As the year 1768 drew to a close, the people of Georgia were informed by the *Georgia Gazette* that their new agent, "Dr. Franklin," was "indefatigable in his endeavours to convince the Ministry of the loyalty of the Colonies" and to assure the ministers that "a tenderly and motherly behaviour" by Britain would work more effectively on the colonies than "all her forces by sea and land."[25] That was exactly the tack that Georgians preferred their agent to use, for they, like many other protesting Americans, still saw themselves as loyal British subjects who were demanding nothing more than their just rights under the British Constitution.

Since Franklin wanted to remain in England to promote the Illinois colony, it was fortunate for him that he received the appointment as Georgia agent. He had no reason to stay any longer for Pennsylvania, because for three years there had been little hope of securing royal government for the province and because Lord Hillsborough would soon kill all remaining hope of its ever being achieved. Besides, by this time Franklin probably had serious doubts about royal government. His public mission since 1764 had been to oust the Penns, and he had been unable to accomplish it. His private mission—to reconcile the colonies and the mother country in matters of revenue and taxation—had also ended in failure. Franklin was facing the prospect in 1768 of returning home without having accomplished either mission, but at least he had managed to turn disaster into triumph with regard to the Stamp Act. He might be an *American* hero, but he could offer no royal government to Pennsylvania and no reconciliation of British and American interests in the matter of revenue and taxes. What triumph could he present to the Pennsylvania Assembly, a body which had eschewed Stamp Act radicalism in 1765 and 1766?

Not only was Lord Hillsborough about to close the door forever on the royalization of Pennsylvania, the new Secretary of State for the American Department was busy redefining the nature and functions of colonial agents. His lordship took the position that a colonial lower house

---

[24]*Noble Wimberly Jones to Benjamin Franklin, 24 December 1768. Franklin Papers,* XV, 294.

[25]Georgia Gazette, 28 December 1768.

could not appoint an agent on its own. Agents, contended the secretary, had to be appointed by both houses of a colony's legislature and be approved by the governor. As for petitions to the Crown, Hillsborough wanted them presented by the governors and not by agents. His lordship told Dennys DeBerdt, agent for the Massachusetts lower house, that DeBerdt was no agent at all. The Crown adopted this view, which was generally accepted from 1769 onward. Franklin went to England in 1764, it should be remembered, by leave of the Pennsylvania Assembly. He had neither the sanction nor the good wishes of the proprietors or their governor.[26] If Hillsborough had his way—and he intended to—there would be no need for the Pennsylvania Assembly's agent to remain in London. Under the new ground rules laid down by the secretary, Franklin's appointment by both houses of the Georgia legislature, with the governor's approval, gave him both a legitimate reason to stay in London and some official status at Whitehall.

As Franklin went about his official business for Pennsylvania in 1767 and 1768 and for Georgia beginning in the summer of 1768, he doubtlessly discussed many subjects with British ministers. Among them, of course, were Pennsylvania's petition for royal government and the Currency Act of 1764, but none seems to have claimed more of his attention than the Illinois venture. George Croghan sent the Pennsylvania agent some alarming news on 27 January 1767. Croghan, one of the main instigators of the Illinois scheme, had heard that General Thomas Gage, commander of the British forces in America, had advised the British ministry to relinquish possession of the Illinois country. The general's assessment of Illinois was that "it was more expensive than beneficial to the Crown," since forts would have to be built there to secure trade if the territory was retained. Such expense, the general asserted, would go for nought, as fur traders in the Illinois country were more likely to sell their furs at New Orleans to French buyers who paid higher prices. Thus, His Majesty's government would be spending money on an area that would

---

[26]Benjamin Franklin to Dennys DeBerdt, 31 August 1768. *Franklin Papers.* XV. 196-99, 196 n. 6, 197 n. 7, 198 n. 8; Kammen, *Rope of Sand*, 233-34; Lonn, *Agents of the Southern Colonies*, 107-108; *Pennsylvania Archives*, IV, 311.

Pennsylvania did not have a bicameral legislature. The Pennsylvania Council served the governor in an advisory capacity only. However, the governor's approval was needed to pass laws, and Hillsborough's position could have been construed to mean that the Pennsylvania governor's approval was also required for the official appointment of an agent.

produce no revenue for Britain. Obviously, Croghan disagreed. He doubted that the French paid more for pelts, but, he noted, if it was true, the matter could be easily remedied by changes in British trade laws. Besides, Croghan asserted, Britain's failure to hold on to Illinois would give rise to Indian wars in the area. Franklin's task was clear. He had to convince the ministry that General Gage was wrong, but the Doctor warned Croghan that the ministers were often slow to heed the recommendations of Americans and that he doubted matters would improve until the ministry was "a little better settled."[27] As was his *modus operandi* by this time, Franklin thus provided himself with an excuse in case his efforts failed.

At the same time the Doctor attempted to convince the ministers of the merits of a colony in the Illinois country, his application for a grant of 20,000 acres in Nova Scotia was approved. The approval, given on 26 June 1767, carried with it the condition that Franklin settle the area within ten years. William Franklin believed something would come of this grant, provided the settlement could be "well managed." He gently warned his father that settlement must be handled differently from his venture with Alexander McNutt and John Hughes in the same vicinity, for that grant had been grossly mismanaged. The younger Franklin worried needlessly about any mismanagement of the new grant, for his father would never attempt to settle it. The Doctor's failure to fulfill the terms of the grant meant that the land was supposed to revert to the Crown, but there is no record showing that the British government ever officially reclaimed it.[28]

While Franklin seems to have made no effort to promote settlement on his land in Nova Scotia, he did work diligently to gain approval for a colony in the Illinois country. In August 1767, when Lord Shelburne was preparing to lay out his interior policy for America, the Doctor dined with his lordship and Henry Conway, Secretary of State for the Northern Department. The Pennsylvania agent sought to convince the two secretaries of state that a settlement in the Illinois country would reduce expenses for military outposts, since the settlers there could form a militia

---

[27]George Croghan to Benjamin Franklin, 27 January 1767; Benjamin Franklin to George Croghan, 14 April 1767. *Franklin Papers*, XIV, 13-15, 121.

[28]Acts of the Privy Council, IV, 816-17; V, 598; William Franklin to Benjamin Franklin, 23 October 1767. *Franklin Papers*, XIV, 202, 291-92; *Journals of the Board of Trade, 1764-1767*, 380, 390, 392.

to protect themselves and their colony. Franklin pointed out that Sir William Johnson, Indian agent for the area, approved of the project. Finally, the Doctor worked to convince Shelburne and Conway that the company requesting the grant could bring about settlement "with very little expense to the crown." The two secretaries of state were persuaded and proceeded to recommend the venture to the other ministers. Not only that, but both men led Franklin to believe that they could and would bring about the repeal of the Currency Act of 1764 at the "next session" of Parliament.[29]

Over the next few months, Shelburne promoted his new policy. Convincing some ministers was not that difficult, but Lord Hillsborough, who was president of the Board of Trade at the time, was another matter. He was not at all enthusiastic about the proposed new colony, and he tried to stall it by seeking opinions of London merchants who traded in America. Undoubtedly, his lordship was disappointed to find that the merchants approved of the Shelburne program. It appeared to be well on its way to implementation, until the ministerial shakeup of January 1768 made Hillsborough Secretary of State of the newly created American Department.[30]

As the Shelburne program began to bog down in ministerial wrangling and political jockeying after Hillsborough took charge of the American Department, Americans who lived in colonies bordering on the lands acquired from France in 1763 grew apprehensive over Indian unrest in the newly ceded territory. The Pennsylvania Assembly's Committee of Correspondence urged the province's two agents "to obtain, as soon as possible the Accomplishment and final Ratification" of the boundaries the Indians had agreed on with Croghan and Johnson three years earlier. As the Assembly saw it, ratification of those boundaries was "so necessary to the future Safety of the Colonies." Croghan and the Whartons continued to raise the specter of a frontier Indian war if the Crown did not quickly ratify Johnson's 1765 agreement with the Indians. Thomas Wharton claimed that Croghan's life was in danger from Indian haters who wanted no settlement with the Indians. If Croghan was killed, Whar-

---

[29]Benjamin Franklin to William Franklin, 28 August 1767. *Franklin Papers*, XIV, 242-43.

[30]See letters between Benjamin Franklin and a variety of correspondents in the *Franklin Papers*, XIV, 255-60, 269-72, 275, 302-303; Sosin, *Whitehall and the Wilderness*, 157-61, 163-64, 169, 173-75, 180-81.

ton contended, it would be disastrous, for he alone had the full confidence of the western Indians. Only he could achieve peace with them.
Croghan himself pointed out that Britain's dilatoriness in ratifying the
1765 boundaries had nearly convinced the Indians that the British had
driven out the French so that they could take over the land without
paying the Indians for it. Why, Croghan asked, had the ministry ordered
William Johnson to negotiate the boundaries and then refused to ratify the
agreement?[31]

There can be no doubt that pacification of the Indians had to take
place before the Illinois scheme could move forward. Shelburne had been
ready to take the steps that would have opened the door for a horde of
land speculators (including Franklin and his cohorts) to absorb the
territory west of the Appalachians. Hillsborough, on the other hand, had
merely pretended to go along with Shelburne's plans while erecting
barriers with questions about the management of Indian affairs in the
territory. A little later, according to one historian, Hillsborough came to
fear that white settlement west of the mountains would draw Britain into
a "general Indian War, the expense whereof will fall on this Kingdom."
Perhaps his lordship thought this, without saying so, in 1768, or perhaps
he was indeed worried about new colonies in the American west luring
workers out of Ireland. One issue that emerged during the wrangling was
whether to keep the two superintendents of Indian affairs, William
Johnson in the north and John Stuart in the south, or eliminate their posts
and turn Indian affairs over to the separate colonies that bordered the
western territory. That issue was not resolved, and no clear-cut policy
emerged. In effect, Hillsborough caused a postponement in arriving at a
policy until a new agreement was worked out with the Indians. Johnson
was ordered to negotiate a new treaty with them. Acting on this order, the
superintendent, with the help of George Croghan and with William
Franklin, Samuel Wharton, and other "commissioners" looking on,
negotiated the Treaty of Ft. Stanwix with the Iroquois in November 1768.
Thus were the boundaries between whites and the western Indians settled,
or so it seemed. All the British government had to do was ratify the
Treaty of Ft. Stanwix, and the main obstacle to a colony in the Illinois

---

[31]Pennsylvania Assembly's Committee of Correspondence to Richard Jackson and
Benjamin Franklin, 17 January 1768; George Croghan to Benjamin Franklin, 12 February
1768; Thomas Wharton to Benjamin Franklin, 27 March 1768. *Franklin Papers*, XV, 21-
22, 42-44, 88-92.

country would vanish. Unfortunately for interested speculators, Hillsborough stalled ratification again, an action that eventually helped bring about his ouster as head of the American Department in 1772. The treaty would never be ratified, but, of course, Franklin had no way of knowing that. For as long as he was in England, the Doctor continued to work for the approval to proceed with the colony.[32]

For a man now past sixty years of age, Benjamin Franklin was extraordinarily active. Carrying out his responsibilities as agent and trying to promote the Illinois colony would have kept most men busy enough, but the Doctor was involved in a variety of other activities, too. Sometimes he was called upon to serve when it was not possible for him to do so. For example, on 26 June 1767, George III appointed him and twelve others to determine the boundary between New York and New Jersey. Another of the appointed commissioners, William Allen, was Franklin's mortal enemy. The appointment of the Pennsylvania agent to help decide the boundary must have been made on the assumption that Franklin would soon return to America. Since he did not, he played no part in settling the boundary.[33]

When he could, Franklin continued to do favors for those who asked and for others whom he chose to help or honor. For the Reverend Samuel Cooper of Boston he secured an honorary Doctor of Divinity degree from the University of Edinburgh in the summer of 1767. As a favor to his son William, the Doctor obtained for Jacob Kollock, Jr., the appointment as collector of customs at Lewes, Delaware. For friends in Philadelphia, Franklin purchased, from time to time, books for the Philadelphia Library Company.[34]

Two very unusual matters claimed some of Franklin's attention in 1767. In the spring of that year Dr. John Pringle, the Doctor's usual sum-

---

[32]Benjamin Franklin to the Pennsylvania Assembly's Committee of Correspondence, 13 March 1768; William Franklin to Benjamin Franklin, 22 January and 10 May 1768; Thomas Wharton to Benjamin Franklin, 9 February 1768; [Samuel Wharton] to Benjamin Franklin, 2 December 1768. Ibid., XV, 29, 38-41, 80-82, 124, 275-79, 279 n.9; Woody Holton,"The Ohio Indians and the Coming of the American Revolution in Virginia," *Journal of Southern History* 60 (1994): 453-67; Skemp, *William Franklin,* 101-106.

[33]*Franklin Papers, XIV, 196-201; New Jersey Archives,* IX, 581-82, 591.

[34]Benjamin Franklin to William Franklin, 19 March 1767; Benjamin Franklin to Mr. [?] Pomeroy, 1 August 1767; Benjamin Franklin to Richard Price, 1 August 1767; Charles Thomson and Thomas Mifflin to Benjamin Franklin, 5 November 1768. *Franklin Papers,* XIV, 92-93, 218-20; XV, 257-58.

mer traveling companion, called upon the renowned experimenter with electricity to administer electrical shocks to the thirteen-year-old daughter of the Duke of Ancaster at Chelsea. Whatever Franklin did, failed to help the girl, who was suffering from "spasms and convulsions." She was soon taken to a spa near Bristol, where she died on Palm Sunday. The other unusual matter was his presentation to the Royal Society of some huge bones, presumably the remains of a prehistoric creature, that George Croghan had found near the Ohio River and had sent to the Doctor and Lord Shelburne. Franklin and his scientist friends at the society carried on much speculation over the bones, as well as two large tusks and some teeth, which were also part of Croghan's find.[35]

As had become his custom, Franklin continued to maintain a busy social schedule. He dined with a variety of people, including Thomas Pownall, William Denny (the former Pennsylvania governor), William Strahan, and, perhaps most frequently, Dr. William Heberden. On at least one occasion in 1768 he dined with James Boswell, the great Samuel Johnson's alter ego. In the fall of 1768 the Doctor had the honor and pleasure of dining with Christian IV, the nineteen-year-old king of Denmark and Norway. Franklin apparently made a most favorable impression on the young king, for Christian promised to visit the Doctor at his Craven Street residence.[36] There is no evidence that Christian kept the promise.

Besides following the dinner circuit, Franklin corresponded with his friends Richard Price and Joseph Priestly, and, of course, Polly Stevenson, who still lived with her aunt outside of London. The Doctor also remained active in the affairs of the Royal Society. In 1767 he helped investigate an "ugly affair" at the society—namely, the embezzlement of £1,300 of the society's money by its clerk, Emmanuel Mendes da Costa. Franklin continued to be active, too, in the work of Bray's Associates, working in 1768 to help that organization buy land around Philadelphia for the establishment of a Negro school.[37]

---

[35]Sir John Pringle to Benjamin Franklin, [March 1767]; Benjamin Franklin to George Croghan, 5 August 1767. *Franklin Papers*, XIV, 25-28, 95-96, 95 n. 9, 221-22.

[36]Ibid., XII, 425-31; XIV, 3; XV, 224-27; Labaree, "Franklin's British Friendships," 426-27.

[37]Carl B. Cone, *Torchbearer of Freedom: The Influence of Richard Price on Eighteenth Century Thought* (Lexington: University of Kentucky Press, 1952) 53-54, 63-65; see various letters to and from Franklin in 1767 and 1768, *Franklin Papers*, XIV,

Franklin's correspondence with Polly Stevenson during the time of the Townshend Duty crisis was especially interesting. It must have afforded him a pleasant and much-needed diversion. On 15 June 1767, he wrote a poem for Polly's birthday and sent it to her. One reading of the poem provides sufficient evidence of why the Doctor never became known for his verse. In 1768 Franklin involved Polly in an experiment using a phonetic alphabet of his design. The two went so far as to exchange several letters using the Doctor's bizarre spelling. Even though Polly tried it, she thought that phonetic spelling was a bad idea. "I believe we must let people spell on in their old way," she said in a letter to her mentor. Franklin argued that changing was a good idea, and he persuaded her, at least for a while, to go along with the experiment. Occasionally, Polly returned to Craven Street for a visit, and she may well have been the young woman Charles Willson Peale found sitting on the Doctor's knee, when the famed painter walked in unannounced in 1767. Although Peale sketched what he saw, he did not do so in clear enough detail to make the young woman identifiable.[38]

By this time Franklin had become accustomed to taking a vacation in August and September. He and Dr. John Pringle set out for Paris in late August 1767. This was a particularly pleasant trip, and the Pennsylvania agent might well have stayed in France longer than the six weeks that he did stay if Pringle, the royal physician, had not rushed back to England to deliver the pregnant queen of her fifth child. Although Franklin experienced sea sickness while crossing the English Channel on the way to France, he loved the trip. He visited Versailles and was introduced to King Louis XV and his queen. The king, Franklin reported, was a handsome man and younger looking than the Doctor thought he would be. Before the colonial agent had been in France a week, he wrote Polly Stevenson that his "Taylor and Perquier had transform'd" him into a Frenchman. Franklin claimed that he made quite "a Figure" in a "little Bag Wig and naked Ears!" He almost went as far as the French, he joked to Polly, when he "was once very near making Love to my Friend's

---

339-42; XV, 30, 244-45; Labaree, "Franklin's British Friendships," 427.

[38]See letters between Franklin and Mary Stevenson during 1767 and 1768. *Franklin Papers*, XIV, 187-88; XV, 174-78, 215-20, 244-45.

For the Charles Willson Peale episode see: Randall, *A Little Revenge*, 172. Randall cites Lopez and Herbert's *Private Franklin* as his source, but he embellishes considerably the account they give on page 27.

Wife." Upon returning to London in October, the Doctor wrote Deborah that he had "an exceeding pleasant journey" and had recovered his health.[39]

Two personal matters, which were awkward to resolve from such a long distance, emerged during the time that Franklin was caught up in the Townshend Duty crisis and the Illinois venture. They were not matters of life and death, but they were deeply personal, as one concerned his daughter and the other his longtime printing partner David Hall. In the spring of 1767 Deborah informed the Doctor in a roundabout way that their only daughter Sally had a boyfriend and that she was serious about the young man, Richard Bache, a native of England. Franklin responded in May 1767 that he was too far from the scene to investigate Bache and would, therefore, leave the matter of Sally's marriage to Deborah and William. The Doctor did not want to "occasion a Delay of her [Sally's] Happiness," he assured his wife. A few months later, however, Bache wrote his soon-to-be father-in-law concerning a financial setback. Franklin quickly informed Bache that if he could not afford to provide for Sally, he should not marry her until he could, for he could expect no help from his future father-in-law. The Doctor suggested a postponement of the wedding, but, over his objections, it took place on 29 October 1767. By January 1768 evangelist George Whitefield had heard about it and wrote his old friend, "Your Daughter I find is beginning the world. I wish you joy from the bottom of my heart." Franklin, however, seems to have felt no joy. On 21 February 1768, he wrote Jane Mecom, "I thank you for your Congratulations on my Daughter's Marriage. She has pleas'd herself and her Mother, and I hope she will do well: but I think they should have had some better Prospect than they have, before they married, how the Family was to be maintain'd."[40]

Deborah was miffed over the attitude of her perpetually absent husband, and it is hard to see how anyone could blame her. By the end of the summer of 1768 Franklin had calmed down, and he wrote his new

---

[39]Benjamin Franklin to Deborah Franklin, 28 August and 9 October 1767; Benjamin Franklin to Mary Stevenson, 14 September 1767. *Franklin Papers*, XIV, 241, 250-55, 274.

[40]Deborah Franklin to Benjamin Franklin, [April 1767]; Benjamin Franklin to Deborah Franklin, 23 May 1767; Benjamin Franklin to Richard Bache, 5 August 1767; George Whitefield to Benjamin Franklin, 21 January 1768. *Franklin Papers*, XIV, 136-37, 166-67, 220-21; XV, 28-29.

son-in-law to extend the olive branch. The Doctor explained that his misgivings had stemmed from Bache's financial circumstances, which were now better. Franklin expressed pleasure regarding the match and promised to be an affectionate father. He even addressed Bache as "Loving Son."[41]

The other matter that caused Franklin some personal anguish in 1767 stemmed from the sponsorship the year before of William Goddard and the *Pennsylvania Chronicle* by Joseph Galloway and Thomas Wharton in collusion with William Franklin. Goddard, who was set up in business to publish Franklin's views, could not get along with Galloway and Wharton. Consequently, the two sponsors defaulted on their share of the newspaper's financial obligations, and Goddard eventually ended up in debtor's prison. As late as 1772 William Strahan was still trying to collect from Galloway on a bill for £172, fifteen shillings, and two pence, which represented the cost of materials the London publisher had sent to Goddard at Galloway's request five years earlier. Strahan tried to enlist Franklin's help in collecting the debt, but the Doctor ignored the request. Nor was Strahan the only one who became disenchanted during this unfortunate episode. David Hall was both dismayed and bitter. He said he could not believe that Benjamin Franklin was a partner in the *Chronicle* enterprise, because the Franklin-Hall partnership agreement provided, or at least implied, that Franklin would not again enter the printing business in Philadelphia. Hall also denied all allegations by William Franklin that the Doctor's longtime partner had joined Franklin's enemies. That Hall felt hurt and falsely accused is clear, and he urged Franklin to settle all accounts before they both died.[42]

Franklin, having been put in an awkward position by those who were trying to protect his interests, responded. He explained to Hall that Galloway, Wharton, and the younger Franklin had thought it necessary to found the *Chronicle* because Hall would not print "Party Pieces." While this had caused Franklin's allies to conclude that Hall had gone over to the other party, the Doctor assured his old partner that he did not share that conclusion, for he had always regarded Hall as neutral. The Doctor had declined a share in the *Chronicle*, he informed Hall, and

---

[41]Benjamin Franklin to Richard Bache, 13 August 1768; William Franklin to Benjamin Franklin, 10 May 1768. *Franklin Papers*, XV, 123, 185-86.

[42]David Hall to Benjamin Franklin, 27 January 1767; William Strahan to Benjamin Franklin, 21 August 1772. Ibid., XIV, 16-20; XIX, 266-67, 266 n. 3.

expressed hope that he would never have to join with Goddard. However, the Pennsylvania agent denied ever making any agreement to stay out of the printing business in Philadelphia after the Franklin-Hall partnership ended. Yet he assured Hall that as far as he was concerned, the two men still enjoyed "a settled Friendship, that . . . will not easily be shaken on either side." Franklin also promised to send his observations on Parker's proposed settlement of the partnership at the "very next Opportunity."[43] He never did.

As in previous years, Franklin continued to write Deborah promises that he was about to come home or that he would like to, but that he must "have Patience a little longer." It was not he who needed patience, but Deborah. After so many empty promises, she had to have been impatient as well as sad. In February 1768 the Doctor wrote that he would leave England in May or June. On 25 May he wrote that he would be sailing for home in "a few Weeks" and that he was "impatient" to be with his wife. His sincerity in this matter is in grave doubt, since at that very time he was still trying to land a position in the British government. A few weeks after writing to Deborah of his impending return, the Doctor told Grey Cooper, secretary to the lords of the Treasury, that he was willing to stay in England the rest of his life. Cooper, at that very moment was trying to persuade the Duke of Grafton, first lord of the Treasury and acting head of the Pitt-Grafton ministry, to give Franklin a place at Whitehall. The optimistic Cooper kept assuring the Pennsylvania agent that Grafton had something "handsome" for him, but his lordship kept dodging Franklin. The Doctor never talked to Grafton, but he did talk to Lord North, Chancellor of the Exchequer, who said he hoped the ministry could make it worthwhile for Franklin to remain in England. No offer was ever made, but Franklin's appointment as Georgia's colonial agent provided him with reason enough to again break his promise to Deborah. Also helping to persuade the Doctor to remain was the urging of Dr. John Fothergill to stay "another winter" and "render America and its friends all possible assistance."[44]

---

[43]Benjamin Franklin to David Hall, 14 April 1767. Ibid., XIV, 126-28.

[44]John Fothergill to James Pemberton, 16 September 1768. Corner and Booth, *Letters of Dr. John Fothergill*, 286; Benjamin Franklin to Deborah Franklin, 20 February, 25 May, and 9 August 1768; Benjamin Franklin to Grey Cooper, 24 June 1768; Benjamin Franklin to William Franklin, 2 July 1768. *Franklin Papers*, XV, 53, 138-39, 158-64, 185; "F. B." On Smuggling, *London Chronicle*, 21-24 November 1767.

One is compelled to wonder if the devious Dr. Franklin himself knew what he really wanted. He had bitterly criticized the British political system a few months earlier, having expressed almost total disgust with it and with ministers who were unsympathetic to American views. After all that, would he have abandoned his personal convictions and remained in England for a government job? No one knows definitely, and perhaps the Doctor himself did not know. He worked so hard to keep his image intact in America, it is highly doubtful that he would ever have severed all his ties with family and friends in the colonies for even the most desirable sinecure at Whitehall. It seems certain, however, that he intended to stay in England as long as he could, and he probably convinced himself that London was where he could do the American colonies the most good. Historian Thomas Wendel has argued that Franklin was losing his admiration for everything English by 1767, as he observed the "workings of a government in disarray." He became thoroughly disgusted because of ministerial "cabals, factions, and intrigues." Verner Crane, one of the most thorough Franklin scholars ever, has contended that the Doctor's experience during the Stamp Act crisis caused him to develop "advanced ideas" with regard to American rights and that those ideas were further refined by the Townshend Duty crisis. Franklin began, so Crane contends, to reveal his pro-American sentiments, at least privately, in 1768. Both historians probably have given Franklin too much credit for being a prophet and spearhead of the revolutionary movement, but they are certainly correct about Franklin's pro-Americanism and his growing dissatisfaction with the arrogance and corruption of British political leaders and their failure to understand American sensitivities.[45]

While Franklin was ready as early as 1768 to question the right of Parliament to pass any legislation for the colonies, he still considered the colonies firmly attached to Britain through the Crown. Over the following six years his thinking about the empire led him finally to the point where he could see no hope of preserving the imperial relationship. Would he

---

A government appointment for Franklin was never much of a possibility. In fact, Lords Hillsborough and Sandwich were already trying to find a plausible reason for taking away Franklin's job as deputy postmaster general of the colonies. See: Butler, *Franklin, Postmaster General*, 146-52 and Franklin's 2 July 1768 letter to William Franklin cited immediately above.

[45]Crane, "Franklin and the Stamp Act," 77; Crane, *Franklin: Englishman and American*, 110-111, 124-25; Crane, "Certain Writings," 26-27; Wendel, *Politics of Liberty*, 137.

have reached that point if he had been offered a lucrative post in the British government? That question, as noted above, can never be answered with certainty, but it is obvious that Franklin enjoyed living in London more than he did in Philadelphia and that he planned to remain at his residence on Craven Street until there were compelling reasons for returning to America.

# 7. "Point of Right":

## The Making of an American Radical

The Townshend Duty crisis was pivotal for Benjamin Franklin, for, during it, he came to have doubts about quietly whiling away his last years as a bureaucrat in the British government. It can be argued, of course, that such doubts stemmed from the realization that no government appointment was ever going to be offered to him. On the other hand, it can also be argued that he increasingly came to regard the British political order as corrupt and ultimately held it in profound contempt. The vileness he saw in British political life could well have caused him to exaggerate the virtue that presumably existed in American politics.

When Franklin had captured the imagination of the American colonists in 1766 with his dramatic anti-Stamp Act performance in the House of Commons, he had no idea that he had accomplished far more than he ever intended. He had meant only to rescue his political reputation and regain favor with his fellow Americans. Instead, Franklin had taken the first step toward becoming the primary representative of American views in Great Britain. He moved a step closer to that role in 1768 with his appointment as Georgia's colonial agent. In 1769 he became New Jersey's agent and then the agent of the lower house of the Massachusetts legislature in 1770. As agent for four colonies by the close of 1770, the Doctor was well on his way to being recognized as the chief spokesman of the American cause in London. No longer the agent of a single colony on a special mission, his new task was that of protecting at least four colonies from a misguided imperial policy and the perceived British encroachments on American constitutional rights. Franklin was forced constantly during 1769 and 1770 to define and refine his views on imperial issues because of American actions and British reactions. A devious but still moderate man by nature, he cautioned his fellow colonists against violence. Yet as American attitudes and actions became more radical, so did Franklin. In private correspondence and propaganda pieces for the press, he expressed understanding, if not approval, of American violence. He had learned during the Stamp Act crisis the consequences of ignoring his countrymen's convictions and proceeding as if those principles would gradually fade away. Remembering that lesson, he was forced into a more confrontational position once he accepted the job as agent for the very radical lower house of the Massachusetts legislature. Although the imperial crisis over the Townshend duties continued to claim most of Franklin's attention, he also took time to promote official approval of the Illinois colony, by which he and other land speculators hoped to profit.

Franklin and Richard Jackson remained co-agents for the Pennsylvania Assembly, but their instructions began to say less and less about securing a royal government. Their reappointment letter in October 1769 did, however, direct them to continue following the instructions of prior years. A year later, only Franklin was reappointed. Jackson, having become legal adviser to the Board of Trade, felt obliged to give up the Pennsylvania agency. In 1770 Franklin was once more advised to abide by his earlier instructions, but the emphasis was clearly different. The Doctor was to exert his "utmost Endeavours to obtain Redress of every Agrievance which in any wise" affected "the Rights and Liberties of the Colonies, and to promote the Welfare of this Province."[1]

The political sands were unquestionably shifting in Pennsylvania, undermining Franklin and Galloway's political partnership and, along with it, the Quaker coalition they had put together to control the Assembly. Although the two men remained cordial in their correspondence with one another, they said little about the dead issue of royal government and gave more attention to such viable questions as paper money, the quartering of soldiers in private dwellings, boycotts, and the repeal of the Townshend duties. Franklin was especially concerned about bills that would require the quartering of British troops in American homes. When Lord Barrington, Secretary of War, attempted to insert such a quartering clause in the American Mutiny Bill in early 1769, the Doctor and other colonial agents protested so vigorously that the disagreeable clause was ultimately omitted.[2]

While Franklin and Galloway continued to agree philosophically that Britain's tight money policy was most ill-advised, the increasingly radical Franklin had come to see a positive side to the Currency Act of 1764. It reduced the amount of money Americans had to spend on luxuries and

---

[1]Pennsylvania Assembly's Committee of Correspondence to Benjamin Franklin and Richard Jackson (and another to Benjamin Franklin only), 17 October 1769 and 19 October 1770; Joseph Galloway to Benjamin Franklin, 21 June 1770. *Franklin Papers*, XVI, 219-20; XVII, 177-79, 256; Kammen, *Rope of Sand*, 265.

[2]Benjamin Franklin to Joseph Galloway, 21 March 1769. *Franklin Papers*, XVI, 69-70.

thus put a dent in the pocketbooks of British merchants. If Franklin's countrymen followed his advice, the Doctor informed Lord Kames early in 1769, they would not ask again for the repeal of that law. Galloway, who had few radical bones, if any, in his body, continued to view tight money as an arguable grievance. In 1770, when the Board of Trade recommended disallowance of New York and New Jersey acts issuing paper money, Galloway labeled the action "really ridiculous" and claimed that the British ministry was determined to see to it that "Americans shall not have any Paper Medium at all." As for Franklin, he had given up completely on the issue by mid-1770, seeing no hope of the ministry's changing its policy. He informed Galloway that former Pennsylvania agent Robert Charles had committed suicide over the policy by slitting his throat with a razor. Charles, who had become the agent for New York, was unable to persuade Parliament in 1770 to pass a paper money bill that New York could accept. Unable to achieve what he knew New York officials required of him, Charles took his life—at least that is why Franklin said Charles killed himself.[3] Whether or not Franklin was correct about the reason for Charles's suicide, apparently he believed he was. His reporting the tragedy was likely the Doctor's way of saying that he would not allow the money issue to drive him crazy and was, therefore, finished with it.

Although the situation regarding paper money was not encouraging, there was good news about the determination of Americans to defend their rights. Galloway wrote Franklin in the spring of 1770 that the boycott against British goods was holding in Pennsylvania, and this greatly heartened the agent. The Doctor hoped that the tea duty would be repealed "next Winter," and he took credit for preventing the presentation of a bill that would have punished American merchants involved in the boycott. At this point, Franklin began complaining about not hearing from the Assembly, noting "Your Votes and Laws are rarely sent me."[4] Clearly, the Pennsylvania Assembly's urgency and excitement about Franklin's work in England had dampened.

---

[3]Benjamin Franklin to Lord Kames, 1-[16] January 1769; Benjamin Franklin to Joseph Galloway, 11 January and 11 June 1770; Joseph Galloway to Benjamin Franklin, 21 June 1770. Ibid., XVI 1-2; XVII, 23-26, 168-72, 177-79.

[4]Benjamin Franklin to Joseph Galloway, 11 and 26 June 1770; Joseph Galloway to Benjamin Franklin, 21 June 1770. Ibid., XVII, 168-72, 177-80.

While the Assembly lost enthusiasm for Franklin's work as agent and corresponded with him less frequently, the Doctor's new Georgia constituents called on his services quite often. On 3 April 1769, Franklin wrote Noble Wimberly Jones to report that he had given Lord Hillsborough "the Address of your Commons House of Assembly to the King." The secretary had promised to present it to the king immediately. Word had reached Franklin from unofficial sources that Hillsborough had sent the king's answer to Governor James Wright. What the agent had heard was true. His lordship not only had sent the king's response to Wright, he had told the governor that the king would receive petitions thereafter only through governors. His Majesty, claimed the secretary, regarded any other conveyance as disrespectful and irregular. Already, Hillsborough had begun to insist that petitions from colonial legislatures be sent through governors and not agents, for the secretary thought "Agents unnecessary (perhaps troublesome)," Franklin noted. The Doctor doubted, however, that the colonies would accept the secretary's plan for petitioning the Crown through governors only. The Georgia agent also noted that it would do no good to send petitions to Parliament. Pennsylvania and New York had attempted to do that, and their petitions had been ignored.[5]

Franklin assured Jones that the Doctor and all other American agents were doing everything possible to secure the repeal of the Townshend Duty Act and to restore harmony in imperial relations. Even so, he pointed out that there was a division of opinion as to the proper strategy to pursue. Some argued that repeal would come if America was quiet for a year, while others feared that silence would be regarded as consent and thereby permanently prevent repeal. The Doctor informed Jones and Joseph Galloway, too, that all of the colonial agents had protested Lord Barrington's attempt to quarter British troops in private dwellings and that the ministry had backed away from that plan.[6]

In addition to guarding Georgia's *political* interests, the Doctor was also working in the province's *economic* interest by promoting a bounty on raw silk and by pressing for an act that would permit the exportation of rice from South Carolina and Georgia. Franklin had a longstanding interest in silk culture. He had read widely on the subject, and he

[5]Benjamin Franklin to Noble Wimberly Jones, 3 April 1769. Ibid., XVI, 78-80; *Georgia Colonial Records*, XV, 26-28; XXXVII, 394-95.
[6]Ibid (all sources cited).

demonstrated considerable knowledge of it. Efforts had been made for years to produce silk in Georgia; hence, Franklin's lobbying for a bounty on colonial silk must have pleased Georgians. An act that provided for a decreasing bounty during the years 1770–1777 was finally passed, in part because of the Doctor's efforts.[7]

Franklin worked to serve Georgia in every way he could, but he focused most of his attention on securing the repeal of the Townshend duties. Since that was a Georgia concern, as well as a general American one, Jones, who presumably reflected the sentiments of the lower house, was pleased with the way Franklin spent his time. On 7 June 1769, the Georgia agent wrote to the speaker that the duties would probably be repealed "early in the ensuing Session" of Parliament. His "Majesty and his Ministers" were beginning to have more "favourable Sentiments" toward Americans, Franklin asserted. The ministry had given assurances that there would be no new acts for raising revenue and that the duties on "Glass, Paper, and Painters Colours" would soon be repealed. The Doctor expressed hope that all differences between Britain and her colonies would be resolved, but he thought that complete harmony was too much to expect. Obstacles to achieving the total harmony the Georgia agent desired were, according to Franklin, Britain's pride, the "Point of Right," and the mother country's "Resentment at our disputing it." The agent promised to stay on the job until Parliament convened again and work with other agents for as complete a repeal of revenue measures as was possible. He indicated that he would render Georgia any service he could, even if the colony "should not think proper to continue the Appointment."[8]

Over a year had passed since Franklin's original appointment. No doubt he knew of the legislature's feud over Charles Garth, a dispute which had resulted in the Doctor's selection as a compromise candidate. Perhaps he sensed, because he had not been notified of a second appointment, that the upper and lower houses had renewed their quarrel over the agency. Actually, Franklin's appointment expired on 1 June 1769, and, because Governor Wright dissolved the Assembly at the end of 1768

---

[7]Benjamin Franklin to Peter Templeman, 12 August 1763; Benjamin Franklin to Noble Wimberly Jones, 3 April 1769. *Franklin Papers*, X, 321; XVI, 78-80, 200, 200 n. 2; *Georgia Colonial Records*, XV, 29; Morgan, "Franklin as Georgia's Colonial Agent," 225.

[8]Benjamin Franklin to Noble Wimberly Jones, 7 June 1769. *Franklin Papers*, XVI 151-52; *Georgia Colonial Records*, XV, 29-30.

(until October 1769), no steps were taken to renew the agent's appointment until December 1769. On 27 February 1770, an ordinance extending Franklin's employment through June 1770 was finally passed. He was then reappointed agent in May 1770 for the period from 1 June 1770 to 1 June 1771, but this was done amidst wrangling between the two houses. Provisions were supposedly made at that time for Franklin to collect his salary through John Campbell, the Crown agent for the colony. Since the Doctor later complained that Georgia was several years in arrears on his salary, he obviously was unable to collect from Campbell.[9]

Although the Georgia legislature was negligent in paying Franklin's salary, its members frequently passed resolutions to instruct the agent. At the time of the Doctor's reappointment on 10 May 1770, he was instructed by the legislature to obtain the Crown's approval of a law "for ordering and governing Slaves." Through Richard Jackson, Franklin persuaded the Board of Trade to recommend approval of the statute. He also, in accordance with his instructions, secured the Crown's permission for the Georgia governor "to issue Writs for electing Members to represent the parishes of St. David, St. Patrick, St. Thomas, and St. Mary" in the Georgia legislature. Besides pressing for the approval of various laws, the Georgia agent was supposed to obtain from his predecessor, William Knox, "the plan of the Land claimed by the late Sir William Baker." The recently deceased Baker had been a wealthy London merchant, who had held the offices of London alderman and member of Parliament. Baker's extensive land claims in Georgia had come into conflict with the claims of numerous Georgia settlers. Provincial officers had struggled in vain to arrange a settlement. Franklin worked on this thorny problem for about two years.[10]

The Doctor certainly made every effort to please Georgia, and especially Speaker Noble Wimberly Jones. The agent responded to Jones's request of 21 February 1770 to purchase for the Georgia lower house "a Mace to be made of Silver and double gilt" (to cost no more

---

[9]Georgia Assembly's Committee of Correspondence to Benjamin Franklin, 23 May 1770, and other material. *Franklin Papers*, XVII, 79-81, 137-40, 142, 144-50; *Georgia Colonial Records*, XV, 65-66, 76, 78, 81, 91-92, 95, 108, 185-86, 189-90; XIX, part 1, 499-501; Morgan, "Franklin as Georgia's Colonial Agent," 226.

[10]Instructions to Benjamin Franklin from the Georgia Assembly, 10 May 1770; Georgia Assembly's Committee of Correspondence to Benjamin Franklin, 28 May 1770. *Franklin Papers*, XVII, 137-39, 138 ns. 7 and 8, 139 n. 9, 144-50; Morgan, "Franklin as Georgia's Colonial Agent," 225-26.

than £100 sterling) and two gowns for men 5' 8" and 5' 10" tall—the house speaker and the clerk. Franklin ordered the items almost immediately, and by 6 July he wrote to Jones that the mace and gowns were on their way to Georgia in two boxes marked "N. W. J. No. 1, 2" in the care of "Mr. Crouch" from the colony. By 9 October the items had reached Jones, who was obviously delighted with the articles. The speaker described them as "extremely neat and Ellegant." Altogether the mace and gowns had cost £107, twelve shillings, and six pence—over £7 more than the speaker had wanted to pay. Jones, demonstrating no irritation over the excess cost, remitted two bills of exchange amounting to £120. In thanking the Doctor for rendering the service, the speaker noted that the Assembly was "extra happy" to be represented by a man whose "sentiments coincided with theirs" and "every true American."[11]

Franklin continued to cater to his Georgia constituents. On 10 August 1770, he wrote the Georgia Assembly's Committee of Correspondence to say he had received the committee's letters and other materials and had "carefully perus'd" them all. He promised to "proceed with Diligence in prosecuting every Point" turned over to his care, as soon as government officials returned to London from their summer vacations. The Doctor expressed his gratitude for being reappointed. Two months later, on 10 October, the agent wrote Jones that there was talk in London of settling all differences with the colonies, because Britain was about to go to war with Spain over the Falkland Islands. Franklin always took care to send some news that the Georgia leaders wanted to hear. Already, in June, he had informed them that there was hope for the withdrawal of British troops from America, but that the tea duty had not been repealed.[12]

The Doctor seemed willing to serve Georgia in almost any way, and the colony's leaders called on him to perform some unusual tasks. For example, on 13 December 1770, Jones wrote to ask Franklin's help in securing the ordination of Cornelius Winter to the Anglican priesthood. Winter, a young protege of George Whitefield, had been teaching "Negroes" on the plantation of the now-deceased Rector Bartholomew

---

[11]See numerous letters exchanged between Benjamin Franklin and Noble Wimberly Jones about this business, February-December 1770. *Franklin Papers*, XVII, 77-78, 133-34, 159-60, 184, 241-43, 243 n. 1, 298-99.

[12]Benjamin Franklin to Noble Wimberly Jones, 7 June and 10 October 1770; Benjamin Franklin to the Georgia Assembly's Committee of Correspondence, 10 August 1770. Ibid., XVII, 160, 203, 243, 243 n. 1.

Zouberbuhler. Georgia officials wanted Winter to be ordained in England so that he could return to the province and render additional service to slaves, teaching them Christianity and instructing them in Anglican principles. Unfortunately, the Bishop of London looked upon Winter with suspicion because of the young man's association with Whitefield, who was regarded by many in the Anglican hierarchy as a maverick Anglican priest. Franklin, who had been a close friend of the evangelist from 1739 until Whitefield's recent death in late 1770, was outraged when the bishop refused to ordain young Winter. The Doctor vowed to change the bishop's mind or find another bishop who would perform the ordination. Just how hard Franklin worked on this matter is not clear, but Winter was not ordained and did not return to Georgia.[13]

Even before Franklin was appointed Georgia agent in 1768, he had attracted the attention of political leaders in New Jersey. Governor William Franklin naturally fanned the flames of interest in his father. Samuel Smith, a New Jersey friend of the Franklins, advocated making the Doctor agent for all the American colonies. The Franklin advocate said that the various colonies "ought to join to make it worth" the Doctor's while to reside in England as long as he lived (something the Georgia and Pennsylvania agent appeared to be bent on doing anyway). William Franklin reported in June 1767 that the people of New Jersey were "much pleased" with his father's struggle against Britain's tight money policy. They especially appreciated his mention of New Jersey as one of the colonies that had carefully guarded against excesses in the issuance of "paper currency." The New Jersey governor revealed that the citizens of his province had become disenchanted with Henry Wilmot, their agent since 1766, because he was doing nothing about paper money or any other "American Affair." It was likely, William informed his father, that Wilmot would be removed as agent at the next meeting of the provincial assembly.[14]

The dissatisfaction in New Jersey with Henry Wilmot, "the Giant of Gray's Inn" and Thomas Penn's solicitor, and the popularity of Benjamin

---

[13]Noble Wimberly Jones to Benjamin Franklin, 13 December 1770; Benjamin Franklin to Noble Wimberly Jones, 5 March 1771. Ibid., XVII, 299-300, 299 n. 4; XVIII, 52-54; Morgan, "Franklin as Georgia's Colonial Agent," 225; Morgan, "A Most Unlikely Friendship," 212.

[14]William Franklin to Benjamin Franklin, 10 June 1767. *Franklin Papers*, XIV, 176; *New Jersey Archives*, IX, 625-28.

Franklin, presumed champion of paper money, led to the ouster of Wilmot and the appointment of Franklin as New Jersey agent on 8 November 1769. As Georgia did, New Jersey had laws awaiting Crown approval at Westminster, and the New Jersey legislators were eager for the Doctor to secure the seal for those statutes. The agent's new constituents immediately burdened him with some difficult tasks. Besides securing approval for two election laws, they wanted him to win the Crown's consent to an act "making current One Hundred Thousand Pounds in bills of credit, to be let on loan at five per cent." The New Jersey lawmakers lamented the lack of currency in their province, and, knowing of Franklin's familiarity with their problem, they believed the Doctor could defend their bill against all objections at Whitehall. The Committee of Correspondence for the New Jersey Assembly also urged the colony's new agent to be prepared to help solve a complicated boundary dispute with New York. As a gesture of good faith, the Assembly advanced Franklin a bill of exchange in the amount of £200 for expenses.[15]

The disputed boundary between New Jersey and New York, which had recently been unsatisfactorily resolved by royal commissioners (including Franklin, who was unable to participate), was not the only land trouble New Jersey had. An attempt was made in 1769 to settle "the several rights, titles and claims to the Common Lands of the Township of Bergen." Richard Stockton, an attorney and a member of the New Jersey Council, warned Franklin about William Bayard, "a considerable Merchant of New York and Freeholder of Bergen." Bayard had left for England ostensibly on business unrelated to Bergen land but really, according to Stockton, to seek disallowance of the act the New Jersey Assembly had passed in the interest of settling all claims in Bergen township. Stockton urged the Doctor to stop Bayard and secure royal approval of the act.[16]

In the spring of 1770 Franklin did his best to fulfill the wishes of the New Jersey legislature by arguing for the provincial acts before the Board of Trade on 11 April. He locked horns with Lord Hillsborough over the "Bergen Act" and the "Paper-money Act." His lordship called the Bergen

---

[15]New Jersey Assembly's Committee of Correspondence to Benjamin Franklin, 7 December 1769. *Franklin Papers*, XVI, 253-56; Kammen, *Rope of Sand*, 134-35; *New Jersey Archives*, X, 135-38; XXVII, 578-79.

[16]Richard Stockton to Benjamin Franklin, 22 December 1769. *Franklin Papers*, XVI, 265-68.

Act unjust and condemned the Paper Money Act as a violation of Parliament's prohibition against legal tender issues. Franklin promised his New Jersey constituents that he would attempt some legal and political maneuvers to offset Hillsborough's opposition to the acts. However, because the New Jersey laws had been forwarded to the Privy Council, he doubted that he would succeed. As he expected, the Privy Council disallowed the Paper Money Act, as well as the Bergen Act, on 6 June 1770. Both the New Jersey legislators and the new agent were angered by the decision. Yet Franklin hinted at better days ahead, mainly because Richard Jackson, the Doctor's longtime friend and colleague, was about to become counselor to the Board of Trade. After Jackson assumed his new post, Franklin suggested, Americans might not "be pestered with ignorant frivolous Objections to our Laws, as heretofore has sometimes been the Case." In spite of the Doctor's failure to secure royal approval of key New Jersey laws, his new employers seemed satisfied with his efforts.[17]

Among American colonists, Franklin's star was definitely rising in 1769. People all over America—even in extremely radical Massachusetts—were highly pleased with this colonial agent who had gone from goat to hero during the Stamp Act crisis and who was continuing to promote the American cause in the struggle to repeal the Townshend duties. The Doctor had acquired new agencies in 1768 and 1769, and on 24 October 1770, a majority in the Massachusetts House of Representatives chose him as their agent. This meant that Franklin represented four colonies concurrently, but only in Georgia and New Jersey had he been approved by both the upper and lower houses and the governors, or by what Thomas Penn called the "whole Legislature." As agent for the Massachusetts lower house, the Doctor succeeded Dennys DeBerdt, recently deceased. It should be remembered that Lord Hillsborough had bluntly called DeBerdt no agent at all. His lordship would soon make a similar pronouncement to Franklin with regard to the Doctor's new Massachusetts agency, for the secretary was determined to impose his definition

---

[17]New Jersey Assembly's Committee of Correspondence to Benjamin Franklin, 27 March 1770; Benjamin Franklin to [Joseph Smith?], 12 April 1770; Benjamin Franklin to the New Jersey Assembly's Committee of Correspondence, 11 June 1770; Joseph Smith to Benjamin Franklin, 8 December 1770. Ibid., XVII, 119-22, 172-74, 295; *Journals of the Board of Trade, 1768–1775*, 184-85; *New Jersey Archives*, XVIII, 170; Sosin, "Imperial Regulations of Colonial Paper Money," 193-94.

of an agent on the British government and the colonies. Thus, in Hillsborough's mind, Franklin legally represented only Georgia and New Jersey and had no official standing as spokesman for Massachusetts.[18] Pennsylvania, of course, was unique with its unicameral legislature, which assumed the right to appoint agents—with or without approval from the governor or the proprietor.

Franklin was by no means a unanimous choice for the Massachusetts agency. Samuel Adams and James Otis led a faction in the lower house that favored Arthur Lee, a Virginian who had studied medicine in Scotland and law in London. As a sop to the pro-Lee faction, the lower house named Lee an alternate agent, to serve in the event of Franklin's absence or death. Lee, high strung and perhaps paranoid, resented playing second fiddle to the Doctor. He soon labeled Franklin as Hillsborough's tool, charging that the new Massachusetts agent tried to please both Americans *and* the ministry. Besides Lee, the Doctor also had to work with William Bollan, agent for the Massachusetts upper house.[19]

The fact that Franklin received the appointment as agent of the Massachusetts lower house prompts the serious student of Dr. Franklin's devious nature to study carefully Ezra Stiles's observations, which were discussed in an earlier chapter. Stiles's scenario of Franklin's plans in the late 1760s might well be valid, for the evidence suggests that Franklin did worm his way into the position of Massachusetts agent. Once he realized that the Penns could not be ousted as proprietors of Pennsylvania, Massachusetts became a likely place of refuge to which he could retire—if family connections or political loyalties forced his return to America. At least Deborah could move to Massachusetts without crossing the ocean. Franklin would most certainly have been reluctant to return to Pennsylvania as a man who had failed in his mission. That could possibly have led to his becoming a political has-been, a status Franklin's ego could never have tolerated. Even though his ally Joseph Galloway was still speaker, he and Galloway were clearly taking different forks in the road of imperial politics because of the Townshend Duty crisis. If Franklin had to leave England—and the evidence indicates that he intended to do so

---

[18]*Franklin Papers*, XVII, 257-58, 265, 274-75; Thomas Hutchinson, *The History of the Province of Massachusetts Bay From 1749–1774*, Volume III (London: John Murray, Albemarle Street, 1828) III, 316; Kammen, *Rope of Sand*, 130, 153-54.

[19]*Franklin Papers*, XVII, 257-58; Hutchinson, *History of Massachusetts*, III, 316; Kammen, *Rope of Sand*, 150.

only if he had to—facing up to his failure to achieve royal government for Pennsylvania and harboring nothing but total disgust for Thomas Penn were good reasons for not living in Philadelphia anymore. It is altogether likely that he did regard refuge in Massachusetts as an option and prepared for it by securing honors for people like Ezra Stiles and Samuel Cooper. That Franklin took every opportunity to please Massachusetts people of influence and keep them aware of his work in England seems clear.

Thomas Hutchinson, acting governor of Massachusetts at the time of Franklin's appointment (Hutchinson would be appointed governor in late 1770 and receive his commission in 1771), claimed that selection of the Doctor as the lower house's agent, came as no surprise, for Franklin "had corresponded with the principal conductors of the controversy with Parliament in Boston from the first stir about the stamp act; and they professed in all the important parts of it, to govern themselves by his advice." No doubt Hutchinson exaggerated in reporting Franklin's influence with the Boston leaders, but the Doctor did insure that his correspondence contained statements pleasing to those who had influence in the legislature and in Boston society. In a letter to the Reverend Samuel Cooper on 8 June 1770—a letter in which Franklin expressed views far more radical than were usual for him—he contended that the original colonial charters constituted the colonies as "distinct States." Moreover, the Doctor claimed that, since the Stuart Restoration in 1660, Parliament had "usurp'd an Authority of making Laws for them which before it had not." Thomas Hutchinson soon learned of the letter and asserted that it "contradict[ed] the whole course of historical facts." While Hutchinson criticized Franklin's remarks, members of the Massachusetts lower house relished them. In fact, those remarks soon led the representatives to believe in the Doctor's "abilities and integrity," and "a majority readily confided the affairs of the province, at that critical season, to his care." Cooper, the influential minister of the Brattle Street Church, spread abroad the contents of the 8 June letter and, consequently, offset the opposition of the pro-Lee faction in the Massachusetts house to Franklin's appointment as agent. Whether he actually turned the tide or not, Cooper at least claimed credit for playing a major role in the Doctor's selection over Arthur Lee.[20]

There is no reason to doubt Hutchinson's assertion that Franklin was at least indirectly involved with Massachusetts radicals before his appointment as agent or that the appointment stemmed from that involvement. The governor's contention that the Boston radicals followed the Doctor's advice in every particular does not ring true. Consistently, Franklin cautioned against the use of violence, and violence erupted more than once in Massachusetts. In spite of the failure of the hot-tempered Massachusettsites to follow his advice, the Doctor always managed to conjure up some excuse for their radical ideas and occasional violent deeds. The *London Chronicle* carried in the 6–8 February 1770 issue a piece by "N. N.," one of Franklin's pseudonyms. In it, the Doctor tried to correct the image in England of the Massachusetts provincials as "factious, quarrelsome, averse to government, &c." Under cover of his pseudonym, Franklin pointed out that Thomas Pownall, governor of Massachusetts before Francis Bernard (sarcastically called "Saint Francis" in Massachusetts) had gotten along beautifully with the people of the province. Upon leaving the colony Pownall had praised its people and was continuing to do so at that very time, as a member of Parliament. Bernard, governor in between Pownall and Hutchinson, had called the Massachusettsites ungovernable "to excuse his own inability or mis-management," according to "N. N.".[21] While it is quite likely that Franklin made sure the right people in Massachusetts knew the identity of "N. N." and what "N. N." was saying in London, there is no proof of it.

Even so, a "Committee of the Town of Boston" somehow knew that the Doctor could be counted on to promote the Massachusetts cause in London, and in a letter dated 13 July 1770, its members asked Franklin to help correct the record with regard to the Boston Massacre. Such Boston luminaries as Thomas Cushing, Samuel Adams, John Hancock, and Joseph Warren were among the members of that committee. They alleged that Boston's reputation had been smeared by secret letters, conspiracies by the Board of Customs Commissioners in the city, and distorted accounts in British newspapers. A troublesome pamphlet entitled

---

[20]Benjamin Franklin to Samuel Cooper, 8 June 1770; Samuel Cooper to Benjamin Franklin, 6 November 1770. *Franklin Papers*, XVII, 160-65, 274-75; Hutchinson, *History of Massachusetts*, III, 317-18.

[21]*Franklin Papers*, XVII, 61; *London Chronicle*, 6–8 February 1770.

*The Case of Capt. [Thomas] Preston* had been published and had, in their view, totally distorted the event. Although British troops had been withdrawn from Boston to Castle Island in the harbor following the massacre, the committee wanted it known that British authorities had delayed in ordering the withdrawal. The troops had been brought into Boston in two days, while it took eleven days to move them to Castle William after the massacre. As enraged as the populace was over the bloodshed they blamed on the redcoats, the Bostonians took no revenge on the dwindling troops as they departed "in the Slowest order." Moreover, the families of several soldiers remained in the city, going about their business without being harmed. There was no doubt in the minds of the committee members that Bostonians had exercised unusual restraint under extremely provocative circumstances. Franklin attempted to publicize the Massachusetts version of the story at every opportunity—a couple of months before his appointment as one of that colony's agents.[22]

Given the reputation Franklin had carefully cultivated for himself in Boston and the relationship he had established with certain influential citizens, it was predictable that the Massachusetts lower house would choose Franklin as its agent, as it did on 24 October 1770. Did this mean that Franklin was now a thoroughgoing radical and was chosen because of his radicalism? Or was he still at heart a moderate forced into a more extreme position because of his appointment by one of the most radical legislative chambers in America? As is so often the case with Franklin, there is sufficient evidence to argue the case either way. The preponderance of evidence, however, indicates that the Doctor had become, at the very least, a reluctant radical, even though he continued to deplore violent acts and said so publicly and privately. However much he decried violence, he could scarcely serve Massachusetts faithfully in any capacity without being tarred with the brush of radicalism by British authorities.

Soon after Franklin's appointment, the Massachusetts lower house sent him a long list of grievances for which he was to seek royal redress. According to the Massachusetts legislators, the British government had provoked the Boston Massacre by needlessly sending redcoats into the city. House members feared that Britain was moving toward "an absolute Subjection" of Massachusetts, and they blamed "the administration," making no distinction between king and Parliament. They could see no

---

[22] A Committee of the Town of Boston to Benjamin Franklin. 13 July 1770. *Franklin Papers*, XVII, 186-93.

reason for Britain's refusal to restore the colonies "to the State they were in before the passing [of] the obnoxious Stamp Act."[23] If Franklin truly represented the views of such people, he had to bear the radical label. There can be little doubt that the Doctor's appointment as agent of the Massachusetts House of Representatives brought about a drastic alteration in his image and represented a definite turning point in the controversy between Britain and her colonies. In his correspondence with his new constituents, Franklin gave every indication that he consistently adhered to the Massachusetts hard line (something the devious agent did not do in his correspondence with Georgia or Pennsylvania), and two years later he would send the Hutchinson-Oliver letters to Boston.[24] Thomas Hutchinson almost surely overstated the case by contending that Franklin's conveyance of those letters precipitated the American Revolution. Yet it was an action that most certainly played a part in the final deterioration of the relations between the mother country and her North American colonies.

To the utter irritation of many Americans, the Townshend duties remained on the statute books through 1769 and into 1770. Franklin, now well on his way to becoming the unofficial-but-recognized spokesman of the American cause in England, moved steadily toward the more extreme position that he assumed by late 1770. Verner Crane's contention that Franklin set out in a radical direction almost immediately following the resolution of the Stamp Act crisis is based in part on the "marginalia," or notations, the Doctor made in the margins of several contemporary polemical pamphlets. Although some of those pamphlets were published in 1766, the editors of the *Papers of Benjamin Franklin* have argued persuasively that Franklin did not make the notations until 1769 and after. If the editors are right, as seems to be the case, the Doctor did not reveal definite signs of a radical drift until 1769 (not 1766). Even then, he tried to remain a closet radical, for, in most cases, the "marginalia" were for his eyes only. The notations clearly demonstrate that Franklin, by 1769, had come to hold the following views:

1. Only the king, not Parliament, was sovereign over both the colonies and Great Britain.

---

[23]Massachusetts House of Representatives' Instructions to Benjamin Franklin, 6 November 1770; Massachusetts House of Representatives' Committee of Correspondence to Benjamin Franklin, 17 December 1770. Ibid., XVII, 275-83, 301-304.
[24]Benjamin Franklin to Thomas Cushing, 24 December 1770. Ibid., XVII, 308.

2. Americans had the right not to be taxed, except by their own provincial assemblies.

3. Virtual representation was unacceptable, because British and American interests were not necessarily the same.

4. That Parliament knew best for the whole empire was clearly debatable.

5. Britain caused the hostility between the colonies and herself by sending troops to Boston in 1768.

6. Americans were *willing*—contrary to the views of British writers —to contribute to the "general Exigencies of the State," but they wanted to grant their own money through their own representatives.[25]

Although Franklin had expressed some of these views in his earlier propaganda pieces, he asserted them with greater conviction and forthrightness beginning in 1769. In his marginalia he frequently waxed polemical, not minding to depart from the truth on more than one occasion. For instance, his notations on Thomas Pownall's *State of the Constitution in the Colonies* (and he did share those comments with Pownall) indicate that the Doctor strongly doubted that Parliament had a right to legislate for the colonies in any case at all, much less in "all cases whatsoever," as the Declaratory Act of 1766 asserted.[26] Franklin's argument in this instance was rather ridiculous, since Parliament had been legislating for the colonies at least for a century and a half.

A consistent theme of the "marginalia" was that an Englishman's property should not be taken from him except by his consent. Taxes, then, could be imposed upon him only with his approval or that of his representatives. Franklin's margin comments indicate that he had a good general, though somewhat distorted, view of British history. His contentions that under the "ancient Constitution . . . all had a Right to vote," that Americans voluntarily agreed to be the king's subjects by taking charters and remaining within the "King's Dominions," that Americans were subjects only of the king, and that the original colonists left England to escape the "Power of Parliament" were questionable and misleading, to say the least.[27]

By 1770 Franklin had assumed positions that were as radical in theory (though not action) as any ideas that circulated in Boston. This

---

[25]Ibid., XVI, 276-98.
[26]Ibid., XVI, 298-304.
[27]Ibid., XVI, 304-326.

was obvious in comments he made about a pamphlet that had been written in 1766. Entitled *A Letter from a Merchant in London to His Nephew in North America*, the tract was the work of Josiah Tucker, the economist and theologian with whom Franklin had a number of verbal battles. In the work, Tucker asserted that Parliament's sovereignty in the empire was unlimited and that Americans, who were *virtually* represented in that body, could certainly be taxed by it. He clearly held Americans and their constitutional arguments in contempt, thus infuriating Franklin. Not until after the Boston Massacre (5 March 1770) did the Doctor read the pamphlet and make comments on it. He refuted (secretly, of course) all of Tucker's views and called the Anglican clergyman a "lying Villain!". Franklin's rage and gradually emerging extremism were plainly revealed in the contention that Americans were outside the realm and thus beyond Parliament's jurisdiction. Americans, the agent asserted, had been forced to accept Parliament's oppressive laws for years because the colonists had not been strong enough to resist them, but now they were. The Doctor maintained that Americans paid heavy taxes to support their own governments, and yet they had done their part and more in the imperial wars. He also argued that there were ten riots in England for every *one* in America.[28]

Repeatedly in the "marginalia," Franklin contended that *royal* sovereignty—not Parliamentary sovereignty—united the British Empire. England exercised no sovereignty over America, for England, like the colonies, was a dominion of the king. He condemned British writers for calling Americans "riotous," pointing out that in 1768 England experienced corn riots, election riots, and workers' riots. Yet one incident of mob action and a few broken windows in the colonies caused writers in England to cry "Rebellion." The Doctor noted that Parliament's taxation of the colonies would not achieve its purpose, since Americans would avoid imperial duties by manufacturing taxed items at home. Franklin even used the term "natural Rights," claiming that the colonies departed from Britain in order to settle beyond the "Jurisdiction of Parliament." He saw only one way to resolve the dispute over taxation, and that was for Britain to repeal all "taxing Laws" and return to "Requisitions." Under the requisition system, which the Doctor argued was *the* constitutional one, Americans had done their part during the colonial wars. Britain,

---

[28]Ibid. XVII, 348-80.

however, changed the American "Constitutions" in such a way as to take away colonial rights and subject the colonists to taxation by Parliament.[29]

In opposing the Townshend duties during 1769 and 1770, Franklin did much more than read pamphlets and make private comments in the margins of those works. As previously indicated, he was quite busy as a propagandist, sending numerous pieces to the press. He also talked to influential people in England and wrote openly to friends and relatives in America. Although he sometimes cautioned his correspondents not to show his letters to others, he must have known that what he wrote would almost surely leak out and be circulated. Joseph Galloway was very disturbed in September 1770 about the Doctor's "free Correspondence." The Pennsylvania speaker reported that General Thomas Gage had sent to the ministry a copy of a letter Franklin had written to Charles Thomson. Galloway believed Franklin would be hurt personally by Gage's action, and he was certain that the interests of the American public would be damaged by it. Because this letter's contents were exposed, rumors spread in Boston and other places in the colonies that Franklin would lose his job as deputy postmaster general of the colonies. For a time the removal of the Doctor from the post was a possibility, since the letter was quite direct. In it, Franklin accused Francis Bernard of preventing the total repeal of the Townshend duties (before Bernard was recalled in 1769) by giving the ministry some "lying letters said to be from Boston" and saying that the American boycott was crumbling because of a shortage of British goods. The Doctor also condemned the "Bedford Party" in the British government for preventing "more moderate Measures" from passing and for sending soldiers to the colonies "to make a Massacre among us." Franklin observed that Americans had their friends in high places in Britain—Rockingham, Shelburne, and Chatham —but they were out of power and not likely to return. The Doctor expressed disappointment in British merchants and manufacturers for their slowness to protest the duties or, in the case of many, for not protesting them at all. He expressed the view that the American boycott should continue until all duties were repealed and Britain abandoned its tax schemes forever.[30]

After the publication of the Thomson letter, the Doctor's stock rose to astronomical heights in America, while in England it plummeted. His

---

[29]Ibid., XVII, 317-48, 380-400.

[30]Benjamin Franklin to [Charles Thomson], 18 March 1770; Joseph Galloway to Benjamin Franklin, 27 September 1770. Ibid., XVII, 110-113, 228-29.

deputy postmaster's job was saved only because he had influential friends like Lord LeDespencer (one of the postmasters general over the whole British postal system), who apparently intervened and forestalled his removal. Franklin insisted that he would never resign, for he believed he had turned the colonial postal service into a successful operation and had "some kind of Right to it." The ministry would have to take the post from him, he asserted, since he would never voluntarily surrender it.[31]

More than a year before Franklin's letter to Thomson was revealed, the Doctor's radical views were slowly becoming known. It happened because of his own unguarded statements in private conversation and the identification by friends and relatives of his propaganda pieces, which he had been unable to camouflage by the use of pseudonyms. On 9 January 1769, Franklin wrote Galloway that he had been asked "by a noble Lord if no Plan" of conciliation could be devised to resolve Anglo-American differences. The agent responded that indeed there was a very simple plan that would do the trick: "*Repeal* the Laws, *Renounce* the Right, *Recall* the Troops, *Refund* the Money, and *Return to the old Method of Requisition.*" The inquirer answered that he might be able to accept all the points except "*Renounce* the Right." Franklin claimed that this was no problem. The mother country could claim the right forever, as long as she never attempted "to execute it." This was, and continued to be, the crux of the matter. Americans denied Britain's right to tax them, while even a genuine American sympathizer like William Strahan could not accept such an extreme position.[32]

Besides Franklin's occasional unguarded remarks in conversation and correspondence, those who knew him well saw through the pseudonyms he employed. William Franklin wrote that he had seen several pieces in "the [London] Chronicle" that he was sure his father had written. The younger Franklin warned the Doctor that the propaganda he penned and the letters that his enemies secured and published gave him "great Credit in the Colonies," but not in England. In fact, William himself was "out of Favour" with Lord Hillsborough, and he seemed to suspect that his

---

[31]Benjamin Franklin to Lord LeDespencer, 26 July 1770; Benjamin Franklin to Jane Mecom, 30 December 1770. Ibid., XVII, 199-201, 313-16. Also see: Ibid., XVII, xxvii.

[32]Benjamin Franklin to Joseph Galloway, 9 January 1769; Philadelphia Merchants to Benjamin Franklin, 18 April 1769. Ibid., XVI, 17-18, 115-16.

father's activities helped to cause it, although he did not say so forth-rightly.[33]

Throughout his struggle to secure repeal of the Townshend duties, Benjamin Franklin consistently called for continued colonial economic pressure until *all* duties were repealed. He argued that Americans should be frugal and manufacture needed items for themselves instead of relying on Britain's industry for their goods. The Doctor wanted to show the British that Americans did not need the manufactures of the mother country. To Samuel Cooper, he wrote that, if Americans would remain "fix'd" in their "Resolutions of Industry and Frugality," he would almost wish that the duties were never repealed. Franklin's desire to see Americans stand on their own economic and financial feet caused him to have second thoughts, too, about the Currency Act of 1764. After working for three or four years to have that law repealed, he abruptly did an about-face on the measure in January 1769. He told Lord Kames that scarcity of money would reduce American extravagance and promote more industry and frugality in the colonies. The prospect of that happening made him, he said, indifferent to the repeal of the Currency Act. If his country would accept his advice, Franklin wrote, they would request repeal no more.[34] His constituents, of course, particularly those in New Jersey, continued to seek approval for a more flexible money supply, and their new agent was compelled to support their paper money acts. While Dr. Franklin, by early 1769, was already quietly advocating what amounted to American *economic* independence, he did not inform the New Jersey legislature of the modifications in his views on the Currency Act. Franklin's advocacy of political independence was still years down the road.

The struggle that the Doctor—and to a lesser extent some of the other American agents—carried on against the Townshend duties ended with a partial victory in the spring of 1770. In a five-to-four vote the ministry supported a proposal by Lord North, new chief minister, to repeal the duties, except for the one on tea, which was retained to "keep up the

---

[33]William Franklin to Benjamin Franklin, [31 January 1769]. Ibid., XVI, 34-38; Skemp, *William Franklin*. 91.

[34]Benjamin Franklin to Lord Kames, 1-[16] January 1769; Benjamin Franklin to Joseph Galloway, 9 March 1769; Benjamin Franklin to Samuel Cooper, 27 April 1769, and 8 June 1770; Benjamin Franklin to Philadelphia Merchants, 9 July 1769. Ibid., XVI, 1-2, 64-65, 117-20, 174-75; XVII, 164.

right" to tax the colonies. The king approved the new policy on 12 April. Franklin was disappointed and irked by partial repeal, informing Samuel Cooper that the tea duty remained "to continue the Dispute." In his letter to Cooper, written on 8 June, the Doctor expressed radical views regarding imperial relations, knowing full well that they would be warmly received in Boston. By this time he was saying more of what Boston radicals and Charles Thomson wanted to hear and less of what the equivocating Joseph Galloway desired from his mouth. The political sands were indeed shifting. Franklin knew it, and he changed his ground. Galloway, on the other hand, stood fast, only to be buried politically over the next five years. Thomson and the Philadelphia merchants had declared near the end of 1769 that they were determined to establish the constitutional fact that Parliament had no right to tax the colonies— period. "A partial redress will little avail to allay the heats and quiet the minds of the people," Thomson had written. Fully aware of the new direction America was taking, even if his friend Galloway was oblivious to it, Franklin made sure that colonial leaders in key colonies like Massachusetts and Pennsylvania (as well as Georgia and New Jersey, of course) knew where he stood on the issue of taxation. He was for total repeal, and he urged non-importation of British goods until all taxes imposed on America by Parliament were eliminated. Parliament, the Doctor insisted, had no right to tax Americans. As a matter of fact, Parliament had usurped the Crown's prerogative in governing the colonies by making laws that should have been made by provincial legislatures and approved by the Crown. Franklin had no doubt that his view would be condemned by Parliament as treason.[35] What he refused to admit, but undoubtedly knew, was that the Crown, whose sovereignty he ostensibly championed, would also label it as treason. By the summer of 1770 the Doctor was a full-fledged radical in his views regarding the imperial relationship. His standing as an American hero, which had been gradually mounting since

---

[35]Benjamin Franklin to Joseph Galloway, 9 March 1769; 11 and 29 January, 21 March 1770; Benjamin Franklin to Philadelphia Merchants, 9 July 1769; Benjamin Franklin to Joshua Babcock, 26 February 1770; Benjamin Franklin to Samuel Cooper, 8 June and 30 December 1770; Samuel Cooper to Benjamin Franklin, 3 August 1769; and letters to the press by Benjamin Franklin under pseudonyms. Ibid., XVI, 54-55, 54 n. 2, 174-75, 182-84, 237-40; XVII, 5-8, 23-26, 29-31, 78-79, 114-19, 160-65, 197-200, 310-13; Kammen, *Rope of Sand*, 185; Newcomb, *Franklin and Galloway*, 208-209.

the Stamp Act crisis, received another substantial boost from his efforts to repeal the Townshend duties.

With the interests of four colonies to protect by late 1770, Franklin obviously spent more time monitoring legislation before Parliament than he had when he had served as the agent of the Pennsylvania Assembly only. Of course, the Townshend Duty crisis, like the Stamp Act crisis before it, was an abnormal situation, when one compared it to the first century and a half of Anglo-American relations. The Townshend duties were so much a matter of American concern that Franklin spent most of his efforts in and out of Parliament during 1769 and 1770 to effect their repeal. Still, he somehow found time to continue promoting the Illinois colony and to carrying on a social life.

The Illinois scheme, which Lord Hillsborough seemed determined to block, took several complicated twists and turns while Franklin was wrapped up in the fight over the Townshend duties. Hoping to expedite ministerial approval, Samuel Wharton and William Trent, headed for England in 1769. Once in London, Wharton made contact with Thomas Walpole, influential banker and member of Parliament, as well as a cousin of the famous Horace Walpole. Since the Illinois venture had been successfully delayed by Hillsborough, various interests, including Walpole, Wharton, and Franklin, merged to form the new Grand Ohio Company in the summer of 1769. The group was also known as the Walpole Associates and the "Vandalia Company," since the new company intended to name its colony "Vandalia." This name was chosen in honor of Queen Charlotte (George III's wife), who was said to be descended from the Vandals. Among the members of the Grand Ohio Company were most of the men who had been associated with the Illinois Company, plus three Walpoles (Thomas and two cousins), William Strahan, Richard Jackson, Anthony Todd (one of Franklin's bosses in the post office), John Foxcroft, Thomas Pownall, and John Sargent.[36]

In June 1769 the new company petitioned the king for the right to purchase the 2,400,000 acres that the Indians had ceded to the British government in the Treaty of Ft. Stanwix. The petitioners offered to pay the government the £10,640 it had agreed to give to the Indians for the cession and asked the king to waive the payment of quitrents for twenty years. Included in the petition was a promise by the company to sponsor

---

[36]Abernethy, *Western Lands*, 40-41; *Franklin Papers*, X, 217 n. 5; XVI, 163-69; Randall, *A Little Revenge*, 224-25; Skemp, *William Franklin*, 105-106.

a settlement in the territory, which was bounded by the Greenbriar River on the East and the Ohio on the west. The settlement, claimed the company, would bring in revenue to the government, as a strenuous effort would be made to promote British commerce with the Indians who lived in the area. On 24 July the Privy Council referred the petition to the Board of Trade, which finally considered it on 13 December. Franklin expected Hillsborough to block the petition, but instead his lordship surprised the agent by pretending to support it. The secretary went even further by encouraging the company to ask for 20,000,000 acres instead of 2,400,000, believing all the time that the Walpole Associates would be unable to raise the purchase price of £100,000 for the greater number of acres.[37]

The company took Hillsborough's bait by requesting the 20,000,000 acres and presenting the request to the lords of the Treasury on 4 January 1770. Although the lords claimed to like the idea, they insisted on more information from the Board of Trade and asked the opinions of some other government departments. Thus the project, as the Illinois scheme had, bogged down in bureaucratic wrangling, and a final decision on it would never be made. Besides Hillsborough's secret opposition, the ministry was confronted by the protests of Virginia speculators, who laid claim to some of the same land being sought by the Grand Ohio Company. Among those laying claim to part of the Illinois country were the Ohio Company of Virginia and the Mississippi Company, the agent of which was Arthur Lee. The Virginia company had received a grant of a 500,000 acres from the Virginia Council, and the company's agent, George Mercer, fought unsuccessfully against the encroachment of the Walpole Associates. Mercer ended up buying two shares in the Grand Ohio Company. Samuel Wharton, who gathered impressive support from a number of influential Englishmen, was mainly responsible for the Grand Ohio Company's outmaneuvering the Virginia-based companies in 1770. Franklin, already at odds with Hillsborough, attempted to keep a low

---

[37]*Franklin Papers*, XVI, 163-169; XVII, 8-11; *Journals of the Board of Trade, 1768–1775*, 152; Skemp, *William Franklin*, 105-106; Sosin, *Whitehall and the Wilderness*, 184-88.

profile, although he was instrumental in luring such people as Thomas Pownall, Richard Jackson, and William Strahan into the venture.[38]

In addition to doing the work required by his agencies, now numbering four, and promoting the new Grand Ohio Company, Franklin continued to give occasional attention to the American post office. He and John Foxcroft, his fellow deputy postmaster general, corresponded from time to time, and in 1769 Foxcroft joined the Doctor in England. He remained long enough to be married in August 1770 and did not return to America until the autumn of that year. Thus through personal contact, as well as correspondence, with Foxcroft, Franklin helped manage colonial postal affairs. The Doctor kept ample notes on the accounts of various post offices in America. Whenever sensitive issues involving Franklin's postal appointees arose, Foxcroft nearly always deferred to his colleague in resolving them.[39]

As in the past, Franklin continued to do favors for a wide variety of people who approached him in London. When "Miss Farquarson and Miss Smith," one a "Milliner" and the other a "Mantuamaker," decided to sail to Philadelphia to ply their trades in that American city, the Doctor wrote and asked Deborah and Sally to show them "Civility" and to give them "Advice and Countenance in the Prosecution of their Design." He also recommended two young men, George Spencer and Theodorus Swaine Drage, to the Society for the Propagation of the Gospel in Foreign Parts for ordination and missionary work. Both were ordained, and both turned out to be controversial characters who were hardly model missionaries. A seemingly endless stream of young men from America knocked on the door of Franklin's Craven Street residence, seeking his help in one endeavor or another. In most cases he gave it. He even persuaded the blind music teacher John Stanley to come out of retirement to teach Josiah Williams, Franklin's blind nephew from Boston. Josiah had reached London wondering if his uncle would balk at appealing to Stanley and then send his nephew home. The young blind man was pleasantly surprised when the Doctor gladly gave his assistance. Franklin

---

[38]Benjamin Franklin to William Franklin, 17 March 1770, and other material. *Franklin Papers*, XVI, 163-69; XVII, 8-11, 97, 135-36; Sosin, *Whitehall and the Wilderness*, 188-95, 198-200.

[39]John Foxcroft to Benjamin Franklin, 21 February 1769; [Joseph Chew] to Benjamin Franklin, 12 December 1769, and other material. *Franklin Paper*, XVI, 48-50, 157-58 n. 1, 173 n. 8, 259-63; XVII, 4.

also honored the request of the Royal Society in 1769 when he was appointed by it to serve on a committee to give advice on lightning rods for St. Paul's Cathedral to protect it "from the Effects of Lightning." Interestingly enough, the committee's investigation provoked a controversy over the merits of pointed versus round-knob lightning rods. Franklin favored the pointed rods and thereby incurred the displeasure of King George III, who was an advocate of round-knob rods. Royal physician John Pringle, because he sided with Franklin in the controversy, was forced to resign as president of the Royal Society.[40]

Other matters, which affected Franklin personally, came up during this time. Joseph Galloway came under attack. The common people of Pennsylvania turned against him, and some derisively called him "pope." According to historian Benjamin Newcomb, Galloway was no more than "a rotten borough member of the Assembly" after 1770. William Strahan, another of Franklin's confidants, had become "a great Courtier" during the Townshend duty crisis. This troubled the Doctor, but his personal friendship with Strahan remained intact, as was evidenced by Franklin's bringing Strahan into the Grand Ohio Company. Sir John Cust, speaker of the British House of Commons and Franklin's friend since 1761, died in 1770. So did the Doctor's "dear old Friend" George Whitefield, the man who had moved thousands to repent by his stirring oratory. Franklin and Whitefield had known and admired each other since 1739. Though far different in their theological views, they had maintained a close relationship since their first meeting. A few months before Whitefield died, Franklin's devoted friend, James Parker, had died in Burlington, New Jersey, on 2 July 1770. The Doctor's former printing partner, David Hall, still lived, but he sensed that his time was short and expressed considerable anxiety over his longtime friend's failure to settle the accounts of their partnership. On 17 March 1770, Hall wrote Franklin to say that he had heard nothing from him for three years. Hall's letter was friendly, but he made it clear that he was eager to settle the accounts. On 11 June, Franklin responded by offering a variety of excuses for not writing and

---

[40]See various letters to and from Benjamin Franklin, as well as other material. Ibid., XVI, 38-39, 70-72, 70 n. 2, 145-51; XVII, 125, 212-13, 243-50, 313; Kammen, *Rope of Sand*, 251.

for not resolving matters concerning the partnership. He promised to return to Philadelphia "next Spring at farthest, if not sooner."[41]

In March of 1770, before his letter to Hall in June, Franklin told Jane Mecom that he would return to Philadelphia in the summer of 1770. Deborah was probably sad—and irked, too—that summer, when she found out that her husband had once more put off his return to her. "When will it be in your power to Cume home?" she wrote in obvious frustration. Yet she was still the loving wife. Her husband had written to her about the first "Fit of Gout" he had in five years, and she answered that if she were "near aneuf," she would "rube it with a lite hand." Deborah, by this time, realized that she was having trouble with her "memerey," but her main problem, since 1764, had been loneliness. That was somewhat relieved by the birth of Benjamin Franklin Bache on 12 August 1769. "King bird," as Deborah called Sally's firstborn, became the center of Deborah's life until her death in 1774. Franklin quickly saw in her letters that his wife's "Happiness" was "wrapt up" in her new grandson, for she constantly gave "the History of his pretty Actions."[42]

Along with matters concerning his real family during this period, Franklin was also caught up in events associated with his surrogate family in England. The Doctor was very attentive in the late summer of 1769 when Polly Stevenson met a physician with whom she was obviously enamored. She thought him quite clever, she told Franklin, because "he thinks as *we* do." The young physician was Dr. William Hewson, with whom Polly thought she might—she warned Franklin—"run off." The Doctor responded that he might "have Reason to be jealous of this insinuating handsome young Physician." Franklin refused to give Polly any direct advice on whether or not to marry Dr. Hewson, telling her that she alone could make the decision and that he had complete confidence she would make the right one. On 10 July 1770, Polly married William Hewson. In September the newlyweds visited the Stevenson residence on Craven Street to take care of Franklin while Margaret Stevenson and young cousin Sally Franklin were away. During the Hewsons' visit,

---

[41]See several letters to and from Benjamin Franklin with a variety of correspondents. *Franklin Papers*, XVII, 98-101, 172, 175, 185, 204-205, 255, 284; Kammen, *Rope of Sand*, 210, 248-49; Newcomb, *Franklin and Galloway*, 216, 218-20, 227. Also see: *The Autobiography*, 178, and Morgan, "A Most Unlikely Friendship," 208-218.

[42]See Benjamin Franklin's correspondence with Deborah Franklin and Jane Mecom. *Franklin Papers*, XVII, 95, 166-68, 205-208, 239-40.

Franklin engaged in some nonsensical literary fun by writing "The Cravenstreet Gazette. No. 113." In it the Doctor referred to the newly-weds as "Lord and Lady Hewson" and called himself the "*great* Person," because of his "enormous Size."[43] Thus, it appears that Franklin, as occupied as he was with serious business during the Townshend Duty crisis, found time to handle many personal matters and to give at least some attention to family and friends.

By the end of 1770, after a struggle of more than two years over the Townshend duties, Franklin's destiny was fixed. His future was inexorably bound up with that of the American colonies. When he accepted the post of agent for the Massachusetts lower house, he passed the point of no return. He was representative for four American colonies, and he had made himself the chief propagandist of the American cause in England. He could not expect, especially as the Massachusetts agent, ever again to find favor in the eyes of the men who held power in England. Even those high-ranking political figures who felt kindly disposed toward the colonies looked askance at the radical notions that emanated too frequently from Boston. From his secret writings and some of his unguarded correspondence, it appears that Franklin joined the radical campaign deliberately. His days of walking the political tightrope of moderation were over, and all hope of landing a sinecure in the British bureaucracy was *certainly* over. Indeed, his job with the colonial post office was at risk. Still, the Doctor hoped that somehow the British leaders who viewed the imperial relationship as he did would regain power. That hope kept him in England for over four more years.

---

[43]Benjamin Franklin to Mary Stevenson, 2 September 1769; 31 May and 18 July 1770; Mary Stevenson to Benjamin Franklin, 1 September 1769, and other material. Ibid., XVI, 187-94, 191 n. 6; XVII, 152-53, 185-86, 185 n. 7, 194-95, 220-26.

# 8. "Between the Cup and the Lip":
## A Discouraged and Disenchanted Agent

In the spring of 1771 William Strahan accused Benjamin Franklin of idleness, while the disgruntled Arthur Lee called him Hillsborough's tool.[1] Given the hostility that existed between Franklin and the American Secretary, Lee's charge was absurd. Strahan's assessment, on the other hand, was partly true. Franklin, whose standing with members of the ministry in general and Hillsborough in particular was on the decline, had begun to wonder if colonial agents were still useful. The Doctor had become a marked man, and in 1771 and 1772 he took actions that could only damage his reputation at Whitehall even more. He could hardly have hurt himself more in the eyes of the British leaders, if he had deliberately set out to make himself *anathema* to them. He continued to fight with Hillsborough, who finally resigned as Secretary of the American Department in August 1772. The secretary quit following a Cabinet showdown that found his lordship on the losing side. In addition to Franklin's squabbling with Hillsborough, the agent engaged in a great deal of posturing to prove his radicalism to the Massachusetts lower house. This ultimately caused him irreparable damage at Westminster, but he did not yet know it. When Hillsborough departed and was replaced by Lord Dartmouth, who was considered a friend to the colonies, the Doctor thought that American affairs would take a ministerial turn for the better. His optimism, however, was short-lived, because, in 1773, it would be revealed that Franklin had sent the Hutchinson-Oliver letters back to Massachusetts. That one deed would destroy the Doctor's credibility forever with the entire ministry and render him useless as a colonial agent at Whitehall.

If the truth be told, Franklin appeared to be a man in a political daze during 1771 and 1772. Although he continued to carry out the requests of the four colonies he served as agent, he had clearly lost his enthusiasm for the job. There can be little doubt that Hillsborough's enmity was the main reason for Franklin's disenchantment, but to a great degree the agent brought his woes upon himself. As soon as the Doctor could strike out for Hillsborough's residence to inform him of the appointment by the

---

[1]*Franklin Papers*, XVIII, 119.

Massachusetts lower house, Franklin did so, claiming that Strahan urged
him to do it. Surely the agent was looking for an argument, and he went
to the right place to find one. According to Franklin's own account (the
only one available), the secretary received him graciously, until the agent
brought up the Massachusetts appointment. Hillsborough contended that
the bill appointing Franklin to that agency had been vetoed by Governor
Thomas Hutchinson. The Doctor shot back that there *was* no bill, only a
vote of the house, and then he showed Hillsborough the recorded vote.
His lordship insisted that such information should be sent to the Board of
Trade and not to his office, but he warned that he personally would
prevent its being entered in the Board's minutes. Angrily, the secretary
asserted that the lower house could not appoint an agent and that he
would take no notice of such appointments. At this point Franklin left,
saying that Hillsborough's acknowledgment made little difference, since
an agent could not be of any use to the colonies at that time. This confrontation took place on 16 January 1771, and the Doctor seems to have
invited it to impress his new constituents of the Massachusetts lower
house. Otherwise, he would simply have informed John Pownall, secretary of the Board of Trade, of the appointment.[2]

Lord Hillsborough's standard for appointing agents eventually prevailed. A little over a year after the confrontation with his lordship,
Franklin wrote to William Franklin and noted that the Board of Trade had
resolved not to accept agents anymore, unless they had been appointed
by act of both houses of a colony's legislature and had the approval of
the governor. The Doctor was convinced that this would "put an end" to
agents, since assemblies would regard agents appointed by Hillsborough's
rules as too much under ministerial influence to do them any good.
Franklin was ready to leave "this infallible minister to his own devices."
What sense did it make to put a colony to the expense of sending an
agent to London, the Doctor wondered, if the American Secretary, could
displace that agent by what amounted to "a repeal of the appointing act"?
Franklin claimed that he could not serve under such circumstances.[3]

The gulf between Franklin and Hillsborough continued to widen.
After 16 January 1771, the agent stopped going to the American

---

[2]Franklin's Account of His Audience with Lord Hillsborough. Ibid., XVIII, 9-16. Also
see: Benjamin Franklin to Samuel Cooper, 5 February 1771. Ibid., XVIII, 24-25.

[3]Benjamin Franklin to William Franklin, 30 January 1772. *New Jersey Archives*, X,
330-34.

Secretary's levees. In the summer of 1771 it appeared for a brief moment that the estrangement between the two men might end. Traveling with Richard Jackson, Franklin visited Ireland, and at Jackson's insistence the two men called upon Lord Hillsborough at his estate. When the travelers paid their respects, the secretary received them most hospitably. He insisted that they spend a few days with him. They visited for four days, and his lordship entertained them with "great Civility." The Doctor was genuinely surprised, since in London Hillsborough had called him "a Republican, a factious mischievous Fellow and the like." Now, however, the secretary was most agreeable, acknowledging England's narrowness toward Ireland and expressing the view that the colonies should have a free hand to manufacture their own goods. He even presented himself as a friend of American interests. His lordship's oldest son, Arthur Hill (Lord Kilwarling), drove Franklin forty miles around the country. When the Doctor and Jackson said farewell, Hillsborough used his own cloak to cover Franklin, lest the agent catch cold. Knowing that his lordship liked neither him nor the colonies, Franklin's suspicions were aroused by all the attention the secretary bestowed on him. He suspected that Hillsborough, seeing a storm looming on the political horizon, was trying to mend a few fences with his enemies, even agents whom his lordship usually had trouble tolerating.[4]

Even if Hillsborough had acted from an ulterior motive, the hospitality he heaped upon Franklin in Ireland must have led the Doctor to think that the secretary would be more cordial in their future relations. If so, he was wrong. Some time in the summer of 1772, Franklin tried to see Hillsborough in London to discuss, among other matters, "a Georgia affair." The secretary refused to see the agent. According to Franklin, on five occasions, following his trip to Ireland, he attempted without success to see Hillsborough. The secretary told a different story. Franklin, so said his lordship, had repaid Hillsborough's hospitality in Ireland by shunning him in London. Obviously, the two men were still estranged in the summer of 1772. The secretary's attitude and his domination of American affairs with what Franklin considered wrongheaded policies had the Doctor on the verge of leaving England earlier that year. As ever, Franklin was torn between his love for life in England and his family

---

[4]Benjamin Franklin to Thomas Cushing, 13 January 1772; Benjamin Franklin to William Franklin, 30 January 1772. *Franklin Papers*, XIX, 16-24, 47-53; Kammen, *Rope of Sand*, 256-58, 270-71.

connections in America. Having reached the age of sixty-six and suffering some infirmities, he wanted to go home and settle his business affairs. His fear that he might not be able to return to England caused him to hesitate.[5]

Finally, Hillsborough's stubbornness and domineering ways caught up with him. After the political showdown mentioned above, he was ousted in August 1772. Just prior to his lordship's overthrow, Franklin wrote a polemic attacking the American Secretary as the fountainhead of all that had gone wrong in American affairs since 1768. Hillsborough's cardinal sin, according to the disenchanted agent, was his interruption of petitions sent to the Crown. Such actions by the secretary, Franklin argued, deprived Americans of any hope that their grievances would be heard by His Majesty. Furthermore, the Doctor asserted, the secretary had tried but failed to force Americans into submitting to his will. Hillsborough's policies were both imprudent and unconstitutional, according to Franklin, and the agent accused his lordship of pursuing bad ends through improper means. On this occasion, the disgruntled agent signed himself "A Well-Wisher to the King and all his Dominions."[6]

Franklin reported Hillsborough's resignation with obvious delight in a letter of 17 August 1772 to William Franklin. Hillsborough was out, and Lord Dartmouth was in. This was good news for Americans, the Doctor asserted. Reports that Hillsborough had fallen because of the Ohio land scheme were viewed by Franklin as an oversimplification. He saw the secretary's overthrow as more personal than anything else. Hillsborough's fellow ministers disliked him and had supported the Ohio scheme because he opposed it. The king, too, according to Franklin, was tired of his lordship, but there is no evidence to support that opinion. While Hillsborough's departure seemed to be a prelude to bringing the Ohio scheme to fruition (especially since the Privy Council had approved it three days before Franklin wrote to his son), the Doctor refused to be overly optimistic. In words that proved prophetic, he told William that the scheme might be "suffered to linger, and possibly may yet miscarry." Even so, Hillsborough was gone and, because Franklin's longtime friend,

---

[5]Benjamin Franklin to William Franklin, 30 January 1772, and other material. *Franklin Papers*, XIX, 47-53, 257, 257 n. 5.

[6]Ibid., XIX, 216-26.

Lord Dartmouth, now ran American affairs, the disenchanted agent took hope that the colonies were finally in store for some favorable treatment.[7]

Franklin was immeasurably more comfortable as agent after the ascendancy of Dartmouth as American Secretary. He hoped for a return to normal Anglo-American relations, but he had observed enough disarray in the British government not to rejoice too soon. While informing his son in New Jersey that he had been received cordially by the new secretary, Franklin emphasized that he had done what he could to promote William's interests. By 1772 William was the senior royal governor in America and wanted badly, for the sake of a bigger salary, to be appointed governor of the island colony of Barbados. His father thought William's chances of securing that appointment were good, now that Dartmouth was American Secretary. Yet the Doctor was cautious, warning the New Jersey governor that "Time will show" the depth of Dartmouth's cordial feelings toward the controversial agent, his son, and America. Of one thing Franklin seemed sure; Dartmouth would not intercept and read the correspondence between the New Jersey agent and the governor, as he was certain Hillsborough and undersecretary William Knox had done.[8]

Although Franklin was discouraged about his agencies as long as Hillsborough remained in power, he continued to serve his constituents. The level of his enthusiasm, however, was far below what it had been in prior years. His efforts for Pennsylvania were minimal in 1771 and 1772, when Hillsborough seemed most unbearable. The Assembly, too, lost enthusiasm, once it was certain that a royal government for the province was unobtainable. Perhaps to nudge Franklin into giving up the agency, the Assembly cut his salary from £500 per year to £400 upon reappointing him in October 1772 for the "ensuing Year." The Doctor's lone accomplishment for Pennsylvania during this two-year period was the promotion of silk culture in the province. He corresponded on the subject with John Bartram and Humphrey Marshall, but especially with Cadwalader Evans, all of whom were Pennsylvanians interested in

---

[7]Benjamin Franklin to William Franklin, 17 and 19[-22] August 1772; Benjamin Franklin to Noble Wimberly Jones, 7 October 1772. Ibid., XIX, 243-44, 243 ns. 6 and 7, 257-60, 323-24, 332-37.

[8]Benjamin Franklin to William Franklin, 3-[4] November 1772, and 2 December 1772; William Franklin to Benjamin Franklin, 13 October 1772. Ibid., XIX, 332-37, 360-61, 416-18.

agricultural and economic progress. Franklin urged Evans to win the Assembly's support for the project. When the Assembly failed to act, the Doctor persuaded the American Philosophical Society to promote it. Franklin was easily the leading advocate in London for an American silk industry.[9]

While Franklin's fretting over Hillsborough's hostility was at its height, events that were of great moment to Pennsylvanians occurred on both sides of the Atlantic. On 4 February 1771, Richard Penn died. His brother Thomas, old and sick, began preparing his will. Already Richard Penn, Jr., had been tapped to succeed his brother John as governor of the colony. In the spring of 1771, young Richard received his instructions from Uncle Thomas, who was taking the waters at Tunbridge Wells. There were other political changes on the horizon, too. Although Joseph Galloway was reelected speaker of the Assembly in 1771 and 1772, he was in bad health. Galloway realized that political control of the colony was slowly slipping away from him. In 1772 William Goddard, with whom Galloway had had such a bitter squabble, came within only a few votes of being elected to the Assembly as representative of Philadelphia County.[10] Slowly, but surely, Galloway's influence was waning.

Although Franklin did very little for Pennsylvania during this period, his efforts for Georgia were considerable. This is most interesting in view of that colony's perennial squabbling over his reappointment as agent and the low salary it promised to pay him and never did. Throughout 1771–1772 the Doctor worked through Thomas Life, a fellow agent and a lawyer, to unravel the complicated Baker land claims. At the request of the Assembly's Committee of Correspondence, Franklin asked for and received from former Georgia agent William Knox the papers Knox held concerning the claims. By the summer of 1771 the agent presented the matter to the Privy Council, which referred it to the Board of Trade. No record exists of the Board's action, but the Privy Council finally rendered a decision in June 1772—a decision contrary to the desire of the Georgia lower house. In a letter dated 3 August 1772, Franklin reported to Noble

[9]See letters between Benjamin Franklin and a variety of correspondents during 1771–1772. Ibid., XVIII, 31-32, 96-99, 159-61, 180, 188-89, 232-33, 232 n. 2, 245-46, 254-56; XIX, 68-69, 134-39, 338-39, 338 n. 6, 339 n. 7.

[10]Pennsylvania Assembly's Committee of Correspondence to Benjamin Franklin, 16 October 1771; Joseph Galloway to Benjamin Franklin, 12 October 1772. Ibid., XVII, 232-33, 232 n. 2; XIX, 330-32; Nolan, *Franklin in Scotland and Ireland*, 126.

Wimberly Jones that the Privy Council had "not favour'd our Petition" regarding the Baker claims. On 19 June that august body had upheld Sir William's heirs against the Georgia settlers on the lands claimed as part of the Baker estate. The Doctor held out little or no hope of a reversal, pointing out that the Privy Council rarely reconsidered a matter, once it had made a decision. Of course, Governor Wright and the Georgia Council had steadfastly favored the Baker heirs in the dispute, and they were delighted with the ruling.[11]

The Baker land dispute was by no means all that created political contention among Georgia leaders in 1771 and 1772. Several matters drove a wedge between Wright and the lower house. Although Noble Wimberly Jones claimed that the trouble stemmed from *his* reelection as speaker, the political currents ran considerably deeper. The governor dissolved the legislature on 22 February 1771 because the house conducted an independent investigation of the colony's deputy surveyor general for allegedly taking double fees. House members also refused to pass a tax bill that the governor requested. The legislature did not meet again until April 1772, and then it sat for only a few days before adjourning until September. Because there was little time to conduct business, Franklin was not officially reappointed during 1771–1772.[12]

The Doctor was well aware that his support in Georgia came from the lower house, and in 1771 he seems to have decided to leave little doubt about his loyalties in the apparently never-ending political war in the province. The report Jones sent him of the quarrel between the lower house and the governor apparently prompted the agent not to meet with Wright when the Georgia chief executive visited London during the late summer of 1771. Franklin seemingly wanted to emphasize his disapproval of the governor's refusal to accept Jones as house speaker and of his dissolving the legislature. So thoroughly disgusted was Franklin with Wright that the agent deliberately slighted the governor, even though he was convinced that the action would cost him the Georgia agency. Stating that the king would probably not have acted as the governor had, the

---

[11]*Acts of the Privy Council*, V, 295-96. Also see: correspondence between Benjamin Franklin and Noble Wimberly Jones and William Knox. *Franklin Papers*, XVII, 148-50; XVIII, 17-18, 20, 22-23, 158-59, 167-70; XIX, 95-96, 226-27, 227 n. 8.

[12]See various letters between Benjamin Franklin and Noble Wimberly Jones. Ibid., XVIII, 50-52, 51 ns. 9 and 10, 57, 158-59, 169-70; XIX, 54-55, 55 n. 2; *Georgia Colonial Records*, XV, 313, 330, 363.

Doctor noted that "Governors take Greater Liberties, having naturally no Respect for the People, but abundance for Ministers." Arbitrary actions by British officials in America, supported by officials in London, caused great disenchantment in America and could ultimately lead, Franklin suggested, to disunion.[13] If the Doctor entertained the smallest hope of hanging on to the Georgia agency, his refusal to meet with Wright was indeed a huge mistake. At this juncture, however, he was so discouraged and disenchanted because of Hillsborough's attitude and policies that he thought seriously about giving up all of his agencies anyway.

Georgia was not the only province where governor and legislature had political differences. Franklin's own son was beginning to take positions that irritated the New Jersey legislature. This put the Doctor in an obviously awkward position. On 22 June 1771, Stephen Crane, speaker of the New Jersey House of Representatives, wrote the colony's agent to report that the governor and the house had disagreed sharply over raising money to support royal troops stationed in New Jersey. According to Crane, economic depression in the province made it impossible for the people to pay new taxes, unless the legislature could provide some relief through the issuance of paper money. Unfortunately, "his Majesty" had disallowed the legislature's act providing for the needed paper currency. Crane asked the New Jersey agent to help with the rewording of a currency bill so that it would not violate the Currency Act of 1764. This, Crane maintained, was the only way New Jersey could comply with the royal requisition. The speaker criticized William Franklin as rash for "intimating a Want of Duty and Loyalty in the House to his Majesty."[14]

Fortunately for both Franklins, this political storm passed quickly. On 21 December 1771, ten days after the Doctor was reappointed agent for another year, the Assembly's Committee of Correspondence informed him that the dispute over quartering troops had been settled. The troops had been withdrawn, but the Assembly had paid for their housing during the time they had stayed. A few weeks later, on 6 January, Governor Franklin told his father in a letter that quartering troops was not the only issue. He wrote that he had "carried two Points of great Difficulty." The legislature had finally provided for the troops *and* had agreed upon "leaving out those Words in the Support Bill, which the Board of T. look'd upon as

---

[13]Benjamin Franklin to Noble Wimberly Jones, 2 April 1772. *Franklin Papers*, XIX, 95-96.

[14]Stephen Crane to Benjamin Franklin, 22 June 1771. Ibid., XVIII, 134-36.

meant to establish the Assembly's Claim of the sole Right of appointing an Agent." William predicted that the ministry, but not his father, would be pleased. In the governor's mind, the issue concerning the appointment of agents made "no kind of Difference."[15]

Benjamin Franklin was "griev'd" by the "Misunderstanding" between William and the lower house and hoped the differences would be resolved. Like Crane, the elder Franklin was upset by the disallowance of the colony's "paper Money Act." While the agent held out some hope that a rewording might bring approval, he was cautious, noting that the Board of Trade had a "rooted Prejudice" against "paper Money." Although the Doctor was discouraged and nearly ready to quit his agencies, the New Jersey house, which had no inkling of his disenchantment, urged him to push for several laws that the legislature had passed recently. A few dealt with debt recovery, and one, called the "Septennial Act," provided for Assembly elections every seven years. The Septennial Act, passed in 1768, had been tabled by the Board of Trade in July 1770, and it was never brought up again.[16]

As Franklin brooded during 1771 and 1772, halfheartedly approaching his duties as agent, he lamented the limited attention Parliament gave to American affairs. It bothered him that Parliament was consumed by matters such as the Falkland Island crisis with Spain and a dispute with the City of London. Parliament's inattention and Hillsborough's hostility deflated his spirit again and again. Still, he held on to all four of his agencies, all the while wrestling with the decision of whether to go home or stay in England. On 5 May 1772, he wrote William to say, "I am balancing upon a Wish of Visiting at least, if not returning for good and all (as the Phrase is) to America. If I don't do that, I shall spend the Summer, with some or other of those Friends who have invited me, at their Country Houses." He closed by encouraging his son to promote the silk industry in New Jersey.[17] Silk seems to have occupied a great deal

---

[15]New Jersey Assembly's Committee of Correspondence to Benjamin Franklin, 21 December 1771; William Franklin to Benjamin Franklin, 6 January 1772. Ibid., 260-62, 268-71; XIX, 3-5; *New Jersey Archives*, X, 238-65; XVIII, 236, 271.

[16]New Jersey Assembly's Committee of Correspondence to Benjamin Franklin, 21 December 1771; Benjamin Franklin to [Stephen Crane], 6 February 1772. *Franklin Papers*, XVIII, 268-71; XIX, 67-68.

[17]Benjamin Franklin to William Franklin, 20 April 1771 and 5 May 1772; Benjamin Franklin to Joseph Smith, [6 February 1772]; Joseph Smith to Benjamin Franklin, 1 October 1772. Ibid., XVIII, 74-77; XIX, 72-73, 131-32, 313.

of Franklin's attention during the time he floundered in despair over Hillsborough's handling of American affairs.

Perhaps the Doctor was tired of the Pennsylvania, Georgia, and New Jersey agencies and wanted to give most or all of his time to Massachusetts. He certainly seemed more alive when dealing with Massachusetts matters than when conducting the business of the other three colonies during the politically dreary months of 1771 and 1772. Surrendering the other agencies, particularly those of Georgia and New Jersey, might well have cost him recognition by the ministry as a bonafide agent. This could well have been his reason for retaining them. Whatever his motives for holding on to them, he clearly catered more to his Massachusetts constituents—in spite of the fact that he had little likelihood of ever receiving his salary from them. After all, he was appointed by the House of Representatives without the governor's consent, and the house could not appropriate money to pay him without the governor's signature. Not long after he became the agent of the Massachusetts lower house, Franklin began "calling in" at the New England Coffeehouse on Threadneedle Street near the Bank of England. He also arranged a meeting with William Bollan, the Massachusetts Council's agent. Thereafter the two men got together periodically, and Franklin believed there was "a good Understanding" between them.[18]

In February 1771 Franklin hinted to Thomas Cushing, speaker of the Massachusetts House of Representatives, that he might leave England in the summer. If so, he would turn the colony's affairs over to Arthur Lee or Dennys DeBerdt, Jr. Why Franklin considered assigning matters to DeBerdt, who had no kind of appointment from the Massachusetts lower house, is a matter of conjecture. DeBerdt's father was Franklin's immediate predecessor, and the Doctor must have assumed that the younger DeBerdt would have sufficient knowledge of Massachusetts affairs and be acceptable to the lower house. Franklin revealed to Cushing that he contemplated leaving England because of Hillsborough's scheme to gain control over all colonial agents. Although the disenchanted agent was almost ready to depart, he was careful to maintain his radical image for Cushing's benefit. The Doctor asserted that American resistance had to continue until all remaining taxes were removed. He also echoed the

---

[18]Benjamin Franklin to James Bowdoin, 5 February 1771; Benjamin Franklin to Jonathan Williams, Sr., 11 August 1772. Ibid., XVIII, 23; XIX, 232, 232 n. 4.

oft-heard American position that the colonies should be restored by Britain to their pre-Stamp Act status.[19]

Though on the verge of quitting, Franklin continued to say what the radicals in Boston wanted to hear. In referring to British officials in America, he used words such as "proud and insolent," "rapacious," and "malicious." The agent viewed the British customs system as a sinister apparatus that sowed the seeds of "a total disunion of the two Countries." On every issue dividing colonies and mother country, Franklin sided with the Bostonians and lashed out at Hillsborough's "wild Administration." The Doctor asserted that Parliament should pass no laws of any kind that bound Americans without their consent. Still, he urged all Americans to act with forbearance as long as possible so that, when "this Catastrophe" of disunion occurred, it would "appear to all Mankind" the fault of the British and not the Americans.[20]

As Franklin sought to augment his radical image in the eyes of the Bostonians, Arthur Lee tried to portray him as a dupe at best and a double-dealer at worst. On 10 June 1771, Lee wrote some very derogatory remarks about the Doctor to Samuel Adams. The alternate agent understood that, according to Franklin, all designs in the ministry against the Massachusetts Charter had been laid aside. This convinced Lee that Franklin was not merely "the dupe but the instrument of Lord Hillsborough's treachery." His lordship, Lee contended, had postponed—not laid aside—his scheme to revoke the Massachusetts Charter. The overly suspicious Virginian implied that Franklin would sacrifice everything else to secure a royal charter for Pennsylvania. Moreover, Lee insisted that the Doctor had Hillsborough's confidence and trust—a preposterous contention! In words transparently self-serving, Lee claimed that he was not influenced by selfish motives, while Franklin, who seemed compelled to play politics with the ministers, could not be "faithful to his trust."[21]

If the Doctor realized what Lee thought of him and wrote about him to people in Boston, it is no wonder that Franklin continuously flaunted his radical views in letters to Massachusetts leaders. As agent, he was compelled to resist the new imperial policies and to be prepared to

---

[19]Benjamin Franklin to Thomas Cushing, 5 February 1771. Ibid., XVIII, 25-30.

[20]Benjamin Franklin to the Massachusetts House of Representatives' Committee of Correspondence, 15 May 1771; Benjamin Franklin to Thomas Cushing, 10 June 1771. Ibid., XVIII, 102-104, 120-27; Crane, *Franklin: Englishman and American*, 128-29.

[21]Arthur Lee to Samuel Adams, 10 June 1771. *Franklin Papers*, XVIII, 127-29.

present the Massachusetts position to the ministry. This role forced him into a more uncompromising stance than ones he had previously taken. In the summer of 1771 the Massachusetts lower house dragged him into a complex dispute concerning lands in eastern Maine. Massachusetts settlers held grants of land between the Kennebec and St. Croix Rivers, under the authority of the colony's General Court [i.e., legislature]. Those grants had not been confirmed by the Crown. Francis Bernard, former governor, and Thomas Hutchinson, incumbent governor, had attempted to have the lands detached and made into a separate province or have them annexed by Nova Scotia. The lower house, however, sought to preserve the province's jurisdiction in the area. Franklin was instructed to seek the king's confirmation of the land grants. The house was determined to have the Doctor fight the colony's battles and do it in an uncompromising fashion. In response to his 5 February letter, in which he had called for forbearance, a house committee let Franklin know in unmistakable terms that moderation was not high on its agenda. The British needed to beware, the committee asserted, of "forcing a free people by oppressive Measures into a State of Desperation." The people of Massachusetts, the house members warned, would not give up even *one* important point with regard to their rights. Massachusetts, even if abandoned by the other colonies, would "never submit to the Authority of an absolute Government." The people of Massachusetts objected to partial repeal of the Townshend duties, they objected to the Crown's paying British officers in Massachusetts, and they would continue to object until they carried every point.[22] The Doctor had signed on with a colony whose people were adamant in their views and contemptuous of compromise, and this forced him to eschew his natural inclination toward moderation and flexibility. His views differed only slightly from the radicals of Massachusetts, but in spirit he was conciliatory, while they were rigid.

Not until the summer of 1771 did Franklin finally realize the extent of the agitation in Massachusetts over the Townshend Act's provision that put British officials in the colony on the Crown's payroll. At first the agent had cautiously observed that nothing could be done to prevent the king from paying his own servants in America. Although Franklin had seen no cause for alarm in this new practice, the Massachusetts lower

---

[22]Massachusetts House of Representatives' Committee of Correspondence to Benjamin Franklin, 25 and 29 June 1771. Ibid., XVIII, 138-44 and ns. 2-9, 147-53.

house viewed it as a critical matter. The control over salaries seemed to house members to be the only way of keeping arbitrary British officials in check. Samuel Cooper pointed out that removing this restraint on officials created much uneasiness in the colony. The representatives of the Crown had always been supported "by the free Gift of the Province" under the Charter of 1691. The legislature, Cooper noted, had even paid the salary of Francis Bernard, or "St. Francis B." (as Cooper called the former governor), and had never considered denying it to him. The legislature appropriated the salary of Governor Hutchinson in 1771, but the governor declined it. Then, before the new session began in May 1772, the king granted Hutchinson £1,500 per year. The Massachusetts house, infuriated by this turn of events, argued that the colony's charter gave the legislature the power to levy taxes and to support the government. Its members put pressure on Hutchinson to ask the Crown to return to the old practice. The governor not only refused, he prorogued the house as well. Thomas Cushing, acting for the house, sent Franklin a petition protesting payment of the governor's salary from Crown revenues and instructed the agent to present it to the king. The petition reached Franklin in September 1772, just a month after Lord Dartmouth had replaced Hillsborough as American Secretary. Believing that Dartmouth might work to heal the breach between Britain and the colonies, the Doctor sat on the petition as long as he dared—two months—before giving it to his lordship in November and asking him to present it to the king.[23]

Once Franklin saw how alarmed his Massachusetts constituents were over the issue of the Crown's paying British officials in America, he swung over to their side. He was in thorough agreement, he wrote to Cooper on 13 January 1772 that the governor of Massachusetts should be paid by the province. No doubt British leaders wanted to pay Hutchinson so that they could influence him to carry out "arbitrary Instructions." Years before, Franklin had blamed every misguided policy announced in England or Pennsylvania on Thomas Penn. During the Stamp Act crisis, George Grenville had been the culprit. His new scapegoat, of course, was Lord Hillsborough. The Doctor informed Cooper that the practice of

---

[23]Benjamin Franklin to Thomas Cushing, 10 June 1771, and 4 November 1772; Massachusetts House of Representatives' Committee of Correspondence to Benjamin Franklin, 29 June 1771; Samuel Cooper to Benjamin Franklin, 10 July 1771. Ibid., XVIII, 147-53, 172-75, 208-209, 209 n. 1; XIX, 364-65.

paying British officials in America from Crown coffers would likely continue as long as Hillsborough headed the American Department. The best way to defeat the plan, Franklin suggested, was for Americans not to drink tea (which was still taxed) so that revenue would not flow into the American fund that was set aside for such salaries. Then, the depletion of the fund would demolish "the Project."[24] Franklin's failure to forward the Massachusetts petition immediately to Dartmouth in September 1772 suggests that the agent was not being entirely candid with Cooper about the issue of Crown-paid salaries to colonial officials. If he had felt as deeply on this issue as he told Cooper, he undoubtedly would have approached Dartmouth with the petition at once. The Doctor continued to be as devious as he had been throughout his career as a colonial agent.

By 1772 the people of Massachusetts had raised another critical issue—the status of a governor's instructions from the Crown. In England those instructions had long since been regarded as having the force of law. The Massachusetts position, with which Franklin had consistently agreed, was that such instructions were not laws. They were to be disregarded if they conflicted with the charter or laws of the colony over which the governor presided. If a governor obeyed all instructions, whether or not they were consistent with "the Constitution, Laws, and Rights of the Country he governs, there is an End of the Constitution, and those Rights are abolished," the Doctor asserted. While the agent was sincerely concerned about the issue of governors' instructions, he spent more time in early 1772 worrying over the status of American agents. If Hillsborough's policies were continued, Franklin feared, agents would only be able to act as "private Gentlemen" without official standing.[25]

By April 1772 the discouraged agent, in a letter to Thomas Cushing, indicated that he was ready to leave London for America. Since agents had lost their usefulness, the Doctor saw no need to continue sending them to Westminster. Filled with total disgust, Franklin suggested that the Crown could send agents of its own to the colonies "when it wants Aids or would transact Business with us."[26] Thus, the most visible of all American agents had become a bitter and disillusioned man.

---

[24]Benjamin Franklin to Samuel Cooper, 13 January 1772. Ibid., XIX, 13-15.
[25]Benjamin Franklin to James Bowdoin, 13 January 1772. Ibid., XIX, 8-13.
[26]Benjamin Franklin to Thomas Cushing, 13 April 1772. Ibid., XIX, 103-104.

Despite his disenchantment, Franklin remained in England during the summer of 1772, dabbling with the Grand Ohio Company and anticipating the prospect of Hillsborough's overthrow. As soon as Hillsborough was out and Dartmouth was in, the Doctor's spirits rose. After all, Dartmouth was friendly toward Franklin and was generally regarded as an American sympathizer. The agent, as noted earlier, envisioned a dramatic improvement in relations between Britain and her colonies. Now hopeful of reconciliation, Franklin became more moderate—except in his letters to Boston. At last, in November 1772, the Doctor presented to the new American Secretary the Massachusetts petition objecting to the Crown's paying the salaries of royal governors. The agent promised his Massachusetts constituents that he would promote the petition energetically. He failed to keep that promise, for Dartmouth, convinced that such a petition would bring "a severe Reprimand to the Assembly by Order of his Majesty," asked Franklin to withdraw the document. The agent honored his lordship's request. He then asked the lower house for "fresh Orders" and proposed that the petition be reconsidered in Boston.[27]

After changing directions on the petition, Franklin persuaded Lord Dartmouth and Thomas Cushing to engage in an unofficial correspondence so that the American Secretary could gain a clearer understanding of the Massachusetts position. Ironically, the Doctor tried to act as moderator between his lordship and the speaker of the Massachusetts lower house at the very same time he committed the act that dealt the death blow to any future success he might have as an agent and conciliator. In the same note in which he urged the lower house to reconsider the petition regarding governors' salaries, the Doctor informed Cushing that letters would soon be sent to the speaker, letters that, in the agent's opinion, had "laid the Foundation of most if not all our present Grievances." Franklin could not divulge the source of the letters, he said, and he wanted them read only by a handful of "Men of Worth in the Province." According to the agent, the writers of the letters were guilty of "bartering away the Liberties of their native Country for Posts" and of "calling for Troops." The writers were "mere Time-servers, seeking their own private Emolument thro' any Quantity of Public Mischief"—traitors

---

[27]Benjamin Franklin to Thomas Cushing, 2 December 1772; Benjamin Franklin to Lord Dartmouth, 8 December 1772. Ibid., XIX, 409-413, 422-23, 423 n. 4.

to Massachusetts, the British government, and the whole empire. Several times Franklin emphasized that the letters were not to be made public, but surely he knew that his admonitions not to divulge the contents of the inflammatory Hutchinson-Oliver letters would be ignored.[28] The letters, written by Thomas Hutchinson, Andrew Oliver, and several other New England officials during the Townshend Duty crisis, had advocated strong measures by the mother country to curb rebellious actions in the colonies. Assuming that Franklin expected the contents of the letters to leak out, he no doubt failed to anticipate the violent reaction that followed. Once more the Doctor had made a serious miscalculation—one that would soon destroy his effectiveness as an American agent and cost him his job as deputy postmaster general of the colonies.

Pessimism held Franklin firmly in its grasp during most of 1771 and 1772. He saw no hope for a favorable turn in American affairs as long as Hillsborough headed the American Department. Yet, for some reason, perhaps his knowledge that a few powerful ministers favored a western colony in America, he had hopes for the plans of the Grand Ohio Company. He seemed almost overly optimistic in a letter to his son on 20 April 1771. "The Ohio Affair seems now near a Conclusion. And if the present Ministry stand a little longer, I think it will be compleated to our Satisfaction," he wrote. One reason for this, Franklin observed, was the untiring promotion of the scheme by Samuel Wharton. Though quite hopeful, the Doctor remained at least a little cautious, and he admonished William to say nothing definite until "the Event appears," since "many things happen between the Cup and the Lip." About this same time, William Strahan wrote to tell the New Jersey governor that the elder Franklin "could not stir in this Business" because of his alienation from Hillsborough and the "*Ministry in general.*" Strahan warned the younger Franklin to watch his statements, lest he be regarded as a proponent of his father's views.[29]

The Walpole Company dueled with Hillsborough over the Vandalia colony throughout 1771 and 1772. His lordship influenced the Board of Trade, but some powerful members of the Privy Council's Committee on Trade and Plantations and several Cabinet members led by Lord

---

[28]Benjamin Franklin to Thomas Cushing, 2 December 1772. Ibid., XIX, 409-413.

[29]William Strahan to William Franklin, 3 April 1771; Benjamin Franklin to William Franklin, 20 April 1771. Ibid., XVIII, 65, 65 n. 3, 74-77. Also see: *New Jersey Archives*, X, 236-37.

Rochford, Secretary of State for the Southern Department, favored the Grand Ohio Company's plans. Hillsborough was able to snarl the matter up as long as he did primarily because of the several conflicting land claims in the Ohio country. Lord Dunmore, who became Virginia's governor in late 1771, opposed the Vandalia scheme, thus strengthening Hillsborough's hand. The American Secretary threatened to resign when the Privy Council, in the summer of 1772, approved the Vandalia project in the face of the Board of Trade's negative recommendation. The result was the Cabinet showdown that led to Hillsborough's resignation on 1 August 1772. Lord North, who did not want the controversial American Secretary to leave, finally yielded to pressure from the Cabinet's Bedford faction and acknowledged the resignation on 3 August. North, then, promptly appointed his own stepbrother, Lord Dartmouth, to succeed Hillsborough at the American Department.[30]

The ascendancy of Dartmouth caused the Doctor and Samuel Wharton to believe that the huge grant of land to the Grand Ohio Company, along with permission to establish the colony of Vandalia, would surely be approved soon. On 7 October 1772, Franklin expressed his optimism to John Foxcroft about the "Patent." Barring unexpected difficulties, the now hopeful agent thought the Board of Trade would give its approval at its next meeting. Franklin also noted, "Our Friends here are easy about the Virginia Grants, Mr. W. assuring us that they are mostly out of our Bounds." But the Doctor again miscalculated. Although the Board of Trade received an order-in-council regarding Vandalia a few weeks later, on 2 November, its members postponed considering the matter until the following spring. Thus, the Grand Ohio Company's investors were kept anxiously waiting for months, wondering if the bureaucrats would ever make a decision.[31]

---

[30]*Acts of the Privy Council*, V, 203-208; see numerous letters to and from Benjamin Franklin, as well as other material. *Franklin Papers*, XIX, 59-61, 69-72, 123-25, 275-78, 278 n. 4, 290, 294-95, 320, 349-52; Lawrence H. Gipson, *The British Empire Before the American Revolution*, 13 volumes. (New York: Alfred A. Knopf, 1936-1967) XI, 471-75; Holton, "The Ohio Indians and the Revolution in Virginia," 471; Peter Marshall, "Lord Hillsborough, Samuel Wharton, and the Ohio Grant, 1769–1775," *English Historical Review* 80 (1965): 727-33; Randall, *A Little Revenge*, 246-55, 356-58; Sosin, *Whitehall and the Wilderness*, 199-202, 204-208.

[31]Benjamin Franklin to John Foxcroft, 7 October 1772; Benjamin Franklin to William Franklin, 2 October 1772. *Franklin Papers*, XIX, 320-23; Gipson, *The British Empire*, XI, 474-48; Marshall, "Lord Hillsborough and the Ohio Grant," 727-33.

While 1771–1772 turned out to be a time of disappointment and disenchantment for Franklin, mainly because of Hillsborough's American policies, it was not a time of total inactivity for the Doctor (contrary to what William Strahan implied in his letter to William Franklin). Franklin might not have pursued his duties as agent with impressive vigor, but he was busy with many other activities and some personal difficulties. As usual, there were family problems. Richard Bache arrived in England near the end of October 1771, only to find that his famous father-in-law was still on his trip to Ireland and Scotland. The two men met for the first time at the home of Richard's mother, Mary Bache, in northern England. Mrs. Bache, like so many other people, was charmed with the Doctor and invited him to return for a longer stay, as Franklin and Richard, who was suffering from an injured leg, shoved off for London. Once the two men reached Craven Street, Margaret Stevenson carefully nursed Bache's leg. Franklin and Bache warmed to each other almost immediately, so much so that the Doctor made his son-in-law a gift of £200, agreed to set him up in a cash-only dry goods business at the Franklin home in Philadelphia, and gave him a power of attorney to request and receive payment of all debts owed the agent in America—except those owed by William Franklin.[32]

Once Franklin began to confide in his son-in-law and after Bache returned to America, the Doctor began addressing Richard in correspondence as "Dear Son." He also wrote more affectionately of his grandson and namesake, calling him "our dear little Benjamin." Franklin told Deborah to "Give him a Kiss from me with my Blessing." Ultimately, the Doctor started calling his little grandson "Benny boy." On the other hand, the absent patriarch was probably not very pleased when Bache wrote him from Philadelphia on 16 May 1772 to say that business was going slowly. At the time the letter arrived on Craven Street—likely in June or July—Europe was on the brink of a financial crisis, which started in England, spread to Scotland, and eventually engulfed the Continent. Franklin was personally unscathed, breathing a sigh of relief that he was "Out of Debt and out of Danger."[33]

---

[32]See letters to and from Benjamin Franklin with a variety of correspondents. *Franklin Papers*, XVIII, 236-37, 252, 252 n. 6, 256-59; XIX, 41, 41 n. 6, 42-45, 54, 66, 79-80.

[33]William Franklin to Benjamin Franklin, 3 August 1771; Benjamin Franklin to Deborah Franklin, 5 May, 22 August, 7 October 1772; Benjamin Franklin to Richard Bache, 7 October 1772; Deborah Franklin to Benjamin Franklin, [14?-]16 May 1772;

Good relations between Franklin and Bache might have been established at last, but there was other trouble in the Franklin household at Philadelphia. Deborah was declining rapidly. She knew it, and William knew it. She wrote to her husband and expressed approval of his giving Richard the power of attorney, since she had become uncomfortable in trying to manage money. Bache no doubt had alerted the Doctor of Deborah's advancing senility, and William had written that her "Memory has failed her much, and she becomes every Day more and more unfit to be left alone." Deborah herself wrote in the spring of 1772 that she was "very uncapall of dueing aney bisness," as she was "not abell to walke aboute" and her "memerey [was] so poorley and sum times worse than others." Before Franklin realized how pitiful his wife had become, he had promised her—as he had so many times before—that he would return home after one more winter.

Prior to knowing how seriously Deborah had declined, the Doctor had criticized her extravagance and her unkind words to Franklin's friends, who would not give in to her requests for money. Unknown to Deborah, her husband had limited her income to £30 per month, plus what she received from renting "7 or 8 Houses"—for a total of more than £500 per year. In words that must have hurt her deeply, he had written that this amount was sufficient for "the Maintenance of your Family." He had told her not to borrow money from his friends. In a gruff fashion, Franklin had chastised her as one not attentive to money matters during her "best Days" and had suggested that her memory was now "too much impair'd for the Management of unlimited Sums."[34] The letter in which the Doctor scolded his wife is unique in his correspondence with her. Never had he been so blunt, and never would he be again. He might have mistreated Deborah by staying away from home for years, but he was usually kind to her. The reprimand was certainly out of character for him. Perhaps the frustrations caused by Hillsborough's policies bothered him so much that he took them out on the woman who had been devoted to him for forty years.

Besides the problems Franklin had with Deborah, great changes occurred with his surrogate family in London. Just over nine months after

---

Richard Bache to Benjamin Franklin, 16 May 1772. Ibid., XVIII, 195; XIX, 130-31, 141, 143-45, 274-75, 314-16, 321.

[34]Benjamin Franklin to Deborah Franklin, 1 May and 4 July 1771. Ibid., XVIII, 90-92, 161-62.

he had given away the bride at the marriage of Polly Stevenson to William Hewson, Polly gave birth to the Hewson's first child, a son, on 26 April 1771. That summer Hewson and his partner, Dr. William Hunter, asked Franklin to help settle a dispute between them. Hunter complained that Hewson was letting family responsibilities interfere with his work. Even Franklin's wisdom failed to resolve the dispute, and the partnership between Hewson and Hunter was dissolved. After Hewson went his own way in the summer of 1772, he and his family took over Margaret Stevenson's house at 7 Craven Street. Mrs. Stevenson and her prominent tenant moved across the street. While Margaret supervised the moving, Franklin spent sixteen days visiting with Lord LeDespencer at his lordship's home in West Wycombe.[35]

As Franklin dealt with the problems surrounding those who were close to him, he repeatedly received sad new about old friends. His crony John Hughes, who had taken so much abuse as Pennsylvania stamp agent, ended up as a customs agent in Portsmouth, New Hampshire, and then, thanks to Franklin, had transferred (presumably for health reasons) to a similar post in Charles Town, South Carolina. In October 1771 Peter Timothy wrote to Franklin that Hughes was not doing well and that the Doctor should be prepared for the worst. The worst quickly followed, as Hughes died in January 1772. Two months later, John Canton, Franklin's longtime friend and sometimes traveling companion, followed Hughes to the grave. Near the end of 1772, David Hall, after making one last plea for Franklin to settle the accounts connected with their partnership, died on Christmas Eve.[36] Thus, Franklin was saddened in 1772 by the loss of three old and cherished friends.

Through it all, requests for favors and for assistance in carrying out worthwhile projects were directed to the Doctor. Anthony Benezet, a Quaker merchant living in Philadelphia, urged Franklin to take an "effectual step" to help end that "terrible evil," the slave trade. Almost immediately after receiving Benezet's letter, while England was abuzz over the momentous Sommersett decision (which freed all slaves in

---

[35]See numerous letters to and from Benjamin Franklin. Ibid., XVIII, 90-92, 192-94; XIX, 202-204, 314-16, 322-23, 323 n. 4, 353-54, 359-60.

[36]Peter Timothy to Benjamin Franklin, 20 October 1771; David Hall to Benjamin Franklin, 3 February 1772; Benjamin Franklin to David Hall, 20 March 1772; Richard Bache to Benjamin Franklin, 4 January 1773. Ibid., XVIII, 233-35, 235 n. 8; XIX, 57-58, 89, 89 n. 7, 91-92; XX, 4-6.

England), Franklin sent a letter to the *London Chronicle*. He called for an immediate end to the slave trade and for the gradual elimination of slavery in the colonies by "declaring the children of present Slaves free after they become of age." Even so, at that very time, he felt compelled, because of his instructions from the Georgia legislature, to seek Crown approval for that colony's slave code.[37]

There were others who sought Franklin's support. Isaac Smith, Jr., son of a Boston merchant and first cousin of Abigail Adams, asked for advice and letters of introduction before taking a tour of France. The Doctor responded with a letter introducing Smith to Jean Baptiste Le Roy, one of Franklin's closest friends in France. Another who called on Franklin was William Smith. In spite of the enmity long felt between the two men, the Anglican clergyman did not hesitate to ask Franklin to help raise money for the College of Philadelphia. Then, there was Peter Timothy, who wanted help in securing "any Employment in his Majesty's Service" that would not "degrade" him. Franklin advised Timothy not to seek a government post, for such employment often resulted in "Poverty and Distress." The Doctor, who at this point could hardly have influenced British officials to give anyone a job, urged the South Carolina printer to continue with his printing business. Timothy followed that advice and remained a printer until he died in 1782. An unusual request was made of Franklin when the British Army asked for his expert advice on how to protect the new Purfleet Powder Magazine from a lightning strike. The Doctor recommended a number of *pointed* lightning rods strategically placed, thus reviving the old controversy over pointed versus round-knob lightning rods. In the end, Franklin's advice was followed. The most unusual request Franklin received for help during this juncture as colonial agent was one that came from Major Robert Rogers, a soldier and an adventurer, who asked the Privy Council to sponsor a search he wanted to launch for a navigable northwest passage in northern Canada. Rogers urged the Doctor to support the petition. Whether Franklin honored the request is not clear, but the petition was shifted to the Board of Trade and then the Treasury, where it apparently died.[38]

---

[37]Anthony Benezet to Benjamin Franklin, 27 April 1772; Benjamin Franklin to Anthony Benezet, 22 August 1772, and other material. Ibid., XIX, 112-16, 187-88, 269.

[38]*Acts of the Privy Council*, IV, 739; V, 316-317; VI, 417-19, 510; Robert Rogers to Benjamin Franklin [20 February 1772]; William Smith to Benjamin Franklin, 16 May 1772; Peter Timothy to Benjamin Franklin, 24 August 1772, and other material. *Franklin*

In many ways the year 1771 was among the most difficult for Franklin. Not only did he have to endure Hillsborough and worry about Deborah's careless use of money, he had to suffer with the terrible weather. The winter of 1771 was awful in the British Isles. Snow fell in England as late as 20 April. Livestock perished by the thousands. The approach of summer brought prospects of a more pleasant time ahead, as Franklin planned trips away from London. In late May he took a ten-day tour of Birmingham and "some other Manufacturing Towns" in northern England. Traveling with him were his nephew, Jonathan Williams, Jr., John Canton (the friend who died the following year), and Dr. Jan Ingenhouz. Canton, Ingenhouz, and the Doctor had become friends because of their mutual interests in electrical experiments. A few months after Franklin toured northern England with these friends, he traveled to Hampshire to visit with another friend, Jonathan Shipley, the pro-American Bishop of St. Asaph. In late July the Doctor set out for the bishop's home, Chilbolton, near Twyford. The vacationing agent spent three blissful weeks at Shipley's Tudor mansion, which sat on the banks of the Itchen River. Franklin became a great favorite of Shipley's wife and two young daughters. At Chilbolton, during this very visit, the Doctor began writing his *Autobiography*. When he returned to London, he wrote to the bishop, "I now breathe with Reluctance the Smoke of London, when I think of the sweet Air of Twyford."[39]

Franklin's final trip of 1771 was supposed to last a month or six weeks, but it took considerably longer. With Richard Jackson, the Doctor went to Ireland, crossing from Holyhead in Wales and arriving in Dublin on 5 September. Meeting numerous dignitaries, Franklin was heartily weicomed by pro-American political leaders among the Irish. He and Jackson stayed for more than a month, deciding not to leave until after the Irish Parliament convened on 8 October. Upon attending the opening session, the two men were recognized by the speaker and then allowed to sit in the chamber, instead of the gallery. Franklin, because he had a letter of introduction from Jonathan Shipley, was also able to meet Richard Robinson, Baron Rokely, the Archbishop of Armagh and the

---

*Papers*, XVIII, 106-107; XIX, 80, 80 ns. 5 and 6, 146-49, 153-56, 153 ns. 2 and 3, 154 ns. 6 and 7, 232-33, 260-65, 261 n. 7, 262 ns. 2 and 3, 283-85, 283 n. 6.

[39]Benjamin Franklin to Jonathan Shipley, 24 June and 25 July 1771; Benjamin Franklin to Deborah Franklin, 5 June and 14 August 1771. Ibid., XVIII, 113-16, 118-19, 137, 190-91, 199-202, 204-205; Nolan, *Franklin in Scotland and Ireland*, 123-30.

Metropolitan of Ireland. And, of course, because of the unexpected invitation from Lord Hillsborough (at the time they stopped at his estate to pay their respects), Franklin and Jackson were the American Secretary's guests for four days. By the time the travelers left Hillsborough's home on 20 October, they had met and conversed with most of the elite who resided in Ireland.[40]

Six days after bidding farewell to Lord Hillsborough, Franklin arrived in Edinburgh, Scotland. Jackson, no longer accompanying the Doctor, had headed back to London. Once in Edinburgh, Franklin "lodg'd miserably at an Inn," but David Hume, the famous Scottish philosopher, sent for him, insisting that the Doctor become Hume's house guest for the remainder of his stay. While there, Franklin was able to visit all of his friends except Adam Smith and Alexander Dick, both of whom were away from Edinburgh. The traveling agent abandoned Hume's hospitality long enough to spend five days with Lord Kames, who by 1771 resided on an estate called Blair Drummond near Stirling. During most of his stay in Scotland, Franklin was joined by Henry Marchant, the new colonial agent for Rhode Island. Marchant and Franklin became good friends during those days, and the Doctor soon recommended Marchant for an honorary doctorate at the University of Edinburgh. Throughout Marchant's brief tenure as Rhode Island's agent (most of 1771 and 1772), he resided on Craven Street, across the street from Franklin. Together the two men traveled from Edinburgh to the famous Carron Iron Works and to Glasgow, and both enjoyed their five-day stay with Lord Kames at snow-covered Blair Drummond.[41]

Upon leaving Edinburgh and en route to London, Franklin traveled alone to Preston, where he had the meeting (previously discussed) with

---

[40]Jonathan Shipley to Benjamin Franklin, 13 August 1771; Benjamin Franklin to Deborah Franklin, 14 August 1771; Benjamin Franklin to Jonathan Shipley, 14 December 1771; Benjamin Franklin to James Bowdoin, 13 January 1772; Benjamin Franklin to Thomas Cushing, 13 January 1772; Benjamin Franklin to William Franklin, 30 January 1772. *Franklin Papers*, XVIII, 203-205, 266-67; XIX, 8-13, 21-22, 47-53; Nolan, *Franklin in Scotland and Ireland*, 131-32, 146, 148, 151-52, 157, 169.

[41]Benjamin Franklin to William Strahan, 27 October and 17 November 1771; Benjamin Franklin to Alexander Dick, 11 January 1772; Benjamin Franklin to Agatha Drummond, 11 January 1772. *Franklin Papers*, XVIII, 236, 250-52; XIX, 5-6; Kammen, *Rope of Sand*, 141; Labaree, "Franklin's British Friendships," 426; Nolan, *Franklin in Scotland and Ireland*, 136-38, 171-74, 176-85, 187-202.

Richard Bache. The Doctor liked the Bache family well enough to return to Preston for a visit in the summer of 1772.[42]

A few months after returning to London from his trip to Ireland and Scotland, Franklin wrote an account of his travels to Joseph Galloway. The Doctor noted that Ireland was a very poor country, while Scotland made "a better Appearance" and seemed to be improving. Only about half the Scots were poor, he estimated, noting they wore "neither Shoes nor Stockings, or wear them only in Church." Commenting on the miserable conditions among the working poor in England, Franklin concluded that America was better off than any European country he had visited, except Holland.[43]

Though 1771 and 1772 were in many ways dismal years for Franklin, there were some positive developments. He did take that pleasant trip to Ireland and Scotland and two to the north of England. Besides his rewarding trips, he was elected in June 1771 to membership in the Batavian Society of Experimental Science, the Dutch equivalent of England's Royal Society. The following year he was admitted to the French Royal Academy of Sciences. He also renewed his interest in electrical experiments, which prompted him to correspond with a number of scientists in England and on the Continent. Moreover, he began collecting exotic seeds, sending them to his son William, Noble Wimberly Jones, and John Bartram. He urged the three men to plant the seeds and to experiment with them. Finally, he hired a Frenchman named Lewis Fevre to assist him with his work as agent. Fevre became Franklin's clerk in the spring of 1772 and remained in his employee until the agent left for America in 1775. When Franklin departed, Fevre went to work for Lord Shelburne.[44]

As disappointing and frustrating as the two years 1771 and 1772 were for the Doctor, there were a few bright moments, and the American agent would soon learn that there were far worse problems to endure than frustration. During the ensuing months he would come under heavy political fire from powerful British leaders who longed to drag him through the valley of public humiliation. Some even wished to throw him in jail.

---

[42]Benjamin Franklin to Mary Hewson, 8 July 1772; Benjamin Franklin to Deborah Franklin, 14 July 1772. *Franklin Papers*, XIX, 204, 207; Nolan, *Franklin in Scotland and Ireland*, 203-204.

[43]Benjamin Franklin to Joseph Galloway, 6 February 1772. *Franklin Papers*, XIX, 69-72.

[44]*Franklin Papers*, XIX, 45 n. 1, 126, 182, 228, 247-48, 259-60, 438 n. 7.

# 9. "The Very Edge of the Precipice":
## The Collapse of Franklin's Credibility at Whitehall

"Even yet the wounds may be healed and peace and love restored; But we are on the very edge of the precipice."
—Charles Thomson to Benjamin Franklin, 1 November 1774

When Franklin received the letter containing the words above, he was probably ready to agree totally with Charles Thomson's assessment of Anglo-American relations. A year earlier he had been more optimistic. For a time after Hillsborough's fall from power in 1772 the Doctor thought that harmony might be restored between Britain and her colonies and that he could relax again in London. Less than three weeks after his lordship's resignation, Franklin had written to William that nothing could be "more agreeable" than his life in England. He had powerful and learned friends, an active social life, and plenty of publicity and acclaim. Even the king spoke of him "with great regard." If he decided to leave it all and go back to Philadelphia, though, there he would stay. He told his son that the salaries he made as agent did not "fully compensate the disadvantages" of the double expenses he incurred by living in London. The Doctor indicated that he would go home in the spring or fall of 1773. When spring arrived, he wrote, "I grow tired of my Situation here, and really think of Returning in the Fall."[1]

Once again, it is clear that Benjamin Franklin preferred to live in London, but he was torn between the pleasant life he enjoyed there and his obligations in Philadelphia. He seemed genuinely ready in 1773 to go home at last. Again, however, events occurred that worked against his leaving England. Parliament passed the Tea Act on 27 April 1773, and that act, which in effect gave the British East India Company a monopoly on tea in the American marketplace, set the stage for the Boston Tea Party on 16 December of the same year. Just before Bostonians, poorly disguised as Indians, dumped the East India Company's tea into Boston

---

[1]Benjamin Franklin to William Franklin, 19[-22] August 1772 and 15 March 1773. *Franklin Papers*, XIX, 257-60; XX, 109. The letter quoted in the chapter title can be found in Ibid., XXI, 344-45.

Harbor, a scandal began to swirl around the Hutchinson-Oliver letters in London. William Whately, brother of Thomas Whately (to whom the letters were originally written), accused John Temple, a customs official, of sending the letters to Boston. The two men fought an inconclusive duel over the matter on 11 December. To prevent a second duel between the pair, Franklin publicly admitted on 25 December that he and he alone had sent the letters to the Massachusetts lower house. Almost immediately Massachusetts and its agent were under heavy fire from British authorities —the colony for the destructive tea party and Franklin for filching private letters. The Doctor, unable to defend himself effectively, spent the following year, 1774, reeling from the loss of his position with the post office and attempting to defend Massachusetts from the wrath of Parliament and the ministry.

As best he could, Franklin continued his work as agent for the four colonies he served. While he gave some time to them all, he devoted the most time to Massachusetts. When informed that the Pennsylvania Assembly had reduced his salary from £500 to £400 per year, he professed to be happy with whatever "they please to give me." He suspected that the Assembly had reduced the amount because of his services to the three other colonies. The Doctor confided to Joseph Galloway that New Jersey gave him only a small salary, but one that was paid on time. Although Georgia was supposed to pay him £100 per year, plus expenses, that colony had in fact paid him nothing since 1770 because of political squabbling over his reappointment. Massachusetts had never given him "a Farthing" and probably never would, for the governor would not sign an appropriations bill to cover the salary. Franklin claimed he was ready to become a private citizen, for it was costing him too much to serve. In addition to the unprofitability of being an agent, he had already, in his view, had more than his share of "public Bustle." Even so, because he thought there was some chance of helping his country now that Dartmouth headed American affairs, he would stay a little longer. If he could only put matters on a "better Footing" before leaving London, he would happily do it for no compensation, he told Galloway.[2]

By this time, Franklin and Galloway had little in common but their friendship. Although both still opposed British policies, they did so for different reasons. The Doctor objected to the policies on principle, while

---

[2]Benjamin Franklin to Joseph Galloway, 6 January 1773. Ibid., XX, 16-18.

Galloway disliked them because they created political trouble for him in Pennsylvania. In spite of the growing differences between the two men, the Franklin-Galloway friendship endured, and their letters began to reveal even greater affection for one another. At the same time, Franklin's feelings toward the British government were becoming increasingly less cordial. He made this quite clear to the Pennsylvania Assembly's Committee of Correspondence. Writing to the committee on 6 January 1773—the same day he wrote to Galloway that he would stay in England a little longer—he promised to oppose strenuously any act proposed in Parliament that might adversely affect the commercial rights of the colonies. Still, he pledged to do all in his power "to restore that harmony between Great Britain and her Colonies so necessary . . . to their mutual Safety and Happiness." He reported that he had presented thirty Pennsylvania laws, passed in March and September of 1772, to the government on 22 December 1772, and promised to keep a watchful eye on them while they were being considered for approval. The agent pointed out that it had become extremely important "to keep an exact Note of the Time of Presentment," since the Privy Council increasingly failed to pass judgment on the colony's laws within the six months required by the Pennsylvania Charter. In this case, however, the Board of Trade reviewed the laws in January and forwarded them to the Privy Council, which, in April, approved all but two.[3]

Presenting Pennsylvania's statutes to the King in Council was about all that Franklin did for the colony during 1773 and 1774. Fifteen laws passed by the Assembly on 26 February 1773 were long delayed in reaching the agent, and he was unable to present them until 26 January 1774. One of the fifteen laws provided for a loan office to handle issues of paper money, and Franklin was pleasantly surprised by its allowance. He knew the Assembly had that bill "much at Heart," but there had been "some Circumstances in the course of its Consideration" that made him "apprehensive for the Fate of it." Actually, the way for a favorable decision on the Loan Office Bill had been prepared in 1773, when Parliament had amended the Currency Act of 1764 to allow colonial assemblies to issue notes as legal tender for duties and taxes at colonial treasuries.

---

[3]*Acts of the Privy Council*, V, 365-68; Benjamin Franklin to the Pennsylvania Assembly's Committee of Correspondence, 6 January 1773. *Franklin Papers*, XX, 18-19; *Journals of the Board of Trade, 1768–1775*, 334, 344, 347; Newcomb, *Franklin and Galloway*, 234-36.

Since the notes were redeemable at the treasury, they circulated freely at face value. Twelve more of the fifteen laws were allowed, while two were disallowed. Franklin was in attendance on 5 May and 12 May at the Board of Trade's deliberations on the fifteen laws. On 6 July 1774, the Privy Council allowed the thirteen laws recommended by the Board and disallowed the two that the Board had refused to endorse.[4]

Franklin, now in no mood to shrug off any setbacks, was displeased by the Privy Council's failure to approve the two Pennsylvania laws. One of the two provided for severe penalties against anyone damaging sea markers that marked the Port of Philadelphia, while the other imposed high duties on slaves, in order to discourage their importation. The agent was convinced that the Pennsylvania Charter described the types of laws the Crown could disallow, and he contended that neither of the disallowed laws was included in that description. Since 1768 or 1769 the Doctor had argued privately that Parliament could pass no laws of any kind for the colonies without their consent. He now concluded that the king, too, was limited in matters of legislation where the colonies were concerned.[5]

There was a curious turn of events during the Board of Trade's deliberations on the fifteen Pennsylvania laws in 1774. On 21 April John Pownall, secretary to the Board, asked Franklin if he had any authority to act as Pennsylvania's agent. The Doctor responded by sending to the secretary the Assembly's resolution appointing Franklin agent for "the current Year." The Board began its consideration of the laws that day, but did not ask Franklin to attend. On 26 April, Pownall informed the Doctor that the Board was proceeding on the laws and that he had not been told to require Franklin's presence.[6] Nonetheless, after John Pownall alerted the agent, Franklin took it upon himself to attend the deliberations on 5 and 12 May.

---

[4]*Acts of the Privy Council*, V, 398-99; Ernst, *Money and Politics in America*, 314-17; Benjamin Franklin to Samuel Rhoads, 5 January 1774; Benjamin Franklin to the Pennsylvania Assembly's Committee on Correspondence, 2 February 1774, and [7 May 1774]. *Franklin Papers*, XXI, 9-10, 77, 212-13, 212 n. 14; *Journals of the Board of Trade, 1768–1775*, 386, 393-95; Sosin, "Imperial Regulations of Colonial Paper Money," 198.

[5]Benjamin Franklin to the Pennsylvania Assembly's Committee of Correspondence, [7 May 1774]. *Franklin Papers*, XXI, 212-13.

[6]John Pownall to Benjamin Franklin, 21 and 26 April 1774; Benjamin Franklin to John Pownall, [on or after 21 April 1774]. Ibid., XXI, 202-204.

Apparently the Pennsylvania Assembly was satisfied to let Franklin remain in England, indefinitely, as its agent—at his new, reduced salary, of course. Other than presenting and promoting the colony's laws at Whitehall, the Doctor was doing very little for the Assembly. Even so, its members showed no inclination to recall him. On 15 October 1774, the Assembly appointed Franklin again for the coming year.[7] Before the year of 1775 was out, however, the Doctor would be back in Philadelphia.

Franklin's efforts for Georgia in 1773 and 1774 were no greater than those on behalf of Pennsylvania. Understandably, he had lost some of his enthusiasm for Georgia. No *official* word from that colony was directed to him between 28 May 1770 and 14 March 1774. He did, however, keep in touch *unofficially* through Noble Wimberly Jones, and he had continued to serve—such service as he provided—without official status and without pay. The matter of Franklin's reappointment, which had been a bit controversial in the legislature during 1771 and 1772, produced a dispute in 1773 and a political donnybrook in 1774. For the first nine months of 1773 the two houses fought over the appointment. A bill was proposed. Both houses attempted to amend it. Out of this maneuvering came the appointment of Grey Elliott as co-agent. He was to serve if Franklin left Great Britain—something the Doctor had said more than once that he might do. Elliott, a former Georgia planter and legislator, had only recently moved to London. Both houses favored him as the man to back up Franklin at Whitehall. An acceptable compromise appeared to have been reached with Elliott's appointment. On 29 September 1773, Speaker of the House William Young, President of the Council James Habersham, and Governor James Wright signed an ordinance reappointing Franklin as agent and appointing Elliott as substitute agent. Wright, however, appears to have had a change of heart soon thereafter and rescinded his action. On 30 December 1773, he noted in a letter to the Board of Trade that he had refused to assent to Franklin's reappointment. On the other hand, he did approve Grey Elliott's appointment as "a kind of Conditional Agent." The governor advised the Board that he expected a new ordinance from the legislature in January.[8]

---

[7]Ibid., XXI, 335, 471.

[8]Georgia Commons House Committee of Correspondence to Benjamin Franklin, Ibid., XXI, 142-45, 142 n. 7; *Georgia Colonial Records*, XV, 369-70, 378, 383, 496; XVII, 679-681, 685, 735, 746, 758-59, 768; XIX, part I, 249-52, 506-508; XXVIII, part 2, 393;

If Wright assumed that the new ordinance would settle the controversy, he was mistaken. When, in January, the lower house passed a bill providing for Franklin's reappointment, the upper house announced that it would investigate the Doctor's record of service between 1768 and 1771. A committee appointed for that purpose by the upper house reported back that nothing had been heard from the agent during those years except that he was satisfied with the salary he was to be paid and that he would do his best for Georgia. Following the negative report, the upper house refused to concur in Franklin's reappointment, in spite of the fact that it had voted to reappoint him the previous September. Not to be outdone, the lower house appointed its own investigative committee. That committee's report was altogether positive, citing dates of letters from the agent and praising him for his work. According to the report, Franklin had "exerted his utmost abilities to serve his [Georgia] Constituents." In so many words the report accused the upper house's committee of lying, or being "uncandid," and of trying to smear Franklin's reputation. Moreover, the lower house's committee asserted that the Doctor had been "indefatigable in negotiating the affairs" of Georgia, especially in 1768, 1769, and 1770, and recommended thanking the agent and expressing confidence in him. The lower house promptly approved its committee's report.[9] Little was said about Franklin's service for the years following 1771. What was there to say, except that the Doctor's enthusiasm for Georgia's business, not surprisingly in view of the circumstances regarding payment of his salary, had waned?

Worn out with the upper house and the governor for obstructing Franklin's reappointment, the lower house on 2 March 1774 passed a resolution claiming the power to appoint an agent as "a right and privilege which . . . ought to be exclusively lodged in the Representatives of the People." And, in the same resolution, the lower house announced Franklin's appointment as agent. He was to work through a nine-member committee of the house, any five of whom constituted a quorum with the power to act. The house set Franklin's salary at "150 pounds Sterling

---

Morgan, "Franklin as Georgia's Colonial Agent," 227, 229-30.

[9]*Franklin Papers*, XXI, 142-45; *Georgia Colonial Records*, XVII, 777-86; XXXVIII, part 1, 214-22; Kammen, *Rope of Sand*, 181; Morgan, "Franklin as Georgia's Colonial Agent," 229-31.

money of Great Britain . . . over and above his Charges and disbursements."[10]

Highly displeased with the actions taken by the lower house, the upper house contended that Franklin's letters, which had been cited in the lower house's report, had somehow been "mislaid or secreted" from the upper house. Any mistaken conclusion drawn by that house was caused by not having access to the agent's correspondence. The upper chamber flatly denied that its committee's report was "uncandid" and accused the lower house's committee of deliberately attempting to create a division between the two houses. Although the upper house had not perused all of Franklin's letters, its members remained convinced that the Doctor had performed no "real service" for Georgia. Furthermore, the upper house challenged the existence of a letter Franklin supposedly had written on 1 May 1771, hinting that it was a fabrication. Finally, the upper house denied the lower house's right to appoint an agent and called the action unconstitutional. Governor Wright, at the request of the upper chamber, was to ask British officials not to accept Franklin as Georgia's agent "at any of the Publick Boards in Great Britain."[11]

Wright, at odds with Franklin at least since 1771, was only too happy to oblige the upper house. The upper chamber likely was following the lead of the governor in this matter anyway. Wright's correspondence reveals that it was he who had blocked Franklin's reappointment at sometime following 29 September 1773, when, at first, he had assented to it. Franklin almost surely was angered by the political situation in Georgia, and on 2 May 1774, he turned the Georgia agency over to Grey Elliott. The Doctor had already contacted Elliott the previous November and had found him cordial and cooperative. The Georgian gave Franklin much information about the colony's history and commerce. Elliott also provided as clear a picture as possible of the complex Baker claims. The substitute agent referred to the lands claimed by Baker's heirs as "the Barony." Although convinced that the Baker claims were valid, Elliott believed a compromise could be worked out between Baker's heirs and the Georgia settlers. He offered to answer any questions Franklin had regarding Georgia affairs, but the Doctor presently lost all interest in

---

[10]*Georgia Colonial Records*, XXXVIII, part 1, 222-24; Morgan, "Franklin as Georgia's Colonial Agent," 230-31.

[11]*Franklin Papers*, XXI, 142-45; *Georgia Colonial Records*, XXXVIII, part 1, 224-28; Morgan, "Franklin as Georgia's Colonial Agent," 231.

Georgia's business and decided to resign. Upon turning the agency over to Elliott, the Doctor noted that Georgia owed him £219, five shillings, and eleven pence, a sum he never collected. When he tried years later in 1785 to secure payment, Georgia ostensibly granted him 3,000 acres of land in lieu of the money. Some years after that, Temple Franklin, who inherited the grant from his grandfather, attempted to sell part of it to a French emigre. Temple discovered, to his dismay, that the tract did not exist.[12]

As indicated earlier, Franklin had better luck collecting his salary and expenses from New Jersey than from Georgia. New Jersey presented him with problems of a different kind. As his views became more radical, he found himself more and more in sympathy with the New Jersey legislature and less and less in harmony with his son, the governor. On 5 January 1773, William wrote to his father to inform him of a letter the governor had sent to Lord Dartmouth. William had written the letter on behalf of himself and his attorney general, Cortlandt Skinner, to request "an Augmentation" of their salaries. The governor asked his father to help promote the requested increase in pay. The elder Franklin refused, claiming that it might "embroil" William with his "People."[13] In all probability the Doctor feared that the salary issue might cause the kind of reaction in New Jersey that it was already causing in Massachusetts. If so, he wanted nothing to do with persuading the Crown to increase his son's salary. One can only wonder if the agent worried that the wrath of the New Jerseyites might be directed at him rather than at William.

Franklin continued to perform his expected duties for New Jersey, although he was not as prompt sometimes as he might have been. On 18 February 1774, he wrote to the New Jersey Assembly's Committee of

---

[12]Abbot, *Royal Governors of Georgia*, 159-60; Grey Elliott to Benjamin Franklin, 8 November 1773; Benjamin Franklin's Account with the Province of Georgia, 2 May 1774. *Franklin Papers*, XX, 474-79; XXI, 205-206, 205 n. 8, 206 n. 9; *Georgia Colonial Records*, XVII, 774-75, 778-86; XXXVIII, part 1, 208-209.

Elliott served as agent for two years, 1773–1775. In 1780 he wrote to the Georgia legislature to say he had never received his £100 per year salary. Along with his salary he asked to be reimbursed for some expenses he had incurred in carrying out his duties as agent. It is highly doubtful that he ever collected. See: *Georgia Colonial Records*, XV, 602.

[13]William Franklin to Benjamin Franklin, 5 January 1773; Benjamin Franklin to William Franklin, 6 April 1773; Joseph Smith to Benjamin Franklin, 13 May 1774. *Franklin Papers*, XX, 11-12, 147; XXI, 216-17.

Correspondence to say that the New Jersey law for settling the boundary dispute with New York had received the Privy Council's approval. The confirmation had come the September before, at the same time a similar New York law had been allowed. Edmund Burke, the New York colony's agent in London, had acted promptly, immediately informing New York of the approval. Not only was Franklin slow in notifying New Jersey of the action, his tardy correspondence was delayed in reaching the colony. As late as 5 July 1774, James Parker, mayor of Perth Amboy and a member of the New Jersey Council, wrote to Franklin that no notice of the law's confirmation had been received in the colony. Parker, having heard that the agent had sent a letter with the law enclosed, assumed that the letter and its enclosures had miscarried. Settlers who had been "taken in [i.e., annexed] by this Settlement" were generally inconvenienced by the delay in notification, according to Parker. The mayor urged Franklin to send "a Duplicate of the Act and Confirmation . . . by first Opportunity."[14]

When it came to promoting legislation passed by the colonies he served, Franklin's work was never ending. A letter dated 26 July 1774 informed him that the New Jersey legislature had passed thirty-three acts during its last session. His job was to secure "the Royal Allowance to as many as can be had." The legislators were particularly anxious that two of the thirty-three be allowed. One was an act to bring suit against Stephen Skinner, ex-treasurer of the "Eastern division," and the other was for the "Emission of Bills of Credit on Loan." The Doctor promised in a return letter less than two months later that he would work to have all the recently passed acts approved.[15]

While the New Jersey legislature was concerned, as always, about the fate of the laws it passed, something of even greater concern had begun to trouble that body by 1774—the future of American liberty. On 8 February the lower house established the Standing Committee of Correspondence and Inquiry to obtain information about British measures

---

[14]*Acts of the Privy Council*, V, 45-46; Benjamin Franklin to the New Jersey Assembly's Committee of Correspondence, 18 February 1774; James Parker to Benjamin Franklin, 5 July 1774. *Franklin Papers*, XXI, 111-12, 111 n. 3, 239-40, 240 n. 4.

[15]The New Jersey Assembly's Committee of Correspondence to Benjamin Franklin, 26 July 1774; Benjamin Franklin to the New Jersey Assembly's Committee of Correspondence, 7 September 1774. *Franklin Papers*, XXI, 259-60, 260 n. 4, 289-90; *New Jersey Archives*, X, 461-63, 508-513; Skemp, *William Franklin*, 123-29.

and to keep in touch with the other colonies. The new committee asked Franklin in July to send "the most early and authentic intelligence of all acts and resolutions of the Parliament of Great Britain, or the proceedings of administration, that may have relation to, or any way affect, the liberties and privileges of America." On 7 September, Franklin wrote to the committee that its members could count on him to keep them informed. He asserted that the Continental Congress and the American colonies could achieve their objectives through "Unanimity and firmness." Unity was the path to triumph, he believed. "If you [the American colonies] divide you are lost," he wrote to Peter Timothy on the same day.[16]

As the Doctor became more involved in the controversy brought on by the Boston Tea Party and the Coercive Acts, his son William recoiled from the radicalism evident in the New Jersey lower house and the letters of his father. The elder Franklin minced no words with William when writing him on 7 September 1774. Accusing the mother country of extorting "many Thousand Pounds from America unconstitutionally under Colour of Acts of Parliament," the Doctor asserted that Britain "ought to make Restitution." The government should total up what was owed the colonies, deduct enough to cover the cost of the tea dumped into Boston Harbor, and return "the Rest." After blasting the British government, Franklin fired a salvo at his son, calling him "a thorough Courtier" who saw "every thing with Government Eyes."[17] The Doctor, it seems, could not live in peace for long with chief executives. He served four colonies, and in all four he fell out sooner or later with the man in charge— Thomas Penn, proprietor of Pennsylvania, and James Wright, Thomas Hutchinson, and William Franklin, royal governors of Georgia, Massachusetts, and New Jersey, respectively.

Although his views had steadily become more radical, Franklin still hoped to find some means of accommodating Anglo-American differences. Becoming agent for the Massachusetts House of Representatives, however, eventually ended his chances of playing the role of conciliator. Close association with the implacable leaders of the Massachusetts lower

---

[16]The New Jersey Assembly's Committee of Correspondence and Inquiry to Benjamin Franklin, 26 July 1774; Benjamin Franklin to the New Jersey Assembly's Committee of Correspondence, 7 September 1774; Benjamin Franklin to Peter Timothy, 7 September 1774. *Franklin Papers*, XXI, 261-62, 289-92; *New Jersey Archives*, X, 472.

[17]Benjamin Franklin to William Franklin, 7 September 1774. *Franklin Papers*, XXI, 285-89; *New Jersey Archives*, X, 494-96.

house and the firebrands of the Boston mob made him look like anything but a peacemaker. Defending Massachusetts in the wake of the Boston Tea Party started the trouble between him and his son. The Doctor continued to talk about reconciliation, but his unwavering defense of the Massachusetts radicals put him beyond the pale of political redemption in the minds of British officials at Whitehall—even if he had never sent the Hutchinson-Oliver letters.

Ignoring the ministry's growing hostility toward him, Franklin continued to tout Lord Dartmouth as a man with a favorable attitude toward America and, as previously mentioned, encouraged a correspondence between his lordship and Thomas Cushing. The agent tried hard to sell Americans on the idea that Britain would be compelled soon to treat the colonies with kindness and justice because of America's mushrooming population and increasing wealth. The mother country simply had to hold on to America as a strong ally and avoid turning the colonies into an enemy, Franklin argued. With this in mind, Americans should remain quiet, except when defending their rights, and wait to be honored by Britain. The Doctor seemed convinced, at least at times, that Britain would soon face reality. In explaining developments to Thomas Cushing in a letter dated 9 March 1773, the agent indicated that he would remain in England at least until Parliament adjourned, in case his "being on the Spot" could be "of Use" to America. Arguing that violence played into the hands of American enemies in England, Franklin called for patience. Such a strategy made sense, he believed, because anybody could see that "our rapidly increasing Strength" would soon make it impossible for Britain to ignore any longer America's "just Claims to Privilege."[18]

Attempting to mollify the Massachusettsites with suggestions that Dartmouth would set things right and that the colonies would soon be too strong for the mother country to mistreat anymore, resulted in the failure Franklin should have anticipated. Samuel Cooper pointed out to him that news of Dartmouth's ascendancy had been joyously received in Massachusetts—at first. Second thoughts and disenchantment, however, had followed when his lordship had formed a commission to investigate the burning of His Majesty's ship the *Gaspee*, with the intention of bringing the perpetrators to trial in England. Thomas Hutchinson, George III's governor in the province, was another problem. The governor had

---

[18]Benjamin Franklin to Thomas Cushing, 5 January and 9 March 1773. *Franklin Papers*, XX, 7-11, 98-100.

provoked even the provincial Council by asserting in a speech "the absolute Supremacy of Parliament over the colonies." Franklin was quick to condemn "Govr. Hutchinson's Speech." The Doctor assured Cushing that the speech had caused consternation in England. Some people there believed the governor a fool, while others thought he must have been erroneously informed that Hillsborough was again heading the American Department. According to Franklin, Dartmouth had spoken to him of Hutchinson's "Imprudence." Even so, the American Secretary could not ignore the fact that the Massachusetts house had responded to the governor's speech by denying British authority. Dartmouth felt he had to do something to establish British authority, but he did not know what to do. His lordship asked Franklin to persuade the Massachusetts house to retract its response to Hutchinson's speech. The Doctor assured the secretary that the house would never do that, unless Hutchinson retracted the speech. At this juncture both men must have known that there was virtually no hope of restoring harmony between Massachusetts and Great Britain.[19]

Hutchinson, though vilified by radicals in Boston and by Franklin in London, could hardly have been expected to sit quietly by in Massachusetts while the provincial legislature and Boston town meetings blatantly challenged royal authority. In July 1772 the lower house had petitioned the Crown to stop paying Hutchinson's salary. When it was rumored two months later that judges would also be paid by the Crown, a series of town meetings were held in Boston to condemn such unconstitutional innovations. Three resolutions attacking unacceptable British policies were approved at one of the meetings on 20 November. Hutchinson viewed this action as a "declaration of independency." Another petition, condemning the payment of Massachusetts officials by the Crown and demanding a return to the old system of payment by the Massachusetts legislature, was sent to London by the House of Representatives in March 1773. Once these petitions reached Franklin, he, as the house's agent, was obligated to forward them by Dartmouth to the

---

[19]Samuel Cooper to Benjamin Franklin, 15 March 1773; Thomas Cushing to Benjamin Franklin, 20 April 1773; Benjamin Franklin to Thomas Cushing, 3 April and 6 May 1773. Ibid., XX, 110-115, 139-40, 172-75, 199-203; Lord Dartmouth to Thomas Cushing, 19 June 1773. Benjamin F. Stevens, compiler, *Facsimiles of Manuscripts in European Archives Relating to America, 1773–1783,* 25 volumes. (Wilmington DE: Mellifont Press, 1970) XXIV, Doc. no. 2025.

king. In a letter of 2 June 1773, the Doctor reported to Cushing that he had delivered the petitions to the American Secretary and had "press'd his Lordship to present them to his Majesty." When Dartmouth read them to George III, the king was "greatly displeased." George responded to the petitions by reaffirming the absolute authority of the Crown and Parliament "to bind his Subjects in America in all Cases whatsoever." The king said he believed, as did most of the ministers at Whitehall, that the petitions were "the Artifices of a few" who sought to "create groundless Jealousy and Distrust."[20]

By this time Parliament had inadvertently made the situation even more desperate by passing the Tea Act on 27 April 1773. The new law, which went into effect on 10 May, was designed to bail the British East India Company out of financial difficulty. The Company, with warehouses bulging with tea, needed a market desperately. Parliament rushed to the rescue with the Tea Act, which enabled the company, in spite of the tax on tea, to make its tea available to Americans at a price lower than the colonists had to pay for foreign tea. This was made possible by a system of government drawbacks that returned all export duties paid by the company. Franklin was astonished that the ministry seemed to think that American principles could be purchased with cheap tea. He knew that the colonists would not sit still for this new attempt to wring tax money from them and to establish a British monopoly in the American marketplace. The Tea Act, along with the king's response to the Massachusetts house's petitions, shook, at least for the moment, all Franklin's hopes for reconciliation. By July, he saw little chance for redress and despaired of compromise. The steps America would have to take to secure redress would bring the "Dispute to a crisis," he believed. Those steps included a "general Congress," called to formulate a slate of "American" demands. Franklin was convinced that it was worthwhile to take the risk inherent in such a bold move. In his momentary despair, the Doctor seemed resigned to an open break between the colonies and the mother country. He expressed all of these opinions in a letter of 7 July 1773 to the Massachusetts House of Representatives. Dartmouth viewed that letter as an act of treason. Thomas Hutchinson somehow obtained a copy of it and then forwarded it to the American Secretary. If his lordship

---

[20]Benjamin Franklin's Preface to the Declaration of the Boston Town Meeting, 11 June 1773; Benjamin Franklin to Thomas Cushing, 2 June 1773; Lord Dartmouth to Benjamin Franklin, 2 June 1773. *Franklin Papers*, XX, 82-87, 221-24.

had been able to secure the original letter, as he attempted to do in June 1774, he would definitely have prosecuted the Massachusetts agent. Fortunately for Franklin, Cushing, who allowed copies of the letter to be made, never permitted the original to leave his possession.[21]

Although Massachusetts and the British government had reached an impasse, Dartmouth continued to talk of reconciliation. He and Cushing went right on sending flattering letters to one another. The Massachusetts legislature, in no mood to flatter anybody at Whitehall, but feeling misunderstood, flatly denied that it had declared independence, as Hutchinson had asserted and as Dartmouth had concluded. Like Dartmouth, the house's members said they wanted to see harmony restored, and they told the American Secretary how to restore it. All Great Britain had to do to end the trouble was abandon taxation by Parliament and return to the old ways—a solution Franklin had advocated for several years.[22]

In the midst of the summer crisis of 1773 the Doctor came under fire in the Massachusetts house for not keeping that body sufficiently informed of events in England. He was specifically accused of not carefully scrutinizing bills under consideration in Parliament. Cushing was able to rescue Franklin on this occasion by revealing some of the agent's informative letters to the speaker. Later, when he was informed of the criticism, Franklin expressed resentment toward the house for accusing him of "Neglect in their Business." How could he know every clause in every bill before Parliament, when about two hundred bills per session were considered? he asked. Although the Doctor admitted to certain faults, he thought the house was unduly critical, and he considered its censure as "grievous." Even if some house members were displeased with their agent, the chamber attempted several times to appropriate his salary. Governor Hutchinson, of course, blocked payment. Franklin expressed confidence that the house would sooner or later find a way to compensate him, which it eventually did.[23]

Almost continuously Massachusetts kept Franklin busy with unpleasant tasks. In August 1773 he received another petition. It called upon

---

[21]Benjamin Franklin to Thomas Cushing, 4 June 1773; Benjamin Franklin to the Massachusetts House of Representatives, 7 July 1773. Ibid., XX, 226-29, 277-86.

[22]Thomas Cushing to Benjamin Franklin, 30 June[-July 7], 1773. Ibid., XX, 252-255; Thomas Cushing to Lord Dartmouth, August 22, 1773. *Facsimiles*, XXIV, Doc. no. 2028.

[23]Thomas Cushing to Benjamin Franklin, June 30-[7 July] 1773; Benjamin Franklin to Thomas Cushing, 7 July 1773. *Franklin Papers*, XX, 252-55, 271-86, 284 n. 9.

the Crown to remove Governor Thomas Hutchinson and Lt. Governor Andrew Oliver from office. The Doctor sent the petition to Dartmouth and began working with William Bollan to promote its approval, all the while assuring his lordship that Massachusetts wanted to be on good terms with the mother country. In Boston, Cushing continued to praise Dartmouth for his conciliatory attitude and his willingness to correspond with the Massachusetts speaker.[24]

Dartmouth's conciliatory statements to the Massachusetts agent and speaker meant nothing as long as Franklin and Cushing insisted that the only hope of restoring harmony lay in returning to the situation that prevailed before the French and Indian War. This meant Britain's abandoning taxation in favor of the requisition system and ending the Crown's payment of salaries to royal officials in the colonies.[25] The British government, of course, had no intention of turning the clock back. By the end of the year it made little difference what anybody said about reconciliation, since the Massachusettsites were up in arms over the Tea Act and the British government was furious over the conveyance of the Hutchinson-Oliver letters to Boston.

On 10 December 1773, less than a week before the Boston Tea Party, Cushing wrote to Franklin about Boston's rage over the Tea Act. The Bostonians viewed the act as a plot to force unconstitutional taxation upon them. Since they had expected a redress of their grievances and instead had gotten more of what had caused their anguish, they were outraged. Cushing called it "a very Serious Crisis" and stated that only "a radical redress of American Grievances" would "save us from a Rupture with Great Britain." Six days later, on 16 December, the Bostonians held their famous tea party. The next day, Samuel Cooper sent Franklin an account of the event. Cooper told how huge crowds had gathered to protest the arrival of the tea. When 16 December came and Governor Hutchinson would not give the tea ships permission to return to England, two to three hundred "Persons in Dress and appearance like Indians" went to the wharves, demanded the tea, and emptied about 340 chests into the harbor. Putting the best nonviolent face he could on the

---

[24]Benjamin Franklin to Thomas Cushing, 24 August 1773; Lord Dartmouth to Benjamin Franklin, 25 August 1773; Thomas Cushing to Benjamin Franklin, 26 August 1773. Ibid., XX, 374-79.

[25]Thomas Cushing to Benjamin Franklin, 26 August and 18 September 1773; Benjamin Franklin to Thomas Cushing, 1 November 1773. Ibid., XX, 376-79, 406-407, 455-57.

incident, Cooper commented, "This was done without injury to any other Property, or to any Man's Person." After it was over, the perpetrators left in silence, and the town had been quiet ever since—one whole day! Others, including Cushing and the Massachusetts house, wrote the agent about the tea party. Most of the letters were hand-carried to him by Hugh Williamson, an old Pennsylvania political enemy. On his way from Philadelphia to England, Williamson had passed through Boston and was entrusted with several letters addressed to the Doctor. Sailing on 22 December, Williamson arrived at Dover four weeks later. Soon thereafter he delivered the letters to Franklin and gave his own account of the events, which he had witnessed personally at the Boston wharves nearly two months earlier.[26]

By the time Franklin responded to the people in Boston regarding the tea party, he had already suffered public humiliation before the Privy Council for sending the Hutchinson-Oliver letters. Even so, he was aghast at what had happened at Boston Harbor. He did his duty as agent, forwarding to Dartmouth the house committee's letter concerning the event. He was clearly concerned, however, noting that in London "the Clamour against the Proceeding" was "high and general." The Doctor urged conciliatory measures, such as Massachusetts paying the East India Company for the destroyed tea. It was a mistake, he contended, to give England an excuse to make war on the colonies. "A speedy Reparation," he suggested, would "set us Right in the Opinion of all Europe." He pointed out that the ministry, not the East India Company, was to blame for the Tea Act. Franklin was highly embarrassed by the Boston Tea Party.[27] By this time he might well have wondered if he had made a serious mistake by accepting the agency of the Massachusetts House of Representatives.

Although Franklin thought the Bostonians had erred on 16 December, he met on 26 March 1774 with other Americans and their sympathizers at the Thatched House Tavern on St. James's Street. There the pro-

---

[26]Thomas Cushing to Benjamin Franklin, 10 and 21 December 1773; Samuel Cooper to Benjamin Franklin, 17 December 1773; Samuel Franklin to Benjamin Franklin, 17 December 1773; Massachusetts House of Representatives' Committee of Correspondence to Benjamin Franklin, 21 December 1773. Ibid., XX, 494-97, 499-505, 509-512.

[27]Benjamin Franklin to the Massachusetts House of Representatives' Committee of Correspondence, 2 February 1774; Benjamin Franklin to Thomas Cushing, 22 March 1774. Ibid., XXI, 75-77, 152-53, 153 n. 4; Kammen, *Rope of Sand*, 289.

American group signed a petition calling upon the House of Lords not to pass the Boston Port Bill, which would shut down Boston Harbor until Massachusetts paid the East India Company for its destroyed tea. The Lords tabled the petition, just as the House of Commons had tabled a similar one two days earlier. Nor did still another petition, sent to the king, avail anything. The Boston Port Bill became law on 31 March. Franklin joined the same pro-American group in May to petition against the Massachusetts Government Bill and the Administration of Justice Bill, two more pieces of punitive legislation aimed at the rebellious colony. Again, the effort to halt the legislation was futile. In between his fruitless efforts to thwart these "Coercive Acts," the Doctor wrote to Cushing on 16 April to report that General Thomas Gage was being sent to Boston to replace Hutchinson as governor. The agent also noted that copies of his letters to the speaker were getting back to the ministry and that their contents had been labeled treason by some. In fact, Franklin had been informed that he would be prosecuted for treason because of his letters, "if Copies could be made Evidence." He thought that his statements would have to be distorted in order to make treason out of them, but still he intended to be more careful about what he wrote in future letters. The Doctor told Cushing not to be surprised if forthcoming letters contained only "mere Relations of Facts."[28]

By late spring 1774 Franklin knew that there was little chance of Massachusetts paying for the destroyed tea. Every word from the colony's lower house indicated that Massachusetts planned not to budge an inch, but the Doctor continued to defend the province. He was delighted when the great William Pitt, Lord Chatham, publicly condemned the Coercive Acts. The agent soon came up with a rationalization that salved his conscience in the matter of the tea party—a rationalization that might be expected to please the Boston firebrands. He repeatedly argued that Americans should total up all accounts against Great Britain from money unconstitutionally extracted by various acts of Parliament, subtract the cost of the tea from that amount, and demand payment of the difference. Franklin's ultimate stand on the tea party brought on the quarrel (mentioned earlier) with William, who was convinced that the Bostonians should pay for the tea—period. By the time the Doctor came up with his rationalization justifying the refusal of the Massachusettsites to pay for

---

[28]Benjamin Franklin to Thomas Cushing, 16[-17] April 1774, and other material. *Franklin Papers*, XXI, 155-57, 155 n. 2, 156 n. 3, 157 n. 4, 191-93, 214-16.

the tea, he was more concerned about what Massachusetts owed him than what it owed the East India Company. In a letter of 1 June 1774, he noted that he no longer received a salary from the British post office, having been stripped of his position as deputy postmaster general of the colonies. He needed the house, he said, to find some means of paying him.[29]

Although the situation appeared to be completely desperate, Franklin held on to a glimmer of hope. On 28 September he thought he saw the tide turning, as America's friends in England began to speak out. A week later he expressed the view that news of actions taken by the Continental Congress would soon reach London. Then America's friends would "be multiplied and our Enemies diminish'd." American rights would be "acknowledg'd and establish'd."[30] The Doctor appears to have lost touch with reality at that point; at the very least, he was indulging in an enormous amount of wishful thinking. That he entertained the idea of a dramatic turnaround and seemed to long for it to happen is astonishing in view of his ordeal before the Privy Council earlier in the year.

Why Franklin retained even a hint of optimism or even desired reconciliation throughout 1774 is somewhat baffling. On 29 January of that year he suffered the most humiliating experience of his long and distinguished public career—all because he had sent the Hutchinson-Oliver letters to Thomas Cushing. Sending those letters stamped him indelibly as a radical and, along with the Boston Tea Party, made the split between Massachusetts and the mother country almost irreparable. The eighteen private letters that caused Franklin so much grief were written between 7 May 1767 and 20 October 1769 during the time of the Townshend Duty crisis. Thomas Hutchinson, then chief justice and lieutenant governor of Massachusetts, and Andrew Oliver, secretary of the province, plus several other officials, had written the letters to a mutual friend in England. That friend was Thomas Whately, a confidant of George Grenville. Whately had served as secretary to the Treasury, but he had left that office after being elected to Parliament. In one of the six letters written by Hutchinson to Whately, dated 20 January 1769, the

---

[29]See Franklin's letters to and from a variety of correspondents, March-October 1774. Ibid., XXI, 162-68, 227-30, 237-39, 273-76, 279-80, 297-302, 306-308, 323-29; *New Jersey Archives*, X, 494-96.

[30]Benjamin Franklin to Thomas Cushing, 3 September and 6 October 1774. *Franklin Papers*, XXI, 279-80, 326-28.

Massachusetts official called for stern measures by the mother country to make sure that Americans remained dependent on Great Britain. In the letters Oliver wrote, he had argued that royal officials must be paid by the Crown. Both men called for a tough ministerial policy; yet neither advised specific or repressive measures, as Franklin later claimed. After Thomas Whately died in 1772 the letters passed into the hands of William Whately, a London banker and Thomas's brother.[31] How the letters ended up in Franklin's hands remains a mystery, and why he sent them to Cushing remains a matter of controversy.

Franklin undoubtedly realized that the contents of the letters would not be kept secret and that his part in sending them would eventually become known. Samuel Cooper warned the Doctor in June 1774 that his part in sending the letters would leak out sooner or later. Because so many rumors were abroad by the time the letters arrived, Cushing and some of his confidants decided to reveal their contents to the entire lower house. The house condemned the letters in a vote of 101 to 5 as a "Design and Tendency . . . to introduce arbitrary Pow[e]r." Cooper called the arrival of the letters "seasonable" and stated that the people of Boston were indebted to Franklin for sending them. At the time Cooper wrote, Cushing seems to have been making a genuine effort to keep the Doctor's part in sending the letters a secret. The speaker informed the agent that he had revealed it only to Cooper and one member of the house's Committee of Correspondence. It would go no further, Cushing assured Franklin, unless the agent himself divulged it. At this point—in the late spring of 1773—not even Thomas Hutchinson suspected the Doctor. While it was not known who had sent the letters, the presence of the letters and their contents were known all over Massachusetts, and Cushing provided the agent with a lengthy explanation of how that had happened.[32]

The existence of Hutchinson's letters to Thomas Whately had been known long before Franklin ever laid hands on them. Samuel Adams had made an abortive attempt, as early as 1770, to secure them through a friend in England. After the Doctor finally got them and sent them to Cushing, Adams played a big part in releasing their contents to colonial newspapers. When Franklin learned in July 1773 that the letters' contents

---

[31]*Franklin Papers*, XIX, 399-404, 404 n. 2; Gipson, *The British Empire*, XII, 58-59.
[32]Thomas Cushing to Benjamin Franklin, 14 June 1773; Samuel Cooper to Benjamin Franklin, 14[-15] June 1773. *Franklin Papers*, XX, 232-38.

were circulating throughout Massachusetts and beyond, he expressed no particular alarm. He had placed restrictions on the use of the letters because that had been required of him by the person who had delivered them to him. The wily agent believed he could obtain more letters that were "still more abominable," if "too much Noise" was not made. It was not himself he was trying to protect, Franklin declared, but the person who gave him the letters. Although the agent was glad his "Name had not been heard on the Occasion" and hoped it would continue to be unknown, he "hardly expect[ed] it." He assured Cushing that he fully understood why the speaker had been unable to restrict knowledge of the letters to a few people.[33]

By the end of July 1773 Governor Hutchinson had concluded that Franklin was the man who had transmitted the letters to Boston. The governor accused the agent of advising the Boston radicals to push for independence. There were others who believed the Doctor had sent the letters, but some laid the blame on John Temple. William Franklin, for example, suspected Temple. Some other people also thought that Temple was the transmitter, since he was and is the most likely suspect in filching the letters. The other major suspect in the theft of the correspondence is Thomas Pownall. Arguing strictly along logical lines, but without hard evidence, historian Bernard Bailyn in 1974 declared Pownall to be his prime suspect, mainly because Pownall favored reconciliation and hated Thomas Hutchinson. The Bailyn scenario has Pownall trying to put the blame for objectionable British policies on Hutchinson so that the Massachusettsites would turn all their fury on the provincial governor and stop blaming Whitehall. Bailyn's logic is good, but John Temple remains the more likely suspect in stealing the letters. It must be conceded, however, that the available evidence is not conclusive. Temple was the son-in-law of Massachusetts radical James Bowdoin. He was also a pro-American member of the Board of Customs Commissioners in Boston, until he was removed in 1770. Finally, Temple, was a distant relative of George Grenville, who was allied with the Whatelys. Four months after Thomas Whately died in 1772, his brother William apparently allowed Temple to examine Thomas's papers. William Whately

---

[33]Philip Davidson, *Propaganda and the American Revolution, 1763–1783* (Chapel Hill: University of North Carolina Press, 1941) 147-48; Benjamin Franklin to Samuel Cooper, 7 and 25 July 1773; Benjamin Franklin to Thomas Cushing, 7 July 1773. *Franklin Papers*, XX, 268-76, 321-22.

certainly blamed Temple for taking the Hutchinson-Oliver letters, fighting one duel with him over the matter and challenging him to another. Also, Temple was removed from his position as surveyor general of the customs in England after the incident—a good sign that the ministry blamed him for giving the letters to Franklin. It is unlikely that the ministers would have forced him out without some evidence. To prevent the second duel from being fought between Temple and William Whately, Franklin publicly stated that he alone took the letters, but Temple later claimed that he obtained the correspondence and gave it to the Doctor. Franklin never confirmed this, leaving posterity to wonder who really gave the letters to him.[34]

A more important question than who gave Franklin the letters is why the Doctor sent them to Thomas Cushing. Thomas Hutchinson never had any doubts about the answer to the latter question. He saw it as a pure act of malice, for the purpose of wrecking the Massachusetts governor's public career. The governor apparently believed Franklin retaliated against him for refusing to approve the Doctor as agent and for preventing the lower house from paying the agent his salary. There was probably some truth in Hutchinson's conclusions, but the explanation Franklin gave for sending the letters makes sense, too. If Franklin was honest with anybody —even knowing that their views differed from his on imperial relations— it was with his son William and his old political partner Joseph Galloway. He told them that he considered it his duty to send the letters to Boston in order to take some of the heat off the British ministry and turn it on the officials in America. Americans who called for strong measures against the colonies were apparently worse, at least in Franklin's eyes, than anti-American leaders in England. The agent thought that his sending the letters would lead more quickly and easily to reconciliation. Once again, the Doctor had badly miscalculated. In the midst of the uproar caused by the letters, Franklin continued to insist that he had acquired

---

[34]There is an enormous amount of material on the Hutchinson-Oliver letters, and much of it is filled with conjecture. Numerous letters in the *Franklin Papers* and Thomas Hutchinson's *History of Massachusetts* say much on the subject, as do countless secondary works. See: *Franklin Papers*, XIX, 399-404; XX, 331-32, 515-16, 539-80; XXI 108-11, 508; *Georgia Gazette*, 30 March, 13 April, and 11 May 1774; Hutchinson, *History of Massachusetts*, III, 262, 282-83, 328, 394-97, 401-405, 416. Also see: Bernard Bailyn, *The Ordeal of Thomas Hutchinson* (Cambridge MA: Harvard University Press, 1974) 224-38, 225 n. 7, 233 n. 23; Kammen, *Rope of Sand*, 284-85.

them honorably and that transmitting them to Cushing was done with the best of intentions. That Thomas Hutchinson's career as a public official was ended by the deed no doubt pleased the Doctor; that this was his primary motive in sending the letters is unlikely. While Franklin felt justified in what he had done, some of his closest friends, like David Hume and John Pringle, were appalled by the deed and felt hard pressed to defend him.[35]

Apparently Cushing really made a sincere effort to keep Franklin's identity as sender of the letters a secret. As late as 10 November 1773, Samuel Cooper assured the Doctor that only three people in Boston really *knew* who had sent the letters. By the time Cooper wrote these assuring words, the letters were the talk of London. In the *Public Advertiser*, there had been charges and counter charges during September, and this had led to the duel between William Whately and John Temple. Franklin's admission of blame in taking and sending the letters appeared in the 23–25 December issue of the *London Chronicle*. The Doctor stated that Temple had not taken the letters from William Whately, but he did not say that Temple had not taken them from somebody else. The devious agent was at his cunning best in offering his explanation. His statement was very carefully worded. Referring to the letters as "public" letters designed "to incense the Mother Country against her Colonies," the Doctor asserted that the correspondence by right ought to have been made public.[36]

The following month Franklin found out how deeply the ministry disagreed with him. He was notified on 8 January that the Privy Council's Committee for Plantation Affairs would, on 11 January, consider the Massachusetts lower house's petition regarding the requested removal of Hutchinson and Oliver from office. The Doctor was informed that his attendance was required at the hearing. He consulted William Bollan, a lawyer as well as the agent of the Massachusetts Council. It was

---

[35]See Franklin's letters to William Franklin, Joseph Galloway, and Lord Dartmouth, and other material. *Franklin Papers*, XIX, 407-409; XX, 372-73, 372 n. 3, 373 n.5, 380-81, 385-88; XXI, 108-111, 113 n. 7. Also see: Bailyn, *Ordeal of Hutchinson*, 376-77, and Jack Sosin, *Agents and Merchants: British Colonial Policy, 1763-1775* (Lincoln: University of Nebraska Press, 1965) 157.

[36]Thomas Cushing to Benjamin Franklin, 24 March 1773; Samuel Cooper to Benjamin Franklin, 10 November 1773, and other material. *Franklin Papers*, XX, 123-25, 480-82, 515-16; Hutchinson, *History of Massachusetts*, III, 416.

decided that the two together could handle the matters before the committee without additional counsel, since no mention had been made of counsel appearing for the other side. Then, late on 10 January, Franklin was told that Hutchinson would be represented at the hearing by Israel Mauduit, a London merchant and pamphleteer, and that Mauduit's counsel would be the ambitious politician and Whitehall's solicitor general, Alexander Wedderburn. At the hearing on the eleventh the Doctor attempted to give Bollan the floor, but the Massachusetts Council's agent was not permitted to speak. The reason given for denying Bollan the floor was that the petition at hand had come from the Massachusetts House of Representatives, not the Council. When Franklin laid copies of the house's resolutions and letters before the committee, Wedderburn raised questions about the resolutions and brought up the Hutchinson-Oliver letters. Pleading that he had not been properly advised to bring counsel to the hearing, the Doctor asked for a delay so that he could secure counsel. His request was granted, and a second hearing was scheduled for 29 January.[37]

If Franklin was surprised by the ambush on 11 January, he must have been utterly astonished by the frontal assault against him on 29 January. He later remarked that the whole affair "was preconcerted." After the agent's counselors spoke, Wedderburn opened a "new case." The scene was packed with drama. In the first place, the hearing was held in the Cockpit, a "block of buildings opposite Whitehall and erected over an old cockfighting site." Originally, it was the section of Henry VIII's palace where cocks were bred and fed and where they fought. Offices of the Treasury and the Privy Council were housed in it during the eighteenth century. At that time it was part of the complex of buildings where policy was made. It symbolized British governmental power, much as 10 Downing Street has in the twentieth century. Franklin would never forget the place, for he sat there in his suit of spotted Manchester velvet for about an hour, while Wedderburn heaped torrents of abuse upon him. Thirty-five members of the Privy Council listened as Wedderburn relentlessly tongue-lashed the Doctor, and only one of them, Lord LeDespencer, was sympathetic toward the American agent. Other celebrities who witnessed Franklin's humiliation included Lord Dartmouth, Lord Hillsborough (who

---

[37]Stephen Cottrell to Benjamin Franklin, 10 January 1774; Benjamin Franklin to Thomas Cushing, 15[-19] February 1774. *Franklin Papers*, XXI, 18-23, 86-89.

must have relished it!), Joseph Priestly, Jeremy Bentham, and General Thomas Gage.

Wedderburn began by asserting that Hutchinson had been made ineffective as governor of Massachusetts as the result of a conspiracy led by Franklin and a half dozen Boston radicals. The solicitor general accused the agent of stealing the Hutchinson-Oliver letters from the Whately family—Wedderburn had been a close friend of Thomas Whately—and sending them to Boston under cover of an unsigned letter. Since the agent signed his cover letter to Cushing, that part of Wedderburn's accusation was patently untrue. Franklin, Wedderburn suggested, was angling for Hutchinson's job. Over and over, the solicitor general blamed all the trouble in Massachusetts on the conspiring agent and the "factious leaders of Boston," who, according to Wedderburn, had learned their lessons at "Dr. Franklin's school of Politics." Throughout the attack, Franklin remained silent, keeping a fixed, solemn expression on his face and refusing to be examined. The agent's lawyer, John Dunning, tried to defend the Doctor, but Dunning could scarcely be heard and was thus ineffective. Apparently the frustrated barrister had been ill and was exhausted by the hearing. The Privy Council, obviously convinced that Franklin was guilty of creating pandemonium in Massachusetts, dismissed the Massachusetts lower house's petition calling for the ouster of Hutchinson and Oliver.[38]

Franklin's verbal mauling by Wedderburn at the Cockpit and the Privy Council's ensuing unfavorable decision on the lower house's petition were glaring signs that the Doctor's London world was starting to crumble beneath his feet. Talk of the agent's impending arrest on criminal charges began to make the rounds in some London circles. William Whately brought suit against him in the Court of Chancery. This action genuinely irked Franklin, since the Doctor had helped Whately a few months earlier in establishing a claim to a valuable piece of real estate in Pennsylvania. Before the suit could be settled, the agent sailed for America.[39]

---

[38]*Franklin Papers*, XXI, 37-70, 91-96, 281-84; Hutchinson, *History of Massachusetts*, III, 417-18; Kammen, *Rope of Sand*, 284-85; Wendel, *Politics of Liberty*, 183; Henry B. Wheatley, *London Past and Present*, 3 volumes. (London: J. Murray, 1891) I, 437-38.

[39]*Franklin Papers*, XXI, 13-18, 73-75, 78-83, 89-91, 95, 103, 106-108, 106 n. 1, 117-119, 147-49, 181-83, 191, 197-202, 226-27, 414-35.

Two days after his humiliating experience at the Cockpit, Franklin was relieved of his duties as deputy postmaster general of the colonies and told by his old friend and boss Anthony Todd to turn in his accounts as soon as he could "conveniently" do so. When the Doctor did surrender them on 5 December 1774, his figures showed that he owed the post office about £973, and the accounts were judged not to be in order. Franklin wrote about his troubles to John Foxcroft, claiming they were caused by his being too much of an American. The agent warned Foxcroft, who was only a little less of an American, to watch his step. As was the case with David Hall and his heirs, Franklin never settled his accounts with the post office.[40]

The Doctor's troubles in England reflected badly on his son William, and the elder Franklin warned the New Jersey governor that he, too, could be removed from office. Since 1771 Franklin had felt useless as an agent; after 29 January 1774, he became so. His career as an effective lobbyist was over forever, and he knew it. The agent wrote Cushing on 2 April to say that he could no longer serve as the lower house's lobbyist. Franklin wanted to quit immediately, but Arthur Lee was on the Continent and could not take over the agency, probably for some months. The Doctor would continue serving until somebody replaced him, he said. Franklin was ready to stop representing all of his constituencies at Whitehall. Tired of the Georgia agency, he eagerly gave it up, resolving to quit the others as soon as possible. His head was bloody, but only partially bowed. He asserted that the ministry had attempted to disgrace him and honored him instead, for the proceedings against him had clearly demonstrated that he was a firm supporter of his country.[41]

All during the crisis of 1774 Franklin carried on much as he had in previous years. His propaganda pen never rested. In September 1773, before the worst of the storm clouds gathered, the Doctor wrote two satires that appeared in the *Public Advertiser*. One, called "Rules by Which a Great Empire May Be Reduced to a Small One," was published on 11 September under the signature "Q.E.D.". It ridiculed every mistake Franklin thought the British government had made since 1765. On the twenty-second of the same month, he followed "Rules" with "An Edict by the King of Prussia," in which he presented the British as colonists of

---

[40]Ibid (all sources cited).
[41]Ibid.; *Georgia Gazette*, 6 July 1774; Kammen, *Rope of Sand*, 286; Thayer, *Pennsylvania Politics*, 167.

Prussia and portrayed them as being treated by Frederick II as Americans were then being treated by George III. The Doctor kept up his propaganda efforts in 1774, writing numerous letters to the press and using some of his old pseudonyms, as well as some new ones. "Rules" made a second newspaper appearance on 15 April 1774 in the *Gazetteer and New Daily Advertiser*. Franklin's arguments resembled those he had used during the Townshend Duty crisis, as he vigorously attacked the Coercive Acts. Thus, his message of 1774 was the same old one—Britain must abandon unconstitutional taxation in favor of a return to the old requisition system and America should keep up the economic pressure until the mother country realized the error of her ways.[42]

Franklin surely knew that there was little hope of reconciliation. Yet he worked as if peace and harmony could be restored and continued doing what he thought was good for the colonies. All the while he was becoming even more popular at home, in spite of a rumor in Boston that he would desert the cause if the British would give him back his position with the post office. Revolted by that rumor, Franklin called it an "infamous Falsehood." News that the Continental Congress would soon meet encouraged him to believe that concerted economic pressure could be applied against Britain. This, he seemed convinced, would force the desired change in imperial policy. The Doctor was wrong again. Economic coercion was doomed to failure this time, for many British political leaders and merchants had reached the conclusion that yielding to American demands only brought more demands. When, late in 1774, the Continental Congress called upon all American agents in England to present a petition from that body to the king, only three were willing to take on the risky task—Franklin, Arthur Lee, and William Bollan. These same three men had joined together on 5 February 1774 to send a circular letter to the speakers of the various colonial assemblies. Their letter, designed to serve as a status report, had painted a gloomy picture of Anglo-American relations. The three were ready to carry out the wishes of the Continental Congress, when they received the call to action near the end of the year. The other agents, including Edmund Burke, claimed they served individual colonies, not the Continental Congress. Since they had no instructions from their respective colonies, they refused to promote Congress's petition. Realizing that Congress was not fully aware

---

[42]Crane, *Letters to the Press*, 232-33, 236-37, 247-52, 254-64,; *Franklin Papers*, XX, 387-99, 413-18; XXI, 115, 125, 130-38, 177-80, 218-20, 233-34.

of how government matters were conducted in London, Franklin, Lee, and Bollan departed from Congress's instructions to go directly to the king and instead presented the petition to Lord Dartmouth on 21 December. His lordship and the Cabinet studied it before passing it along to George III. On the twenty-fourth the American Secretary informed the three agents that His Majesty would present the petition to Parliament. When he did, Parliament promptly laid it aside, refusing to act on it.[43] Time was obviously running out on a peaceful settlement of differences between Britain and her colonies.

No matter what happened and regardless of how hopeless the situation appeared, Franklin could always find reasons to remain in England a little longer: he might be able to help the American cause, the ministry might change and reverse the current policy, and his friends encouraged him to remain. These were his favorite excuses, but there were others, too. One of the others was the Ohio scheme. Before the year 1774 ended, that venture was dealt the *coup d' grace*. Opponents of the project urged Dartmouth to continue Hillsborough's policy with regard to it. Dartmouth chose, however, to support the Privy Council's decision to establish the colony of Vandalia. The Board of Trade, having been overridden in the matter, finally approved the project on 6 May 1773. Less than two weeks later, the Board's recommendations regarding the huge land grant were made to the Privy Council. In July, the attorney general and the solicitor general were instructed to prepare a draft granting the land to the Walpole Company in accordance with the boundaries ordered by the Board of Trade. Turning the matter over to these two officials, together with news some months later that the Bostonians had destroyed a small fortune in tea, killed the ill-fated project that so many had promoted for so long. Attorney General Edward Thurlow and Solicitor General Alexander Wedderburn opposed the Vandalia colony and caused further delay by raising legal objections. Their legal nit-picking brought the project to a halt. By the time the Privy Council considered the Ohio scheme for the last time—just over a year

---

[43]Bernard Donoughue, *British Politics and the American Revolution: The Path to War, 1773–1775* (London: Macmillan Company; New York: St. Martin's Press, 1964) 147-54; letters between Franklin and numerous correspondents, as well as other material. *Franklin Papers*, XXI 206-207, 235-36, 235 n. 2, 264-65, 289, 317-18, 320-22, 336-41, 392-93, 393 n. 9, 398-99, 472-74; Kammen, *Rope of Sand*, 301-302; Sosin, *Agents and Merchants*, 175-76, 227.

later on 12 August 1774—the whole British government was still fuming over the Boston Tea Party and had no inclination to promote anything in America, except the reestablishment of law and order. The Vandalia project was referred to a committee and was never considered again.[44]

During 1773 and 1774, as the Vandalia project moved slowly through Whitehall to its abortive end, Franklin was more pessimistic than optimistic concerning its fate. He promised his friend Nathaniel Falconer, in a letter of 4 February 1773, that he would protect Falconer's interest in the project as vigorously as his own, if the "Land Affair is ever compleated." The agent added that God alone knew whether or not it would be. The following month the Doctor informed Joseph Galloway that Walpole expected everything to be settled soon, but Franklin observed that "men are too apt to expect what they wish." The Doctor declared himself to be "indifferent about it." A few weeks later, on 6 April, he wrote to William Franklin that he was skeptical of a favorable outcome and hoped soon to be able to ask Dartmouth "where it sticks." When the agent wrote to John Foxcroft on 14 July 1773, he was still pessimistic. Pointing out that the Privy Council had instructed the attorney general and the solicitor general to draw up the grant, Franklin warned that all of those officials might repair to their country estates and not get together again for months.[45]

As the Walpole Company cleared one bureaucratic hurdle after another, only to encounter more obstacles, tempers began to flare between the shareholders. The project's most energetic promoter, Samuel Wharton, fell out with the Franklins in 1773. William had continued to suggest that the land grant sought by the Grand Ohio Company probably encroached

---

[44]*Acts of the Privy Council*, V, 210; VI, 543, 546; B. D. Bargar, *Lord Dartmouth and the American Revolution* (Columbia: University of South Carolina Press, 1965) 71-73; Benjamin Franklin to William Franklin, 25 July 1773. *Franklin Papers*, XX, 325-28, 327 n. 7; Gipson, *The British Empire*, XI, 471-83; *Journals of the Board of Trade, 1768-1775*, 351-52, 354, 356; Marshall, "Lord Hillsborough and the Ohio Grant," 736.

Franklin did continue to pursue the Vandalia project during and after the Revolution. He tried, with the help of sympathizers, to promote it in the Congress of the United States, and he *never* gave up on it completely. See: Abernethy, *Western Lands*, 177, 238, 245, 260.

[45]Benjamin Franklin to Nathaniel Falconer, 14 February 1773; Benjamin Franklin to Joseph Galloway, 15 March and 6 April 1773; Benjamin Franklin to William Franklin, 6 April, 14 and 25 July 1773; Benjamin Franklin to John Foxcroft, 14 July 1773. *Franklin Papers*, XX, 58, 109-110, 109 n. 7, 145-50, 298-99, 298 n. 2, 300-314, 325-28.

on territory claimed by Virginia land companies. The Doctor, urged on by William, kept asking questions, even after Wharton assured the agent that there was no overlapping of the lands claimed by the other companies. Wharton became annoyed, and he made derogatory remarks about the illustrious agent and his governor son. Contrary to what Wharton had been led to believe, he asserted, the Franklins had no influence with the ministry. They were no more than "Bluff and Declamation," Wharton said. In spite of a bitter quarrel with the agent, Wharton told William Strahan that he had satisfied the Doctor with regard to the Virginia claims. If Wharton's partner, George Morgan of Baynton, Wharton & Morgan, can be believed, Wharton was a dishonest and dishonorable man. Nor was Morgan any more complimentary of William Trent, the man who had accompanied Wharton to England to promote the colony in the Ohio country. Morgan called Trent a "contemptible wretch" who was not worth "a Kick." William Franklin became convinced that Wharton intended to cheat the governor out of his share in the company. The elder Franklin, however, assured his son that he had paid the money for William's share and had the receipts to prove it. The Doctor could see no way that Wharton and Trent could drop William from the company.[46]

Although William's place in the company was secure, his father's was not—at least not as a visible partner. After the Doctor admitted sending the Hutchinson-Oliver letters to Boston, his participation in the company became an embarrassment. Walpole was convinced that the agent's association with the venture might cause the ministry to kill the project. An arrangement was made for appearance sake. Franklin pretended to resign from the company in a letter dated 12 January 1774, but written on or after 24 January. He asked not that his shares be canceled but that his "Name" be stricken from "the List of Associates" and that he not be "look[ed] upon as one of them." Actually he retained his shares and clandestinely remained a partner in the enterprise.[47] What did it matter? The project was shelved during the aftermath of the Boston Tea

---

[46]Abernethy, *Western Lands*, 116-22; Benjamin Franklin to William Franklin, 14 February, 6 April, 14 and 25 July 1773; William Franklin to Benjamin Franklin, 30 April 1773; George Morgan to Benjamin Franklin, 8 July 1773. *Franklin Papers*, XX, 60-65, 145-48, 184-86, 185 ns. 7 and 9, 294-96, 295 n. 4, 300-314, 304 n. 7, 325-28; Marshall, "Lord Hillsborough and the Ohio Grant," 734; Sosin, *Whitehall and the Wilderness*, 207 n. 57.

[47]*Franklin Papers*, XXI, 31-34.

Party, as the government turned its attention to the more pressing business of bringing the colonies into line. All official interest in a new western colony vanished.

Cecil Currey contends that Franklin's increasing radicalism stemmed in large part from the agent's frustration over land speculation. The Doctor wanted to be a large landowner and even the proprietor of his own colony. The opposition of Hillsborough and other officials to Franklin's speculative ambitions "fed the fires of his anger and increased his loathing for imperial rule."[48] That Franklin was deeply interested in land speculation and strongly desired to participate in founding a colony is not open to question. On the other hand, this writer cannot find in the evidence that Franklin was as desperately moved by the Grand Ohio Company project as Currey contends he was. Currey seems to have read a great deal more into the evidence than is warranted.

Business matters, along with the crises precipitated by the Hutchinson-Oliver letters and the Boston Tea Party, claimed so much of Franklin's attention in 1773 and 1774 that he did not have as much time for other activities as he had had in prior years. Age had slowed his pace a little, too. Uppermost in his mind, by this time, was finding a way to leave the pleasures of London for the personal responsibilities that awaited him in Philadelphia. At last, he was genuinely homesick, telling Jonathan Shipley, "I long to see my own Family once more. I draw towards the Conclusion of Life, and am afraid of being prevented that Pleasure. Besides, I feel myself become of no Consequence here." Still, he spoke only of "visiting America" in June of 1773. Apparently he planned to go home, but with the intention of returning to England. As he watched his godson, William Hewson, Jr., at play, he wanted to "be at Home to play with Ben," one of the *two* grandsons he had not seen. Sally's second son, William Bache, had been born on 31 May 1773, but Franklin wrote almost exclusively of wanting to see his namesake and tended to ignore "Will." The Franklin and Bache families fully expected the Doctor to be in Philadelphia by September 1773, and when "various Considerations, some publick and some private," kept him in England, Deborah and Sally were extremely disappointed—again. In October, Franklin wrote to Deborah to say that he had to stay "another Winter."

---

[48]See: Cecil B. Currey, *Road to Revolution: Benjamin Franklin in England, 1765–1775* (Garden City NY: Doubleday & Company, 1968) 118-52, 233-65, 332-38, and especially 389-92.

He told her that she could be sure that nothing would keep him from returning home the following spring. Convinced that his good health could not continue much longer, Franklin told his pining wife that he wanted to go home to die.[49]

Franklin's proposed trip home in the summer of 1773 was postponed after he resorted to the use of "Prudential Algebra." In one column he listed nine reasons for staying: a trip to Europe with John Pringle, settling up with Mrs. Stevenson, the Vandalia project, the Pennsylvania Paper Money Act, the "Boston ag[ency]," and four other reasons having to do with his writings and scientific experiments. Another column contained his reasons for going home: settling personal and post office accounts with John Foxcroft, dropping his agencies, getting some rest, settling accounts with David Hall's executors, and stopping the "Waste at h[ome]." Conspicuously absent from his reasons for going home was any reference to reuniting with his family, but, given his correspondence with Jonathan Shipley, that should, perhaps, be taken for granted.[50]

In addition to his family in America, Franklin still had his loved ones in England on his mind. He was proud of the progress that his grandson Temple was making in school. The Doctor wanted to send Temple to "Eaton" and then Oxford—at William's expense, of course—but he feared that the governor could not afford it. Franklin planned to take his grandson with him to America. Then William could judge what to do about the lad's education. In the Doctor's mind, Temple, now fourteen, should study law, although being a portrait painter or a surgeon was acceptable. Also on Franklin's mind were the Hewsons with whom the Doctor dined from time to time, before Dr. Hewson's unexpected death of a fever at age thirty-four on 1 May 1774. A grieving Franklin wrote to Deborah, "Our Family here is in great Distress." A few months later, in August, Polly Hewson's third child, a daughter, was born. Polly's husband had died upset at the prospect of leaving her with limited funds and three children to bring up alone. In a matter of weeks after Hewson died, any money problems Polly might have had evaporated. Aunt Mary

---

[49]Benjamin Franklin to Jonathan Shipley, [June 1773]; Benjamin Franklin to Deborah Franklin, 2 February and 1 September 1773; Benjamin Franklin to Richard Bache, 15 July and 1 September 1773; Sarah Bache to Benjamin Franklin, 2 October 1773, and 2 January 1774. *Franklin Papers*, XX, 34, 255-57, 317, 317 n. 1, 381-84, 436, 452-54; XXI, 5.

[50]Franklin's Use of "Prudential Algebra." Ibid., XX, 336-38 and ns. 10-20.

Tickell also died, leaving a considerable inheritance to the Widow Hewson.[51]

Besides carrying out his duties as agent and self-appointed American spokesman and trying to deal with some very personal matters, Franklin was involved in a limited number of other activities. At William Strahan's request he wrote a few passages for a historical work on the colonies. The Doctor was not at his best as a historian, however, as his accounts were written from memory and were inaccurate in numerous details. He also worked on some scientific experiments and engaged in some other writing. He planned a trip with John Pringle to Italy, but Pringle decided instead to go to Scotland. Once more, Franklin visited Lord LeDespencer at his lordship's plush West Wycombe estate and called the gardens there "a Paradise." At LeDespencer's request the Doctor helped his host amend the Book of Common Prayer by deleting a considerable portion of that revered book. Franklin also made another unsuccessful attempt to settle his accounts with the post office. Too, he secured membership in the American Philosophical Society for Timotheus Mazahn von Klingstadt, the founder of the Free Economic Society and an expert on agricultural and legal matters. The agent also wrote a letter of introduction in the fall of 1774 for thirty-seven-year-old Thomas Paine to carry to Richard Bache in Philadelphia. Franklin asked his son-in-law to help Paine find a job and get established. Uncharacteristically, the Doctor, after years of being called upon to help ne'er-do-well relatives, said "no" in no uncertain terms to helping his nephew Josiah Davenport with landing a government job—as if the embattled agent had any influence left with the British government. He declined, too, a request by the trustees of the Burlington Free School in New Jersey to help them maintain control over Burlington Island in the Delaware River. Apparently Franklin thought the trustees should take their case directly to the Board of Trade, which they finally did.[52]

Throughout 1773 the most visible of American agents grew weary in trying to keep hope for reconciliation alive against mounting odds. He

---

[51]Benjamin Franklin to William Franklin, 14 July and 3 August 1773, and 1 August 1774; Benjamin Franklin to Deborah Franklin, 5 May and 22 July 1774, and other material. Ibid., XVIII, 62; XX, 311-13, 339-40; XXI, 208-209, 246-47, 266.

[52]See various letters between Franklin and a number of correspondents, plus other material. Ibid., XIX, 393, 394 n. 2; XX, 12-14, 13 n. 1, 56-57, 207-209, 306, 339-40, 343-52; XXI 284-85, 325-26, 375-76.

was tired and wanted to go home, but turning loose of England was most difficult for him. Reasons for remaining in London always seemed to prevail whenever he thought of relinquishing his agencies and returning to Philadelphia. Even in 1774, when he had brought about his own ruin in government circles and had begun to observe his London world collapsing around him, he still found it hard to leave. Yet his public humiliation at the Cockpit made it clear to him that his political effectiveness in England was over forever. Sorrowfully and haltingly he made plans to leave; it took him months of agonizing, plus news of Deborah's death, to send him finally on his way. In view of the legal action that was likely to be taken against him, his dilatoriness in departing is indeed remarkable. To the bitter end, though, he hoped—and worked—for a miracle that might bring reconciliation between Great Britain and her colonies.

# 10. "The Impending Calamities": Franklin's Final Months in London

Little by little, without ever being *officially* recognized as such, Benjamin Franklin emerged as spokesman for the American colonies in England. He was the most publicized American residing in the mother country, and he gladly assumed the role of colonial representative. The Doctor gloried in the thought that he had influence on both sides of the Atlantic. He even fancied himself as *the* conciliator, despite his less than impressive efforts at effecting compromise. It was no accident that the First Continental Congress called upon Franklin late in 1774 to rally all American agents for the purpose of laying Congress's petition before George III. The agent of four colonies had skillfully used his agencies to turn himself into an American hero, thus making him Congress's logical spokesman in London.

Although many British politicians saw the agent as a dangerous radical, they also recognized him as a man of great stature and powerful influence in America—a man to whom the colonists would listen. Consequently, prominent Englishmen who wanted to avert the tragedy of war between Britain and her colonies went to Franklin in one last effort to negotiate a settlement of Anglo-American differences. That these eleventh-hour negotiations were doomed from the start seems obvious in retrospect. In the winter of 1774–1775, however, a few would-be peacemakers were willing to grasp even at flimsy straws. The self-appointed English diplomats had no commission from the North ministry or any other agency of the British government to treat with Franklin. By the same token, he had no authority from Congress or any colony to participate in negotiations. Even so, the Doctor and several English parties proceeded to talk for over three months, hoping that they might be able to save the British Empire. Although the agent despaired of a settlement on more than one occasion and all but lost hope, he did not finally give up the effort and leave for home until after word reached him that Deborah was dead. Less than a month after receiving that sad news, the Doctor—at long last—sailed for Philadelphia.

On 5 February 1775, Franklin wrote to his friend Charles Thomson and explained how William Bollan and Arthur Lee had joined him in promoting the petition that had arrived from Congress in December.

Noting that the other agents, particularly Edmund Burke, Paul Wentworth, and Thomas Life, had excused themselves from participating, on the grounds that their constituents had sent them no instructions to do so, the Doctor observed that the three Massachusetts agents had acted according to their best judgment and the advice of America's sincere friends in London. The agent explained to Thomson in detail the steps that the three had taken in handling the petition, including their determination to wait until Parliament reconvened on 19 January 1775, and then to come out publicly with the petition two days later. They made arrangements with printer John Almon to have the petition printed and ready for distribution on the appointed day.[1]

Plans somehow went awry, as another printer, Thomas Becket, secured a copy of the material entrusted to Almon and published it on 16 January. The agents labeled Becket's production "Surreptitious as well as Materially and Grossly Erroneous," but the London press picked it up. Over the next few days three newspapers published Becket's version of the petition. Thus, through no fault of the Massachusetts agents, the petition was all over London before Parliament received it from the king.[2]

The agents were more than a little annoyed by the premature publication of the petition. That it happened actually mattered very little, however, since neither house of Parliament was prepared to treat the petition seriously anyway. George III sent it in "a great Heap of Letters of Intelligence," calling no particular attention to it. To add insult to injury, His Majesty placed the petition "last in the List" of documents. The House of Lords tabled the whole packet of material, while the House of Commons referred it to the committee of the whole. Reflecting on this unsatisfactory experience, Franklin told Thomson that petitions were useless and that only a "firm, steady, and faithful Adherence to the Non-Consumption Agreement" made by the Continental Congress would bring any results. In fact, the longtime agent thought he saw signs that commercial coercion was working, for British merchants and manufacturers had already begun to petition Parliament. The Doctor was convinced that economic pressure would ultimately lead Parliament "into reasonable Measures." The ministry expected Americans to become divided, Franklin asserted, but the agent hoped for continued unity. He was delighted that

---

[1] Benjamin Franklin to Charles Thomson, 5 February 1775, and other material. *Franklin Papers*, XXI, 450-53, 475-79.

[2] Ibid.

several prominent English political figures—Lords Camden, Chatham, and Shelburne, plus the Dukes of Richmond and Manchester—had spoken approvingly of Congress and the actions it had taken.[3]

At the time Franklin reported to Thomson on Congress's petition to the king, he was heartened by the support that appeared to be emerging for America among people in the mother country. Especially encouraging was the effort of the eminent William Pitt, Lord Chatham, once known as the Great Commoner and the man who had led Britain to victory in the French and Indian War. When American affairs were debated in the House of Lords on 20 January 1775, Chatham announced his intention of offering a plan to reconcile Britain and her colonies. A week later, his lordship consulted Franklin, outlined his proposals, and swore the agent to secrecy. Supposedly only the Doctor and Lord Camden were informed of Chatham's proposals before the legendary figure presented them to the House of Lords. Chatham shared his whole plan with Franklin on Sunday 29 January at the agent's residence on Craven Street. His lordship's horses were held in the street outside for two hours while the Doctor and Chatham discussed the matter. Before leaving Mrs. Stevenson's house, the great British leader told the agent that he would offer the plan to the House of Lords on 1 February. Chatham promised Franklin that the Doctor would have an opportunity to offer suggestions on 31 January.[4]

Consisting of nine articles, Chatham's proposal called for numerous concessions to the Americans on constitutional issues. His lordship was willing to limit Parliament's power to tax the colonies and to give ground on the highly controversial Declaratory Act. The once-mighty Chatham planned to call upon Parliament to repeal laws it had passed between 1764 and 1774 because Americans found them objectionable and because he believed the colonists resisted many of them for sound reasons. His lordship was not, however, willing to concede the right of the Crown to commit military troops in the colonies or to pay royal officials there. Franklin gloried in Chatham's efforts on behalf of compromise, and the agent especially appreciated the great one's visit to the Doctor's residence on 29 January—one year to the day after Franklin had been publicly humiliated at the Cockpit.[5]

---

[3]Ibid.

[4]Benjamin Franklin to William Franklin, 22 March 1775, and other material. Ibid., XXI, 459-62, 578-79.

[5]Ibid.

Lord Chatham's decision in January of 1775 to throw his support wholeheartedly into a campaign for Anglo-American reconciliation had been made only after careful deliberation. On several occasions before he made his move, his lordship sought information from Franklin. The first time was late August 1774, when Chatham summoned the agent to Hayes, Chatham's estate. His lordship wanted assurances from the Doctor that there was nothing to charges made in England that the colonists were determined to seek independence. Franklin assured him that the charges were untrue. The agent asserted that he had traveled all over the colonies and had never heard anyone "drunk or sober" express "a Wish for Separation."[6] Of course, the Doctor did not call attention to the fact that he had not set foot on American soil in ten years! The two men conferred again on 20 January in the House of Lords and on the twenty-seventh at Hayes.

At least three times, then, before Chatham's 29 January visit to Franklin, the two men had shared their views with one another. While they did not agree on all points of Anglo-American differences, their ideas were remarkably similar, and both sincerely wanted to find an acceptable formula for reconciliation. Franklin was in the House of Lords to hear Chatham's motion of 20 January. It called for the withdrawal of British troops from Boston. The motion, of course, was rejected. This disappointment was followed by the 27 January meeting at Hayes, the Craven Street conference on the twenty-ninth, and the final meeting two days later before Chatham introduced his plan to the House of Lords on 1 February. At each meeting with Franklin, Chatham seemed to listen to the American agent. Yet he brushed aside most of the Doctor's suggestions. When the great statesman offered his plan to the Lords on 1 February, Lord Sandwich, first lord of the Admiralty, delivered a tirade against it, contending that Franklin was the real architect of the plan. Chatham's peace proposals were voted down 61 to 32. The American agent was extremely disappointed. If the Lords would not heed so great a statesman as Chatham, what hope was there for reconciliation? As the Doctor saw it, most of the Lords had received Chatham's proposal with as "much Contempt" as a "Ballad offered by a drunken Porter."[7]

---

[6]Ibid., XXI, 547-49.

[7]Ibid., XXI, 463-64, 575-84. Also see: Benjamin Franklin to Charles Thomson, 5 February 1775. Ibid., XXI, 475-79.

Even before Parliament began its January 1775 debates on the American crisis and before Chatham took action to save the empire by offering his peace plan to the House of Lords, Franklin was carrying on secret negotiations aimed at bringing about reconciliation. Early in December of 1774 David Barclay, the Quaker banker, and Dr. John Fothergill, Franklin's former Quaker physician, approached the agent about working together on a possible peace plan. The two Quakers assured the Doctor that they had the ear of Lord Dartmouth and Thomas Villiers, Lord Hyde, who was a member of the Privy Council. The banker and physician expressed their willingness—and even eagerness—to serve as peace-brokers between Franklin and Whitehall. They urged the Doctor to list the concessions necessary to satisfy the colonists. Somehow, the two Quakers insisted, they would make those items palatable to Dart-mouth and Hyde.[8]

At approximately the same time Franklin began talking to Barclay and Fothergill, he was introduced to Caroline Howe, a prominent London socialite and sister to Lord Richard Howe, an admiral in the Royal Navy and a man with important government connections. Caroline was the widow of a relative, John Howe, and her house on Grafton Street was only a few doors from her brother's. Franklin was introduced to her as a worthy chess opponent, but their chess matches soon turned into negotiating sessions. On Christmas Day of 1774 Mrs. Howe informed the Doctor that her brother wished to talk to him. When Franklin agreed to meet Lord Howe, Caroline sent for his lordship. The admiral soon appeared and asked Franklin to submit points, in writing, that might constitute a basis for peace. Six days later the agent had a document pre-pared. Thus, the Doctor became involved in additional secret negotiations that paralleled those he was already conducting through Barclay and Fothergill. In both of these clandestine peace talks there was one common figure lurking in the background—Lord Hyde, who was a close friend of Lord Howe. The Privy Councilor was always in a position to compare what Franklin was saying to the two Quakers with what he was telling the admiral.[9]

In both instances the negotiations dragged on until the end of February—over two months. On 6 December 1774, two days after

---

[8]Benjamin Franklin to William Franklin, 22 March 1775, and other material. Ibid., XXI, 360-68, 549-53.

[9]Ibid., XXI, 360-64, 363 n. 5, 565-70.

Barclay and Fothergill prodded Franklin to draft points that might bring peace, the American agent presented the two Quakers with seventeen "Hints or Terms for a Durable Union." Included in the "Hints" were: (1) a promise to pay for the tea destroyed at Boston if the duty on tea was repealed and the duties already collected were repaid to the colonists, (2) a demand that various trade laws, such as the Navigation Acts, be reenacted in the colonies in order for them to remain law, (3) a call for all acts restraining American manufacturing to be reconsidered by the British government, (4) an insistence that the colonies be *asked* for money in time of war and be allowed to raise it themselves from taxes levied by them, (5) a return to the practice of all governors being paid by the legislatures in their respective colonies, (6) the restrictions of admiralty courts in America to the same powers that such courts exercised in England and no more, (7) Parliament's relinquishment of "All Powers of Internal Legislation in the Colonies." The demand calling for repeal of the Coercive Acts proved the most troublesome. Fundamentally, Franklin was insisting that the American part of the British Empire had to be run on American terms. He argued the points forcefully with Barclay and Fothergill, but little ground was given on either side. When Barclay sent the "Hints" to Lord Hyde on 12 December, the Quaker banker included a covering note saying that Franklin's proposals demanded too much. Hyde agreed with Barclay and called for modification. For about two months the banker worked on counter-proposals. By mid-February he felt confident that he had devised terms that both sides could accept.[10] The banker failed to realize that he was faced with reconciling opposing principles—a task tantamount to squaring the circle.

During the month of January 1775 the Doctor was saying privately to English friends that the ministry did not really want reconciliation. Yet the agent pushed on, encouraged by his pro-American friend the Bishop of St. Asaph, who refused to believe what Franklin was saying. The bishop wrote, "I am persuaded that the Government at present would be very glad of a Reconciliation, and if any method could be contriv'd to save their honour I doubt not they would come down to your Terms." What Franklin's dear friend in the church hierarchy did not know was that Barclay and Fothergill were getting nowhere with Dartmouth and Hyde, while the Doctor was receiving regular indications through the

---

[10]Donoughue, *British Politics*, 215-16; *Franklin Papers*, XXI, 360-68, 378-86, 553-64.

political grapevine in London that the American Secretary and the Privy Councilor would yield nothing on the principles at issue. For instance, it became clear to the agent that the ministry would make no concessions that implied a limit on Parliamentary power and would insist on the right to alter colonial charters by acts of Parliament.[11]

By 6 February, Fothergill could see that the negotiations were going nowhere, since Americans insisted on the repeal of the Coercive Acts *before* discussing reconciliation, while the ministry made it clear that the acts would not be repealed. Barclay, less pessimistic than his fellow Quaker, refused to give up and continued to search for some magic peace formula. The banker thought he had the answer on 16 February, when he dangled before Franklin the prospect of suspending the Boston Port Act in return for a promise that compensation would be paid for the destroyed tea. The Doctor was willing to guarantee payment for the tea, but he said that suspending one of the Coercive Acts was not enough; they *all* had to be *repealed*, not suspended.[12]

In the face of the new barrier erected by Franklin, Barclay next suggested the appointment of a peace commissioner and proposed some of the concessions Chatham had called for two weeks earlier. A day later, Barclay and Fothergill told Franklin that the Boston Port Act was the only one of the Coercive Acts that was negotiable. Upon hearing this, the agent gathered up his things to leave. When informed that his views would be reported, he asked for direct negotiations with the men in power. This request soon brought the negotiations to an end, but the three men did meet one last time on 17 March. At that meeting the two Quakers told Franklin that he and his fellow Americans were now on their own. By this time, Barclay and Fothergill had come around to the view that the Doctor had held since January—the ministry never seriously intended to make the concessions necessary to achieve reconciliation.[13]

The other negotiations, which Franklin carried on simultaneously with Lord Howe, seemed to go more smoothly. Unfortunately, they were just as barren of results as those conducted with the two Quakers. No doubt the Doctor felt compelled to be more circumspect in his comments to a prominent admiral and member of the peerage than to Quaker gentlemen

---

[11]Bargar, *Dartmouth and the Revolution*, 137; *Franklin Papers*, XXI, 447-48, 465-68, 479-82, 491-99, 528, 528 n. 2, 531-34, 585-91.

[12]Ibid (all sources cited).

[13]Ibid.

with whom he had long been acquainted. The proposals Franklin offered his lordship on 31 December 1774 contained the essence of the "Hints." They were, however, cast in less demanding terms. Echoing the demands of the Continental Congress, the agent called for repeal of all oppressive acts passed since 1763, withdrawal of British troops from Boston, payment of governors and judges' salaries by the colonial legislatures, and a return to the requisition system for raising money in the colonies. Howe asked if Franklin thought the appointment of a peace commissioner to talk to Congress or the colonies would be helpful. The Doctor answered affirmatively, but he added that all would depend on the right man being selected for the job.[14]

Weeks later, on 18 February 1775, Franklin and Howe met again at the home of the admiral's sister. His lordship announced that he expected to be named peace commissioner to America. Howe wanted the Doctor to accompany him to the colonies. Franklin said that he would leave on an hour's notice if the terms to be offered were acceptable. His lordship suggested that the agent discuss the matter with Lord Hyde and promised to arrange an interview. By this time, however, Hyde had learned from Barclay and Fothergill about Franklin's latest stance on the Coercive Acts, and his lordship saw no need to meet with the agent at that time. The Privy Councilor rightly perceived that Franklin's views and those of the British government were irreconcilable. When a week passed and the Doctor heard nothing further from Howe about the interview with Hyde, he inquired through Caroline Howe if he could be of any further use to Lord Howe. If not, he asserted, he would feel free "to take other Measures."[15]

Upon hearing Caroline's report of this conversation, Lord Howe requested a meeting with Franklin on 28 February, presumably to find out what the agent had meant by "other Measures" and to conduct further negotiations. At this meeting, Howe learned that "other Measures" simply meant that Franklin would leave England, because he had received news of Deborah's death. If, however, Howe was going to America as peace commissioner, the Doctor made it known that he was willing to wait and accompany his lordship. In the course of the conversation the agent explained to the admiral that his remarks to Caroline Howe had apparently been misunderstood. This prompted Howe to prevail upon Lord Hyde to

---

[14]Ibid., XXI, 408-411, 444-45, 499-503, 514-15, 584-85, 590.
[15]Ibid (all sources cited).

see Franklin on 1 March, but that interview achieved nothing. At a final meeting between Franklin and Howe on 7 March, his lordship asked the agent if he could count on the Doctor for help in the event that the admiral was subsequently sent to America as peace commissioner. Franklin assured Howe that he was willing to help at any time—in England or America.[16]

There was never much hope, if any, that Franklin's secret negotiations with Barclay and Fothergill and with Lord Howe would be successful. By early January the American agent was convinced that his diagnosis of the problem was fully accurate. The British government, at least most of those in it who made policy, did not really desire reconciliation. Instead, they wanted to put the colonists in their place. The only true peace-seekers were Dartmouth and North—the "moderate elements" in the ministry—and they were locked in a constant struggle with the "firmness group" in the Cabinet. Even Dartmouth and North did not pursue a steady course, being influenced now and again by those calling for stern measures—particularly the king, who believed that the colonists should submit to British authority and that coercion was the only way to make them submit. At one juncture Dartmouth claimed to be working for reconciliation even after he concluded that military force had to be used against the Americans. Negotiating with go-betweens for a ministry containing only two vacillating voices for peace was altogether unpromising, and Franklin sensed this long before Barclay, Fothergill, and Lord Howe understood it. The Doctor also knew that Americans would never accept Parliamentary authority over colonial legislatures and that Parliament, the ministry, and George III would accept nothing less.[17] The two positions were simply irreconcilable, and the agent knew Americans and Englishmen well enough to know that neither would give up their deep-seated principles.

At the very time Dr. Franklin told friends in England that there was little hope for peace (because of the ministry's inflexible policies and its determination to bridle the Americans), he was saying almost the opposite when writing to people in the colonies. On 28 January 1775, he wrote to Thomas Cushing to urge a defusing of the situation in Boston. The people there should be patient, the agent admonished, until the king acted upon

---

[16]Ibid.

[17]Bargar, *Dartmouth and the Revolution*, 137-42, 145, 147, 149, 164; Donoughue, *British Politics*, 216, 224-25, 230; Newcomb, *Franklin and Galloway*, 264.

Congress's petition and until the friends of America in Parliament—especially Lord Chatham—completed their efforts on behalf of reconciliation. Petitions for reconciliation, the Doctor noted, poured into Parliament from all quarters. Even when reporting that more troops and ships were being sent to America, Franklin did so quite matter-of-factly. As late as 25 February he wrote to James Bowdoin that America's steadfast adherence to the non-consumption agreement made by the Continental Congress would bring down "the adverse Ministry" in less than a year and result in the American colonists carrying their point again. On 13 March—just a little over a week before he sailed for home—Franklin said much the same thing in letters to Humphrey Marshall and Charles Thomson, telling the latter that strict adherence to non-consumption would cause British commercial and manufacturing interests to keep up the pressure on the government. The end result, the agent professed to believe, would be the ministry's being "overthrown and routed, and the Friends of America come into Administration."[18]

Meanwhile, Franklin sent Joseph Galloway some mixed signals. Galloway had introduced a plan of union at the Continental Congress, only to see it defeated by a one-vote margin. At Galloway's request, the Doctor showed the plan to Lords Camden and Chatham and promised to make sure that members of the ministry received a copy of it. Franklin's attitude and comments at this point must have confused and frustrated Galloway. The Doctor wrote of "the impending Calamities," while at the same time he spoke of an American victory over the ministry—if Americans remained steadfast on non-consumption. Although the agent had long favored such a union as the one proposed in Galloway's plan, he now appeared hesitant about it. The Doctor feared that a closer union with the "old rotten State" of Britain might bring "more Mischief than Benefit." He also thought that the colonies should not enter into a union unless Britain first agreed to yield on many of the demands he had made in the "Hints" that he had recently drafted for Barclay and Fothergill. In spite of his growing suspicions about British corruption and injustice, the agent was still ready to "try anything" to avoid war with "such near Relations." Franklin also had a warning for the Pennsylvania politician,

---

[18]Benjamin Franklin to Thomas Cushing, 28 January 1775; Benjamin Franklin to James Bowdoin, 28 February 1775; Benjamin Franklin to Humphrey Marshall, 13 March 1775; Benjamin Franklin to Charles Thomson, 13 March 1775. *Franklin Papers*, XXI, 456-58, 506-507, 520-22.

for Galloway was becoming known around London as a pro-British advocate who provided some of the ministers with "private Intelligence" from America. Claiming not to believe these stories, the agent noted that friendship compelled him to tell his fellow Pennsylvanian about them.[19]

Five days before Franklin wrote to Galloway about London rumors portraying the Pennsylvania legislator as pro-British and just about the time that the Doctor's negotiations with Barclay and Fothergill collapsed, Lord North presented to Parliament a peace plan. Offered on 20 February, with the grudging consent of George III, the North proposal provided for the colonists taxing themselves to raise funds for "the common Defense." After being raised, the money would be placed at Parliament's disposal. The colonies were also to provide "for the Support of the Civil Government, and the Administration of Justice," and the only taxes thenceforth to be levied against them by Parliament were to be "Duties . . . expedient to impose for the Regulation of Commerce." After "a good deal of wild Debate," North's conciliatory motion passed in the House of Commons on 27 February by a vote of 274 to 88.[20]

To most Englishmen the North Proposal appeared to grant large concessions, but not to Franklin. When he met Lord Hyde on 1 March, the Doctor was informed by his lordship that North's plan should be conciliatory enough to bring peace. When the agent disagreed, Hyde asked him what was wrong with the plan. Franklin replied that the reference to taxation was too open-ended. No limits were placed on the amounts Parliament could request. Hence the individual colonies would have no say in what was fair for each of them to pay. Parliament could easily become like "a Highway-man who presents his Pistol and Hat at a Coach-Window, demanding no specific Sum, but if you give all your Money or what he is pleas'd to think sufficient, he will civilly omit putting his own Hand into your Pockets. If not, there is his Pistol." Besides requiring open-ended taxation, North had failed to address the "new Dispute" raised by Parliament's "pretending to a Power of altering our Charters and establish'd Laws." Hyde gently warned Franklin that North and the ministry had gone as far toward accommodating American

---

[19]Benjamin Franklin to Joseph Galloway, 5-[7] and 25 February 1775. Ibid., XXI, 468-71, 508-510.

[20]Bargar, *Dartmouth and the Revolution*, 138-42, 145; Donoughue, *British Politics*, 248-51; Benjamin Franklin to William Franklin, 22 March 1775. *Franklin Papers*, XXI, 592-96.

demands as they could and would go and urged the agent to cooperate. The Doctor insisted that he had already demonstrated his good faith by offering, without instructions, to pay for the tea destroyed at Boston. By doing so, he had risked his "whole Fortune."[21]

As noted earlier, nothing was achieved by this interview. Franklin demonstrated that all the inflexibility was not on the British side. For years the agent had advocated a return to the requisition system, one suspects because it was popular with most Americans. In effect, North's conciliatory proposal would have achieved that goal, and Franklin said a firm "no" to it, distorting North's intentions and contending in so many words that the plan was some sort of trap. The meeting between the agent and Lord Hyde on 1 March ended, for all practical purposes, the Doctor's secret negotiations. When Franklin saw Lord Howe six days later, the admiral admitted that the negotiations had broken down completely.[22]

Franklin was not totally alone in his opposition to North's peace plan. In the House of Commons David Hartley, a member of Parliament who would be involved years later at the negotiations in Paris to end the Revolutionary War, was against North's plan from the outset. Like Franklin, Hartley interpreted the proposal as a plan to coerce Americans into granting money instead of asking them for it as a free gift. A few days after the Doctor's departure from London, Hartley went so far as to introduce a motion in the House of Commons. In it, he called upon Parliament to return to the old requisition system in its traditional form, which meant asking each colony in times of emergency to give what it could to support the king's cause. Hartley based his motion on information that had been furnished him by Franklin. It was, of course, rejected.[23]

By the time Franklin was preparing to leave England, he was growing hostile toward British leaders who, in his mind, were condemning the colonies without justification. On 16 March he went to the House of Lords to hear Lord Camden speak on American affairs. As he watched and listened from the gallery, supporters of the ministry attacked his countrymen as "Knaves" who were looking for a way out of paying their debts. None was more vicious in his verbal assaults than Lord Sandwich. Franklin bristled with anger when he left the chamber. Within hours he had drafted a venomous memorial to Lord Dartmouth. In it, he said that

---

[21] Ibid (all sources cited).

[22] *Franklin Papers*, XXI, 596-97.

[23] Benjamin Franklin to David Hartley, 26 February [1775]. Ibid., XXI, 511-12.

Americans would never again help England in war, unless the British government compensated the colonies for all the injuries they had suffered from Parliament's unjust acts. The agent showed the memorial to Thomas Walpole, who revealed it to Lord Camden. Both men advised the Doctor not to send it. Deferring to their counsel, Franklin left London without delivering his parting insult.[24]

For as long as Franklin remained in England he continued to be called on for representation by Pennsylvania, New Jersey, and Massachusetts, and he supplied his constituents with information almost to the end. As late as 14 and 15 February 1775, he reported to Pennsylvania and New Jersey concerning laws they had under review at Whitehall. Not until 19 March did he turn the Massachusetts agency over to Arthur Lee. Franklin left saying that he might return in the fall, but he promised Lee that, even if he did come back, he would not undertake the Massachusetts agency again.[25]

Thus, even though he left England with the threat of legal prosecution hanging over his head, the embattled Franklin entertained thoughts of returning in a few months. One can only wonder when he finally would have left London, if he had not desperately needed to return home to put his affairs in order. Deborah's death made his departure for Philadelphia absolutely necessary. She had suffered a stroke in 1769 and had grown steadily worse ever since, but Franklin had chosen to take no notice of it. On 14 December 1774, she had suffered another stroke. In less than a week, she had passed on. Dying on 19 December, she was buried on the twenty-second. On Christmas Eve, Richard Bache wrote a letter to explain the sad details to his father-in-law. That same day, William Franklin wrote to his father, and, after reporting Deborah's death, chided the Doctor for delaying so long his return to family and home. William's words of reproach probably provide an accurate explanation for the main reason (besides the agent's love of living in London) why Franklin tarried so long in England when he had needed to go home. William wrote:

---

[24]Ibid., XXI, 526-29, 598.

[25]Benjamin Franklin to the New Jersey Assembly's Committee of Correspondence, 14 February 1775; Benjamin Franklin to the Pennsylvania Assembly's Committee of Correspondence, 15 February 1775; Benjamin Franklin to Arthur Lee, 19 March 1775. Ibid., XXI, 489-91, 491 n. 3, 534-35.

If there was any Prospect of your being able to bring the People in Power to your Way of Thinking, or of those of your Way of Thinking's being brought into Power, I should not think so much of your Stay. But as you have had by this Time pretty strong Proofs that neither can be reasonably expect'd and that you are look'd upon with an evil Eye in that Country, and are in no small Danger of being brought into Trouble [i.e., being prosecuted] for your political Conduct, you had certainly better return.[26]

William was probably right in thinking that his father's principal reason for remaining in England was a vain hope that a dramatic change in the personnel at the top echelons of the British government would sooner or later take place. The New Jersey governor knew his father well, and he was obviously irked at the Doctor for engaging in too much wishful thinking and for not returning home to his family. The younger Franklin must have also wondered why the Doctor was so nonchalant about the "Danger of being brought into Trouble" for securing and sending the Hutchinson-Oliver letters to Boston.

On 20 March 1775, Franklin finally took his leave of London. He spent the day before his departure with his old friend Joseph Priestly. At the time the Doctor left, he owed Margaret Stevenson four years' rent, or £400, plus over £470 she had lent him to cover his obligations. Soon after he arrived in Philadelphia, he sent her £871, nineteen shillings, and one-half pence. The Doctor arrived in Philadelphia on 5 May 1775; the next day he was elected to the upcoming Second Continental Congress, scheduled to meet on 10 May. For weeks he said nothing publicly, while rumors circulated that he had become a British spy. When Franklin began to express his pro-American views openly, the rumors subsided.[27]

The Doctor tried, but failed, to persuade his son William and former political partner Joseph Galloway to endorse his positions on the Anglo-American rift. Galloway, ravaged by poor health and by the political rejection of his constituents, was determined to save the empire—an objective Franklin had finally recognized as futile. Protected by the British army after 1776, Galloway fled to England in 1778 to live out his days in a self-imposed exile, supported by a pension from Parliament. He

---

[26]Richard Bache to Benjamin Franklin, 24 December 1774; William Franklin to Benjamin Franklin, 24 December 1774. Ibid., XXI 400-405.

[27]Benjamin Franklin to Lord Bessborough, 16 March 1775, and other material. Ibid., XXI, 525-26, 526 n.2, 539; Jensen, *Founding of a Nation*, 618-19.

eventually denounced Benjamin Franklin as the "chief conspirator." In so many words, Galloway, like Thomas Hutchinson, blamed the Revolution on the Doctor's sending the Hutchinson-Oliver letters to Boston. Without ever seeing his wife or home again, Galloway died in England in 1803.[28]

William Franklin also died an exile in England. He and his father remained estranged for as long as the Doctor lived. In 1788 the elder Franklin altered his will, leaving to William nothing except some worthless lands in Nova Scotia and some books and papers that were already in William's hands. Franklin senior's reason was simple—revenge. He in effect cut William out of his will because of the "part he acted against me in the late War." In the Doctor's mind, William deserved none of the "Estate he endeavored to deprive me of." As had Galloway, eleven years before him, William passed away in 1814, in the country he had refused to abandon when revolution brought disruption to the British Empire.[29]

Benjamin Franklin, as he had always done (at least in his private convictions and anonymous pieces of propaganda, if not always in public declaration), cast his lot with the colonies. Through it all, he proved himself to be a devious man, one who often sent mixed signals and kept people guessing about his true intentions, but in the end he emerged as a leading spirit of the American Revolution, a hero, and a revered member of the pantheon of the new nation's Founding Fathers.

---

[28]Newcomb, *Franklin and Galloway*, 281-83, 287-91.
[29]Skemp, *Patriot and Loyalist*, 151; Skemp, *William Franklin*, 274-76.

# Conclusion

For almost fifteen and one-half years, between 1757 and 1775, Benjamin Franklin lived on Craven Street in London, not far from the banks of the Thames River. Those years were pivotal in his public career. When he left Philadelphia for London in 1757, as an agent for the Pennsylvania Assembly, he expected to remain in England just long enough to complete his mission—perhaps a few months—and then return to Philadelphia. That mission was to persuade the Pennsylvania proprietors, Thomas and Richard Penn, to help the province with expenses for defense by allowing their estates to be taxed in the same way that the colonists' estates were taxed.

The Penns, as in the past, proved tightfisted, and Franklin was compelled to stay much longer than he expected. As months turned into years, he grew increasingly fond of London. He especially enjoyed the praise and acclaim given him by fellow philosophers and scientists. Already famous in the colonies and Europe for his experiments in electricity, he was delighted to receive the honors that came his way in England—membership in the Royal Society and honorary doctors' degrees from established British universities. On the political front, life was not so pleasant. After five years of fighting with Thomas Penn, Franklin—henceforth called the Doctor by many—could go back to Philadelphia claiming that he had carried out his mission. The proprietors, he proudly proclaimed, would be compelled to contribute to Pennsylvania's defense by paying taxes on their estates. Yet he returned to the City of Brotherly Love with secret plans to return to England. Franklin intended to persuade the Pennsylvania Assembly to call for the overthrow of the proprietors in favor of a royal government for the colony. Furthermore, he planned to manipulate that body into sending *him* back to the mother country to effect that political change. Deviously he maneuvered the Assembly into going along with his wishes, and in late 1764 he sailed for England, carrying with him a petition requesting that the king take over Pennsylvania and turn it into a royal colony. His new mission was doomed to total failure. By 1767 Franklin suspected that there would be no royalization of Pennsylvania, and by the end of the following year Lord Hillsborough, Secretary of State for the American Department, dealt the final blow to the Pennsylvania petition.

Meanwhile, the Pennsylvania agent had become embroiled in the disturbances over the Stamp Act and the Townshend Duty Act. During the

Stamp Act crisis he almost ruined himself politically in America because of his acquiescence in that detested statute. Only after a herculean public-relations campaign did he recoup his reputation as a loyal American. Not only did he recover, but he was able to turn hostile colonial opinion completely around and make himself into a hero as one of the people who contributed significantly to securing the hated law's repeal.

Ever after, Dr. Franklin was quite cautious about acquiescing in a British policy before ascertaining which way the political winds were blowing back home. During the Townshend Duty crisis he stood squarely behind the American position, and he was careful to express all the sentiments that endeared him to his fellow colonists. Franklin was not exactly hypocritical, since he was, in fact, gradually becoming radical in his views. By 1769 he had become convinced that Parliament had no right to make laws for the colonies without the consent of the colonists themselves or of their representatives. In view of the Declaratory Act of 1766, this was indeed a radical stance, since that law claimed for Parliament the right to legislate for the colonies "in all cases whatsoever."

Even though the Doctor was turning into a radical, he still delighted in his life on Craven Street in London, and he recoiled at the thought of returning to Philadelphia without a royal charter. If he went home, he would have to go back as a failure. He would have to live under the proprietary government of Thomas Penn, a revolting prospect, to say the least. Consequently, he considered other alternatives, such as securing a good post in the British government and living out his life in London. He also, it seems, thought of returning to America and moving to Massachusetts, the province of his birth. His attempt to win an important government post in London failed, mainly because the influential political figures who were in power regarded him as too much of an American and suspected him of holding radical views. While he never did anything about moving to Massachusetts, he did become closely identified with that colony by being appointed agent for the Massachusetts House of Representatives in 1770. By that time he had also become agent for Georgia and New Jersey and thus held four concurrent agencies. This made him the most visible of American agents in London and prepared the way for him to assume the role of American spokesman in the mother country. His appointment by the Massachusetts lower house forced him to support the very radical ideas and sometimes violent actions of his Massachusetts constituents. Before long he was marked indelibly in the minds of some

British political leaders as a thoroughgoing radical who was not to be trusted—in spite of his public advocacy of moderation and reconciliation.

As Franklin adopted views and took actions that were applauded by his fellow Americans, he alienated more and more British leaders. There were times when even his close friends found it difficult to defend him. After his part in securing and sending the Hutchinson-Oliver letters to Thomas Cushing became widely known, there were few in England who were willing to speak a good word for him. Indeed, he stood in danger of being legally prosecuted, and many thought he should be. As his reputation in Britain slipped steadily downhill, his star rose precipitously in America. His effectiveness as an agent in London had vanished well over a year before he sailed for Philadelphia, but his political stock had never been higher in the colonies. Upon his return home in 1775 he was rewarded with a seat in Congress, membership on the congressional committee that prepared the Declaration of Independence, and an appointment by Congress to be the first American minister to France. In France he became America's first great diplomat, distinguishing himself in Paris. After nine years among the French, Franklin returned to Philadelphia in time to participate as a member of the convention that produced the Constitution of the United States.

The Craven Street years were crucial in determining Franklin's place in history, for they provided him with the opportunity to assume for himself a prominent place as an *American* (not just a provincial) leader. Through his work as a colonial agent for Pennsylvania, Georgia, New Jersey, and Massachusetts the Doctor was transformed from Pennsylvania politician into spokesman for all the colonies. Had it not been for those years as agent, Franklin would be hurriedly passed over by historians as a fairly obscure scientist, inventor, and early American literary figure. Thanks to his devious nature, which enabled him to conceal his true intentions and motives from most people, and his shrewdness in crafting a public image, which made him a hero to the people who turned out to be on the winning side in the American Revolution, Benjamin Franklin's name has been a household word in the United States from the time of its founding to the present moment.

# Bibliography

## I. Primary Sources
### A. Manuscripts

Baynton-Morgan-Wharton Papers, 1725–1789. Historical Society of Pennsylvania.

Franklin, Benjamin. Account of Expenses of my Voyage to England, 1757–1762. Library of the American Philosophical Society.

_____. Manuscripts. British Museum.

Jones, Noble Wimberly; Papers. Perkins Library, Duke University, Durham, NC.

Ohio Company [William Trent] Papers, Etting Collection. Historical Society of Pennsylvania.

Penn Papers. Historical Society of Pennsylvania.

Thomas Wharton Letter Book, 1773–1784. Historical Society of Pennsylvania.

### B. Published Sources

*Acts of the Privy Council of England*, 6 volumes. Colonial Series. London: His Majesty's Stationery Office, 1908–1912.

*The Burd Papers*. Extracts from Chief Justice William Allen's Letter Book. Selected and arranged by Lewis Burd Walker. n. p., 1897.

Candler, Allen Daniel, and Lucian Lamar Knight, eds. *The Colonial Records of the State of Georgia*, 25 volumes. Atlanta: State of Georgia, 1904–1916 [volumes I-XXVI except XX and typescript volumes XXVII-XXXIX except XXVII and XXVIII, parts 1 and 2, 1937.

Carlyle, Alexander. *Autobiography of the Rev. Dr. Alexander Carlyle*. Edinburgh and London: W. Blackwood and Sons, 1860.

Coleman, Kenneth, and Milton Ready, eds. *The Colonial Records of the State of Georgia*, volumes XX, XXVII, XXVIII, parts 1 and 2. Athens: University of Georgia Press, 1977–1979.

Corner, Betsy C., and Christopher Booth, eds. *Chain of Friendship: Letters of Dr. John Fothergill*. Cambridge MA: The Belknap Press, 1971.

Crane, Verner W., ed. *Benjamin Franklin's Letters to the Press, 1758–1775*. Chapel Hill: University of North Carolina Press, 1950.

[John Dickinson]. "The Reasons on Which Were Founded the Protest Offered by Certain Members of the Assembly to that Body Concerning the Sending of Mr. Franklin to England as Assistant to our Agent there." From the *Pennsylvania Journal* of 1 November 1764. Reprinted: Philadelphia, 1878. Located in the Benjamin Franklin Collection, Yale University.

Egle, William H., ed. *Pennsylvania Archives*. Volumes 1-30. Third Series. Harrisburg: State of Pennsylvania, 1894–1899.

*The Examination of Doctor Benjamin Franklin, before an August Assembly, relating to the Repeal of the Stamp-Act, & c.* Philadelphia: Hall & Sellers, 1766. Located in the John Carter Brown Library, Brown University.

[Benjamin Franklin]. *The Interest of Great Britain Considered With Regard to her Colonies and the Acquisitions of Canada and Guadeloupe.* Second Edition. London: Printed for T. Becket, at Tilly's Head, near Surry-Street in the Strand, 1761. Located in the Rare Book Room, Perkins Library, Duke University.

Hazard, Samuel, ed. *Pennsylvania Archives.* Volumes 1-12. First Series. Philadelphia: State of Pennsylvania, 1852–1856.

Hutchinson, Thomas. *The History of the Province of Massachusetts Bay From 1749-1774,* Volume III. London: John Murray, Albemarle Street, 1828. Located in the Benjamin Franklin Collection, Yale University.

_____. *The History of the Colony and Province of Massachusetts-Bay,* 3 volumes. Cambridge MA: Harvard University Press, 1936.

*Journals of the Commissioners for Trade and Plantations, 1704-1782,* 14 volumes. London: His Majesty's Stationery Office, 1920–1938. (Cited after the first instance as *Journals of the Board of Trade* by appropriate dates.)

*Journals of the House of Representatives of Massachusetts, 1770–1771,* Volume 47; and *1772–1773,* Volume 49. Boston: Massachusetts Historical Society, 1978 and 1980.

Labaree, Leonard W., and others, eds. *The Autobiography of Benjamin Franklin.* New Haven and London: Yale University Press, 1964.

_____, and others, eds. *The Papers of Benjamin Franklin,* Volumes 1-14; Willcox, William B. and others, eds., Volumes 15-22. New Haven and London: Yale University Press, 1959–1982. (Cited after the first instance as *Franklin Papers.* Volumes 23 and following go beyond the years of this study and were neither used nor cited.)

Linn, John B., and William H. Egle, eds. *Pennsylvania Archives,* Volumes 1-19. Second Series. Harrisburg: State of Pennsylvania, 1874–1890.

MacKinney, Gertrude, and Charles F. Hoban, eds. *Pennsylvania Archives,* Volumes 1-8. Eighth Series. Harrisburg: State of Pennsylvania, 1931–1935.

_____, eds. *Pennsylvania Archives,* Volumes 1-10. Ninth Series. Harrisburg: State of Pennsylvania, 1931–1935.

Montgomery, Thomas Lynch, ed. *Pennsylvania Archives,* Volumes 1-14. Sixth Series. Harrisburg: State of Pennsylvania, 1905–1907.

_____, ed., *Pennsylvania Archives,* Volumes 1-5. Seventh Series. Harrisburg: State of Pennsylvania, 1914. Index to Sixth Series.

*The Papers of Sir William Johnson,* 12 volumes. Albany: The University Press of the State of New York, 1921–1957.

*Pennsylvania Colonial Records,* 16 volumes. Harrisburg: Published by the State of Pennsylvania, Printed by Theo. Penn & Co., 1838–1853.

Reed, George Edward, ed., *Pennsylvania Archives*, Volumes 1-12. Fourth Series. Harrisburg: State of Pennsylvania, 1900–1902.

Simmons, R. C. and P. D. G. Thomas, eds., *Proceedings and Debates of the British Parliaments Respecting North America, 1754–1783*, six volumes. Millwood, NY and other cities: Kraus International Publications, 1982–1987. Volume VI covers through May 1776.

Stevens, Benjamin F., compiler, *Facsimiles of Manuscripts in European Archives Relating to America, 1773–1783*, 25 volumes. Wilmington DE: Mellifont Press, 1970.

Whitehead, William A. and others, eds., *New Jersey Archives*, Volumes 1-42. Newark and other NJ cities: New Jersey Historical Society, 1880–1949.

## C. Journals, Magazines, and Newspapers

*The Annual Register, 1758–1790.* Located in the Rare Book Room, Perkins Library, Duke University, and in the British Museum.

*The Gazetteer and New Daily Advertiser.* Located in the British Museum.

*The Gentleman's Magazine.* Located in the British Museum.

*Georgia* [Savannah] *Gazette*, 1764–1770. Located in the Georgia Archives, Atlanta, Georgia.

*Lloyd's Evening Post and British Chronicle.* Located in the British Museum.

*The London Chronicle.* Located in the Rare Book Room, Perkins Library, Duke University and in the British Museum.

*The London Evening Post.* Located in the British Museum.

*The London Magazine.* Located in the British Museum.

*The Public Advertiser.* Located in the British Museum.

# II. Secondary Works
## A. Reference Works

Andrews, Charles M. and Frances C. Davenport, *Guide to the Manuscript Materials for the History of the United States to 1783, in the British Museum, in Minor London Archives, and in the Libraries of Oxford and Cambridge.* Washington, DC: Published by the Carnegie Institution of Washington, 1908.

Andrews, Charles M. *Guide to Materials for American History to 1783, in the Public Record Office of Great Britain*: Volume I: *The State Papers*; Volume II: *Departmental and Miscellaneous Papers.* Washington, DC: Published by the Carnegie Institution of Washington, 1912 and 1914.

Buxbaum, Melvin H. *Benjamin Franklin, 1721–1906: A Reference Guide.* Boston: Hall, 1983.

Johnson, Allen, and Dumas Malone, eds., *The Dictionary of American Biography*, 20 volumes. New York: Charles Scribner's Sons, 1928–1936.

Stephen, Sir Leslie, Sir Sidney Lee and others, eds., *The Dictionary of National Biography*. 22 volumes and 7 supplementary volumes. London and Oxford: Oxford University Press, 1921–1981.

## B. Biographies and Monographs

Abbot, William W. *The Royal Governors of Georgia, 1754–1775*. Chapel Hill: University of North Carolina Press for the Institute of Early American History and Culture, 1959.

Abernethy, Thomas P. *Western Lands and the American Revolution*. New York: Russell and Russell, 1959.

Allen, Robert J. *Clubs of Augustan London*. Cambridge MA: Harvard University Press, 1933.

Bailyn, Bernard. *The Ordeal of Thomas Hutchinson*. Cambridge MA: Harvard University Press, 1974.

Bargar, B. D. *Lord Dartmouth and the American Revolution*. Columbia: University of South Carolina Press, 1965.

Burlingame, Roger. *Benjamin Franklin, Envoy Extraordinary*. New York: Coward-McCann, 1967.

Butler, Ruth L. *Dr. Franklin, Postmaster General* Garden City NY: Doubleday, Doran and Company, 1928.

Buxbaum, Melvin H. *Benjamin Franklin and the Zealous Presbyterians*. University Park: Pennsylvania State University Press, 1975.

Carr, William G. *The Oldest Delegate: Franklin in the Constitutional Convention*. Cranbury NJ: University of Delaware Press, 1990.

Carroll, Rachel W. "Benjamin Franklin, Colonial Agent to Great Britain, 1757–1762." Unpublished Master's Thesis, University of North Carolina at Chapel Hill, 1937.

Chancellor, E. Beresford. *The Pleasure Haunts of London*. Boston and New York: Houghton Mifflin Company, 1925.

Clark, Ronald. *Benjamin Franklin: A Biography*. New York: Random House, 1983.

Cone, Carl B. *Burke and the Nature of Politics: The Age of the American Revolution*. Lexington: University of Kentucky Press, 1957.

_____. *Torchbearer of Freedom: The Influence of Richard Price on Eighteenth Century Thought*. Lexington: University of Kentucky Press, 1952.

Conner, Paul W. *Poor Richard's Politicks: Benjamin Franklin and His New American Order*. New York: Oxford University Press, 1965.

Crane, Verner W. *Benjamin Franklin: Englishman and American*. Baltimore: Published for Brown University by Williams & Wilkins Company, 1936.

Currey, Cecil B. *Code Number 72: Ben Franklin: Patriot or Spy?* Englewood Cliffs NJ: Prentice-Hall, 1972.

_____. *Road to Revolution: Benjamin Franklin in England, 1765–1775.* Garden City NY: Doubleday & Company, 1968.

Davidson, Philip. *Propaganda and the American Revolution, 1763-1783.* Chapel Hill: University of North Carolina Press, 1941.

Donoughue, Bernard. *British Politics and the American Revolution: The Path to War, 1773–1775.* London: Macmillan and Co.; New York: St. Martin's Press, 1964.

Ernst, Joseph A. *Money and Politics in America, 1765–1775.* Chapel Hill: University of North Carolina Press, 1973.

Fay, Bernard. *Franklin, The Apostle of Modern Times.* Boston: Little, Brown and Company, 1929.

Fox, Richard H. *Dr. John Fothergill and His Friends.* London: Macmillan and Company, 1919.

George, M. Dorothy. *London Life in the XVIII Century.* New York: Alfred A. Knopf, 1925.

_____. *English Social Life in the Eighteenth Century.* London: The Sheldon Press; New York and Toronto: The Macmillan Company, 1923.

Gipson, Lawrence H. *The British Empire Before the American Revolution*, 13 volumes. New York: Alfred A. Knopf, 1936–1967.

Goodman, Nathan G. *Benjamin Franklin on Religion.* Philadelphia: The Franklin Institute, 1938.

Hanna, William S. *Benjamin Franklin and Pennsylvania Politics.* Stanford CA: Stanford University Press, 1964.

Harlan, Robert D. *William Strahan: Eighteenth Century London Printer and Publisher.* University of Michigan, Ph. D. Dissertation, 1960. Ann Arbor: University Microfilms, 1960.

Hawke, David F. *Franklin.* New York and other cities: Harper and Row, Publishers, 1976.

Henretta, James A. *The Evolution of American Society, 1700–1815.* Lexington MA: D. C. Heath and Company, 1973.

Holmes, Abdiel. *The Life of Ezra Stiles.* Boston: Published according to Act of Congress, printed by Thomas & Andrews, 1798.

Hutson, James H. *Pennsylvania Politics, 1746–1770: The Movement for Royal Government and Its Consequences.* Princeton NJ: Princeton University Press, 1972.

Illick, Joseph E. *Colonial Pennsylvania: A History.* New York: Charles Scribner's Sons, 1976.

Jackson, F. J. Foakes. *Social Life in England, 1750–1850.* New York: The Macmillan Company, 1916.

Jacobson, David L. *John Dickinson and the Revolution in Pennsylvania, 1764–1776.* Berkeley: University of California Press, 1965.

Jensen, Merrill. *The Founding of a Nation.* New York: Oxford University Press, 1968.

Kelly, Joseph J., Jr. *Pennsylvania: The Colonial Years, 1681–1776.* Garden City NY: Doubleday and Company, 1980.

Ketcham, Ralph. *Benjamin Franklin.* New York: Washington Square Press, 1966.

Kammen, Michael G. *A Rope of Sand: The Colonial Agents, British Politics, and the American Revolution.* Ithaca NY: Cornell University Press, 1968.

LeMay, J. A. Leo. *Benjamin Franklin: Writings.* New York: The Library of America, 1987.

_____. *The Oldest Revolutionary: Essays on Benjamin Franklin.* Philadelphia: University of Pennsylvania Press, 1976.

Lincoln, Charles H. *The Revolutionary Movement in Pennsylvania, 1760–1776.* Philadelphia: University of Pennsylvania Press, 1901.

Lonn, Ella. *The Colonial Agents of the Southern Colonies.* Chapel Hill: University of North Carolina Press, 1945.

Lopez, Claude-Anne. *Mon Cher Papa: Franklin and the Ladies of Paris.* New Haven and London: Yale University Press, 1966.

_____ and Eugenia W. Herbert. *The Private Franklin: The Man and His Family.* New York and London: W. W. Norton Company, 1975.

Marshall, Dorothy. *Dr. Johnson's London.* New York: John Wiley & Sons, 1968.

Meyer, Donald H. *The Democratic Enlightenment.* New York: G. P. Putnam's Sons, 1976.

Morgan, Edmund S. and Helen M. *The Stamp Act Crisis: Prologue to Revolution.* Chapel Hill: Published for the Institute of Early American History and Culture by the University of North Carolina Press, 1953.

Mott, Frank L. and Chester E. Jorgenson, eds., *Benjamin Franklin: Representative Selections with Introduction, Bibliography and Notes.* Revised Edition. New York, Cincinnati, etc.: American Book Company, 1962. Originally published in 1936.

Nash, Gary. *Class and Society in Early America.* Englewood Cliffs NJ: Prentice-Hall, 1970.

Newcomb, Benjamin H. *Franklin and Galloway: A Political Partnership.* New Haven: Yale University Press, 1972.

Nolan, J. Bennett. *Benjamin Franklin in Scotland and Ireland, 1759 and 1771.* Philadelphia: University of Pennsylvania Press, 1956.

Parton, James. *The Life and Times of Benjamin Franklin,* 2 volumes. New York: DeCapo Press, 1971. Originally published in 1864.

Randall, Willard S. *A Little Revenge: Benjamin Franklin and His Son.* Boston and Toronto: Little, Brown and Company, 1984.

Riley, Isaac W. *American Philosophy, The Early Schools*. New York: Dodd, Mead and Company, 1907.

Ritcheson, Charles R. *British Politics and the American Revolution*. Norman: University of Oklahoma Press, 1954.

Schlesinger, Arthur M., Sr. *The Colonial Merchants and the American Revolution, 1763–1776*. New York: Atheneum, 1968. Originally published in 1918.

Schwartz, Richard B. *Daily Life in Johnson's London*. Madison: University of Wisconsin Press, 1983.

Shelley, Henry C. *Inns and Taverns of Old London*. Boston: L. C. Page & Company, 1923.

Shepherd, William R. *History of the Proprietary Government of Pennsylvania*. New York: A. M. S. Press, 1967. Originally published in 1896.

Skemp. Sheila L. *Benjamin and William Franklin: Father and Son, Patriot and Loyalist*. Boston and New York: Bedford Books of St. Martin's Press, 1994.

_____. *William Franklin: Son of a Patriot, Servant of a King*. New York: Oxford University Press, 1990.

Sosin, Jack. *Agents and Merchants: British Colonial Policy, 1763–1775*. Lincoln: University of Nebraska Press, 1965.

_____. *Whitehall and the Wilderness*. Lincoln: University of Nebraska Press, 1961.

Thayer, Theodore. *Pennsylvania Politics and the Growth of Democracy, 1740–1776*. Harrisburg: Pennsylvania Historical and Museum Commission, 1953.

Van Doren, Carl. *Benjamin Franklin*. New York: The Viking Press, 1938.

Wendel, Thomas. *Benjamin Franklin and the Politics of Liberty*. Woodbury NY: Barron's Educational Series, 1974.

Wheatley, Henry B. *London Past and Present*, 3 volumes. London: J. Murray, 1891.

Wickwire, Franklin B. *British Subministers and Colonial America, 1763–1783*. Princeton NJ: Princeton University Press, 1966.

Wolff, Mabel P. *The Colonial Agency of Pennsylvania, 1712–1757*. Philadelphia: n. p., 1933.

Wright, Esmond. *Franklin of Philadelphia*. Cambridge MA and London: Harvard University Press, 1986.

## C. Articles

Aldridge, Alfred O. "Benjamin Franklin as Georgia Agent," *Georgia Review* 6 (1952): 161-73.

Bloore, Stephen. "Samuel Keimer: A Footnote to the Life of Franklin," *Pennsylvania Magazine of History and Biography* 54 (1930): 255-87.

Christenson, Merton A. "Franklin on the Hemphill Trial: Deism Versus Presbyterian Orthodoxy," *William and Mary Quarterly* 10 (1953): 422-40.

Crane, Verner W. "Certain Writings of Benjamin Franklin on the British Empire and the American Colonies," *Papers of the Bibliographical Society* 28 (1934): Part 1.

_____. "The Club of Honest Whigs: Friends of Science and Liberty," *William and Mary Quarterly* 23 (1966): 210-33.

_____. "Benjamin Franklin and the Stamp Act," *Colonial Society of Massachusetts, Transactions* 32 (1937): 56-77.

Eddy, George S., ed. "Account Book of Benjamin Franklin kept by him during his First Mission to England as Provincial Agent, 1757–1762," *Pennsylvania Magazine of History and Biography* 55 (1931): 97-133.

Ford, Worthington C., ed. "Franklin's Accounts Against Massachusetts," *Massachusetts Historical Society Proceedings* 56 (October 1922–June 1923): 94-120.

_____. "Franklin and Chatham," *The Independent* 60 (11 January 1906): 94-97.

Gleason, J. Philip. "A Scurrilous Colonial Election and Franklin's Reputation," *William and Mary Quarterly* 18 (1961): 68-84.

Holton, Woody. "The Ohio Indians and the Coming of the American Revolution in Virginia," *Journal of Southern History* 60 (1994): 453-78.

Hutson, James H. "Benjamin Franklin and the Parliamentary Grant for 1758," *William and Mary Quarterly* 23 (1966): 575-79.

Jorgenson, Chester E. "A Brand Flung at Colonial Orthodoxy: Samuel Keimer's Universal Instructor in All Arts and Sciences," *Journalism Quarterly* 12 (1935): 272-77.

_____. "The Source of Benjamin Franklin's Dialogues Between Philocles and Horatio (1730)," *American Literature* 6 (1934): 337-39.

Kammen, Michael G. "The Colonial Agents, English Politics, and the American Revolution," *William and Mary Quarterly* 22 (1965): 244-63.

Kenny, Robert W. "James Ralph: An Eighteenth Century Philadelphian in Grub Street," *Pennsylvania Magazine of History and Biography* 64 (1940): 218-42.

Kerr, Joan P. "Benjamin Franklin's Years in London," *American Heritage* 28 (1976): 14-27.

Ketcham, Ralph L. "Benjamin Franklin and William Smith: New Light on an Old Philadelphia Quarrel," *Pennsylvania Magazine of History and Biography* 88 (1964): 142-63.

Labaree, Leonard W. "Benjamin Franklin's British Friendships," *Proceedings of the American Philosophical Society* 108 (20 October 1964): 423-28.

Marshall, Peter. "Lord Hillsborough, Samuel Wharton, and the Ohio Grant, 1769–1775," *English Historical Review* 80 (1965): 717-39.

Mason, Henry R. "Benjamin Franklin and Religion," *Master Mason* (August 1925): 649-53.

Mathews, Mrs. L. K. "Benjamin Franklin's Plans for a Colonial Union, 1750–1775," *American Political Science Review* 8 (1914): 393-412.

McCoy, Drew. "Benjamin Franklin's Vision of a Republican Political Economy for America," *William and Mary Quarterly* 35 (1978): 605-628.

Morgan, David T. "A Most Unlikely Friendship—Benjamin Franklin and George Whitefield," *Historian* 47 (1985): 208-218.

_____. "A New Look at Benjamin Franklin as Georgia's Colonial Agent," *Georgia Historical Quarterly* 68 (1984): 221-32.

Newcomb, Benjamin H. "Effects of the Stamp Act on Colonial Pennsylvania Politics," *William and Mary Quarterly* 23 (1966): 257-72.

Quinlan, Maurice J. "Dr. Franklin Meets Dr. Johnson," *Pennsylvania Magazine of History and Biography* 73 (1949): 34-44.

Shipley, John B. "Franklin Attends a Book Auction," *Pennsylvania Magazine of History and Biography* 80 (1956): 37-45.

Smith, Paul H. "Benjamin Franklin: Gunrunner?," *Pennsylvania Magazine of History and Biography* 95 (1971): 526-29.

Sosin, Jack. "Imperial Regulations of Colonial Paper Money, 1764–1773," *Pennsylvania Magazine of History and Biography* 78 (1964): 174-98.

Warden, G. B. "The Proprietary Group in Pennsylvania, 1754-1764," *William and Mary Quarterly* 21 (1964): 367-89.

Weaver, Glen. "Benjamin Franklin and the Pennsylvania Germans," *William and Mary Quarterly* 14 (1957): 536-59.

Wecter, Dixon. "Burke, Franklin, and Samuel Petrie," *Huntington Library Quarterly* 3 (1940): 315-38.

Zimmmerman, John J. "Benjamin Franklin and the Quaker Party, 1755–1756," *William and Mary Quarterly* 17 (1960): 291-313.

_____. "Charles Thomson, 'The Sam Adams of Philadelphia'," *Mississippi Valley Historical Review* 45 (1958): 464-80.

# Index

# About the Author

David T. Morgan is professor of history at the University of Montevallo in Montevallo, Alabama. He received his B.A. degree from Baylor University and his M.A. and Ph.D. from the University of North Carolina at Chapel Hill. He has published numerous articles on Benjamin Franklin and has written and edited several books on the American South.